Formed in the Image of Christ
The Sacramental-Moral Theology
of Bernard Häring, C.Ss.R.

Kathleen A. Cahalan

D0869515

M̲
G
A Michael Glazier Book

LITURGICAL PRESS
Collegeville, Minnesota

www.litpress.org

To my parents
David C. and Gloria A. Cahalan

A Michael Glazier Book published by the Liturgical Press

Cover design by David Manahan, O.S.B. Photo courtesy of the Office of Provincial Records, Denver Province of the Redemptorists.

1	2	3	4	5	6	7	8

Library of Congress Cataloging-in-Publication Data

Cahalan, Kathleen A.
    Formed in the image of Christ : the sacramental-moral theology of Bernard Häring, C.Ss.R. / Kathleen A. Cahalan.
        p. cm.
    "A Michael Glazier book."
    Includes bibliographical references (p.) and index.
    ISBN 0-8146-5174-7 (alk. paper)
    1. Häring, Bernhard, 1912– 2. Christian ethics—Catholic authors. 3. Christian ethics—History—20th century. 4. Catholic Church—Liturgy—History—20th century. I. Title.

BJ1249.C14 2004
241'.042'092—dc22   2003061199

Contents

Preface

In many circles of Catholic moral theology Bernard Häring is considered an important twentieth-century historical figure who is now somewhat passé. In recent years his name has appeared in the headlines of the *National Catholic Reporter* when making prophetic or controversial statements about the contemporary Church; yet in academic circles he is rarely considered a source for contemporary moral or pastoral thinking. In my first reading of *The Law of Christ,* I was surprised to discover something much different. The large and weighty three-volume work begins with a discussion of the place of prayer in the moral life and throughout the book the themes of worship and sacraments appear in relationship to the traditional moral categories of agency, conscience, sin, and virtue. Häring reverses the neo-Thomist manualists' notion that sacraments are moral obligations by placing worship at the heart of the Christian life with moral response arising from prayer and worship. Following the Second Vatican Council moral theologians no longer found it necessary to explain the canonical rules of sacramental practice within the discipline; *The Law of Christ*, then, marks the last systematic attempt in moral theology to relate worship, sacraments, and prayer to moral theology and the Christian moral life.

Häring's importance in history, which I recount in chapter 1, cannot be denied and certainly deserves to be told. Only recently have the "minor figures" of the 1940s and 50s begun to receive attention, and Häring's contributions must be considered in the context of theologians preparing the way of renewal in Catholic theology in the mid-twentieth century.[1] But there is more. His theology offers us

---

[1] See, for example, Robert A. Krieg, c.s.c., *Karl Adam: Catholicism in German Culture* (Notre Dame, Ind.: University of Notre Dame Press, 1992); Robert A. Krieg, c.s.c., *Romano Guardini: A Precursor of Vatican II* (Notre Dame, Ind.: University of Notre Dame Press, 1997).

something to consider today. It is a richly textured theology, combining biblical images with personalist anthropology, Christology with theological anthropology, and sacramental theology with moral dimensions of personal and communal life.

There are certainly others who could tell Bernard Häring's story far better. My only relationship to Bernard Häring is through correspondence in the 1990s. When I completed my dissertation, I sent him a copy with a request to visit him in Germany.[2] He wrote back and affirmed my thesis that the sacraments are the key to his moral system. He also welcomed my visit, but warned me of frail health and a failing memory; despite infirmities of body and mind, he noted that "I am still very much spiritually alive." He died only a few weeks later, in July 1998, so I did not enjoy the opportunity of meeting him face-to-face. Of course, over the many hours of studying his work, I have come to know him well.

When I mention to people that I am conducting a study of Häring's work, stories pour forth—his preaching, retreat work, and teaching extended far into the U.S. Catholic community in the 1960s and 70s, and many of his colleagues and students who knew him personally could expand and enrich this story in ways that I cannot. Furthermore, he has written several biographies that provide a portrait of his life and thought as well as his lively faith. In this book I briefly tell that story in the context of understanding what I call Häring's "sacramental-moral theology." My hope is that readers will come to appreciate his importance in Catholic history as well as how his ideas might further the contemporary conversations about the relationship between liturgy and ethics. I hope this book casts fresh light on his moral system—for those who read *The Law of Christ* in their seminary or graduate training and for those who may not know or appreciate this work.

Part One of this book introduces Bernard Häring and his place in the history of Roman Catholic moral theology. Chapter 1 sketches his life and work as a Redemptorist priest and moral theologian. I summarize four well-documented accomplishments of his thought, as well as common criticisms, and point to an area of his work that has yet to be fully examined and appreciated: his understanding of worship and morality. Chapter 2 positions Häring's ideas on the sacra-

---

[2] Kathleen A. Cahalan, "The Sacramental-Moral Theology of Bernard Häring: A Study of the Virtue of Religion" (Ph.D. dissertation, University of Chicago, 1998).

mental and moral life within the history of Catholic moral theology and the liturgical movement. From its beginning the purpose of moral theology has been a mixture of the pastoral and the legal: to assist priests in identifying sins and assigning penance. With the advent of neo-Thomism in the nineteenth century a new wave of moral theology manuals came into Catholic seminaries that strongly emphasized a legal and deductive approach to the moral life. By the 1950s, however, this approach was under attack, and *The Law of Christ* is considered the major effort that would lead Catholic moral theologians in new and different directions. The two major influences on Häring are the Catholic Tübingen tradition and the liturgical movement, which through its theology and practical reforms provides a systematic link for Häring's Christology, anthropology, ecclesiology, and moral theology.

Part Two examines the central concepts of Häring's sacramental-moral theology: responsibility, Christ as Word of God and High Priest, the human person as word and worshiper, and the sacraments as dialogue and response. Responsibility forms the core of Häring's theological anthropology and moral theory and is used to explain both religious and moral experience. Not only does the Christian respond to God through religious acts of worship, prayer, and the sacraments, but moral acts are also responses to God. Through the sacramental formation of the inner life, the Christian is shaped and formed by the Holy Spirit, who enables each person to respond through the imitation of Christ. Häring's understanding of religion is shaped by ideas he gleans and weds from Martin Buber, Max Scheler, and Rudolf Otto; his Christology and sacramental theology are shaped by two major figures of the German liturgical movement, Karl Adam and Romano Guardini.

In *The Law of Christ* Häring extends his understanding of religion and morality as response to the traditional category of the theological and moral virtues. He takes a minor category—the virtue of religion—and places it at the center of the moral life. This much forgotten concept forms the discussion of Part Three. Chapter 5 examines Häring's understanding of the theological and moral virtues and their relationship to the virtue of religion in comparison to Aquinas and the neo-Thomist manualists. Aquinas describes two types of acts that make up the virtue of religion: two interior acts (devotion and prayer) and seven exterior acts (adoration, sacrifice, oblations and first fruits, tithes, vows, oaths, and the use of God's name). Chapter 6 considers Häring's interpretation of the interior acts of devotion and prayer and the exterior acts of adoration and the use of God's name through the categories of his sacramental-moral theology.

To conclude this study I briefly examine contemporary conversations in liturgy and ethics in relationship to Häring's system. In Catholic circles liturgy and social justice has been a central topic since the 1980s; among Protestant authors, particularly narrative theologians, the moral life is defined in terms of community, character, and virtue with worship as a primary arena for virtue formation. Häring's work is in many ways quite distinct from these two conversations. By considering contemporary proposals for the relationship between liturgy and ethics, they provide a helpful critique of his system. In turn, Häring contributes key ideas to the weaknesses found in these proposals.

The life and work of Bernard Häring has had one primary aim: to renew the discipline of moral theology for all Christians—ministers and lay persons—in order to deepen the Church's understanding of the moral life as a religious response to God's initiative. In many ways Häring is first and foremost a pastoral theologian—a devoted priest, committed to teaching, preaching, and caring for souls. His ministry brought him into contact with pressing intellectual and moral concerns of his day—atheism, secularization, and materialism. His unique synthesis of sacramental and spiritual theology into a moral framework dramatically shifts the discipline of moral theology away from minimalist and legal notions of the Christian life. He claims for moral theology a pastoral focus that attends to the ways in which ministers guide the Christian community in seeking faithful response in the world.

There are many people I wish to thank who have supported me in this effort: my professors at the University of Chicago Divinity School, especially Don S. Browning and James M. Gustafson (who introduced me to Bernard Häring); my friend and mentor, Craig Dykstra, Vice President, Lilly Endowment, Inc., who enabled me to have time for thinking and writing; and my husband, Donald B. Ottenhoff, who offers me much-needed editing, critical insight, as well as loving companionship. I dedicate this book to my parents, David and Gloria Cahalan, who have been a constant source of love and support in my life.

Abbreviations

CE	*The Christian Existentialist*
CRCW	*Christian Renewal in a Changing World*
DHG	*Das Heilege und das Gute*
ET	*Evangelization Today*
EW	*Embattled Witness*
FFC	*Free and Faithful in Christ*
HR	*Hope Is the Remedy*
JC	*The Johannine Council*
LC	*The Law of Christ*
MP	*Morality Is for Persons*
MWC	*My Witness for the Church*
SEL	*The Sacraments in Your Everyday Life*
SS	*A Sacramental Spirituality*
ST	*Summa Theologica*

Part I

Bernard Häring
and Roman Catholic Moral Theology

Chapter 1

Reassessing Bernard Häring's Moral Theology

A more biblically oriented approach to the whole of moral theology first appeared in the Tübingen school in Germany and is best exemplified in the manual of Bernard Häring which despite its transitional character stands as the greatest contribution to the renewal of moral theology since the sixteenth century.[1]

——————————— Charles E. Curran, *Catholic Moral Theology in Dialogue*

Roman Catholic theology has undergone significant changes over the past century. Modern political and intellectual developments in the nineteenth century challenged traditional understandings of faith and reason, nature and grace, and individual and religious authority. In response to these perceived threats, neo-scholasticism and neo-Thomism became the official schools of Catholic philosophy and theology. In returning to the metaphysics and theological method of St. Thomas Aquinas, Catholic scholars were discouraged from exploring the emerging developments in historical and biblical studies; these would not be fully integrated into Catholic thought until the middle of the twentieth century. In moral and sacramental theology neo-Thomism viewed both moral action and sacramental practice primarily from the standpoint of duties and obligations and defined each according to the minimum requirements necessary for salvation. Operating within a scholastic metaphysical framework, both moral and sacramental experience was diminished. Concerned that this approach was not adequate to face the challenges of modernity,

[1] Charles E. Curran, *Catholic Moral Theology in Dialogue* (Notre Dame, Ind.: Fides Publishers, 1972) 27.

some Catholic theologians began to explore new insights from historical and biblical studies.

The Redemptorist priest Bernard Häring is considered to be the most significant moral theologian to step outside the neo-Thomist tradition and change the course of moral theology in the twentieth century. He integrates Scripture and dogma into moral theology, explores new philosophical foundations for the discipline, and encourages a more open, pastorally sensitive approach to moral questions. He also brings a renewed understanding of sacramental and spiritual theology into his system, thereby enlarging the image of the Christian moral life beyond the legal and minimal neo-Thomist approach. Häring accomplishes a renewal in Catholic moral theology by introducing the theological theme of invitation and response, which serves as a biblical hermeneutic, a theme that joins together theological anthropology and Christology, and a way of understanding the relationship between worship and the Christian moral life.

Häring's Life and Work: A Brief Synopsis

I told my superior that this was my very last choice because I found the teaching of moral theology an absolute crashing bore. He mollified me with the answer: "We are asking you to prepare yourself for this task with a doctorate from a German university precisely so that it can be different in the future."[2]

— Bernard Häring, *My Witness for the Church*

Born into a Catholic family on November 10, 1912, in Bottingen, Germany, Häring was the eleventh of twelve children.[3] He joined the Redemptorist community in May 1934, to become a missionary, after declining an invitation from the Jesuits to become a professor.[4] He studied at Gars in southern Germany where the Redemptorist community had a theological center affiliated with the University of Munich and was ordained in 1939. The Redemptorists had promised Häring that he would go to Brazil after his ordination; however, just

[2] Bernard Häring, *My Witness for the Church*, trans. Leonard Swidler (Mahwah, N.J.: Paulist Press, 1992) 19, subsequently referred to as *MWC*.

[3] For an extensive account of Häring's family life, see Bernard Häring, *Free and Faithful: My Life in the Catholic Church* (Liguori, Mo.: Liguori/Triumph, 1998) 1–14, subsequently referred to as *FF*.

[4] The Redemptorist order was founded by Alphonsus Liguori in the late eighteenth century for the purpose of preaching and conducting missions among Italian peasants.

before his departure Häring's provincial superior informed him that the community had chosen him to be trained in moral theology, much to his great disappointment.

Häring attended the University of Tübingen, encouraged by Theodore Steinbüchl, a family friend and future professor. He enrolled in September 1940, but his studies were interrupted by World War II, and his dissertation was not completed until 1947.[5] The war experience and the blind allegiance of his fellow Germans to the Nazi regime decisively shaped Häring's intellectual interests and the pastoral focus he later brought to moral theology: "Unfortunately, I also experienced the most absurd obedience by Christians . . . toward a criminal regime. And that too radically affected my thinking and acting as a moral theologian. After the war I returned to moral theology with the firm decision to teach it so that its core concept would not be obedience but responsibility, the courage to be responsible."[6]

In addition, Häring's long-time interest in ecumenism grew out of his war experience. Serving on the eastern front in Poland and Russia, he came into contact with both Protestant and Orthodox Christians and on one occasion was able to assist Jews escaping persecution.[7] After the war Häring desired to continue pastoral work but his community called him back to Tübingen to finish his degree. This did not impede his resolve, however: until 1953 he spent time assisting Catholic refugees in areas of northern Bavaria where no Catholic pastoral work had been organized.[8] Along with his colleague Viktor Schurr, Häring devised an experiment called "Refugees' Mission."

> We wandered from place to place and visited all the families, who often were living in miserable quarters. We shared their poverty, slept with

[5] Häring served in a medical company stationed in France from September 1940 to May 1941. His division was then deployed to the Polish-Russian border until the end of the war. For an account of this experience, see *MWC*, 20–25 and *FF*, 25–51, and Bernard Häring, *Embattled Witness: Memories in a Time of War* (New York: Seabury, 1976) subsequently referred to as *EW*.

[6] *MWC*, 23–24. This experience also made Häring a pacifist. "I find it absolutely laughable and at the same time frustrating that at my age I still have to pour out so much energy on questions like flexibility and inflexibility concerning the forbidding of contraception and in the struggle against sexual rigorism. I am most deeply convinced that my main calling is and must be that of an untiring peace apostle for the elimination of war, for a world culture that is free of violence, for a radical love that will not allow us to become enemies, for a 'transformation of armament' to a nonviolent defense," ibid., 24.

[7] *FF*, 32-35; 69–75.

[8] Viktor Schurr, *Bernard Häring: Die Erneuerung der Moral Theologie* (Salzburg: Otto Mueller Verlag, 1970).

the poorest, often together in a single tiny room. We preached the Good News in rented dance halls. . . . Before this experiment I had carefully worked out fifteen sermon outlines. Not one of them was ever used. After the first home visit it became clear to me that it was not I who should be determining the topics. What should happen was that I ought to respond to the real life problems, fears, hopes, and needs of these men and women. Again and again I learned a responsorial pastoral work went hand in hand with a responsorial moral theology.[9]

This pastoral experience, combined with his education at Tübingen, significantly shaped the young Häring. At Tübingen he was influenced by the work of Karl Adam, Romano Guardini, and Theodore Steinbüchel and was able to listen to the lectures of Protestant theologians Helmut Thielicke and Friedrich Rückert.[10] This brought him into contact with scholars engaged in historical, biblical, and liturgical studies and introduced him to the philosophies of personalism and value theory. Häring's dissertation, *Das Heilige und das Gute (The Sacred and the Good: Religion and Morality in Their Mutual Relationships)*, completed in 1947 and published in 1950, analyzes the relationship between religion and morality in the work of Immanuel Kant, Freidrich Schleiermacher, Rudolf Otto, Max Scheler, Nicolai Hartmann, and Emil Brunner.[11] Following Otto and Scheler, Häring concludes that religion and morality are deeply related to one another yet are distinct and separate realities which must be understood and analyzed as such; much of Häring's early work continued

---

[9] *MWC*, 29; see also *FF* 120.

[10] Tübingen, its renewal of moral theology, and its influence on Häring are discussed in the following chapters. See *FF*, 54-55, for Häring's comments on studying at Tübingen.

[11] The major works which Häring explores in this study, subsequently referred to as *DHG*, include: Immanuel Kant, *Kritik der reinen Vernunft*, in *Immanuel Kants Werke*, ed. E. Cassirer, III (Berlin: Br. Cassirer, 1912–1918); *Kritik der praktischen Vernunft*, in *Immanual Kants Werke V*; Freidrich Schleiermacher, *Uber der Religion*, ed. R. Otto (3d ed.: Gottingen, 1913); Rudolf Otto, *Aufsätze das Numinöse betreffend* (Stuttgart: Gotha, 1923); *Das Heilige* (München: 1936); Max Scheler, *Vom Ewigen im Menschen* (Leipzig, 1921); *Der Formalismus in der Ethik und die materiale Wertethik* (3d ed.; Halle, 1927); Nicolai Hartmann, *Ethik* (2d ed.; Berlin-Leipzig, 1935); Emil Brunner, *Das Gebot und die Ordnungen* (Tübingen, 1932); *Unser Glaube* (Bern-Leipzig, 1935); *Der Mensch in Widerspruch* (Berlin, 1937). Häring's own constructive position on the relationship between religion and morality can be found in Bernard Häring, *The Law of Christ, vol. 1, General Moral Theology* (Westminster, Md.: Newman Press, 1961) 35–49, subsequently referred to as *LC* 1; *The Christian Existentialist* (New York: New York University Press, 1968) 44–46, subsequently referred to as *CE*; and *Evangelization Today* (Notre Dame, Ind.: Fides, 1974) 66–67, subsequently referred to as *ET*.

to examine the issue of how precisely religion and morality are related.[12]

In 1947 Häring became professor of moral theology and moral philosophy on the religious-theological faculty at Gars. Not long after his arrival he began lecturing on the family and religious sociology. Häring's academic career shifted in 1950 when the newly elected Superior General of the Redemptorist order, Leonard Buijs, contacted him regarding "an ancient error in Catholic moral theology." Häring recalls that

> for a long time the religious superiors and bishops had sent all of their prospective professors of moral theology to study canon law or both canon law and civil law in Rome. That served to confirm institutionally the legalism of Catholic moral theology. He envisioned a theology faculty which would specialize in moral theology in its complete thematic breadth and theological-philosophical depth in order to train authentic moral theologians and to prepare them for their real task. He wished to begin on an experimental basis as quickly as possible, starting with a program mainly for Redemptorists. He placed great stock in getting a professor from the Tübingen school—for this he had his eye on me.[13]

From 1950 to 1953, Häring taught one semester at the newly founded Academia Alfonsiana in Rome.[14] He offered two classes, one

[12] Ronald Philip Hamel, "Methodological and Substantive Development in Catholic Medical Ethics: A Critical Study of the Work of Bernard Häring" (Ph.D. diss., Fordham University, 1982) 17. Hamel offers a concise summary of Häring's argument, "Against Kant who upholds the autonomy of morality to which he subordinates religion, Hartmann who negates any role of religion in a totally autonomous morality, Schleiermacher who asserts the primordial nature and irreducibility of religion with no orientation to morality, and Brunner's virtual identification of religion and morality, Häring argues the autonomy of each and their mutual relatedness, much in the manner of Rudolph Otto and Max Scheler." Häring's constructive position on religion and morality is discussed in Chapter 3 of this book.

[13] *MWC*, 31; see also *FF*, 56.

[14] Prior to the formation of the new school, Häring attended lectures in Rome by Franz Xavier Hürth, S.J., and Reginald Garrigou-Lagrange, O.P., in order to survey the theological scene. He heard a case presented by Hürth on whether or not a priest was allowed to say two Masses on workdays even when the people would not be able to receive Communion for a year. Hürth's conclusion that under no circumstances was a priest required to say two weekday Masses led Häring to embrace the vocation his superiors had called him to: "I looked around the lecture hall to see how the students would react. They were all listening in docile silence, so I took my hat and quietly walked out of the hall. That, I thought, must be the limit—to regard the Eucharist purely from the standpoint of a legal requirement. . . . Did I need any clearer proof of the need for an academy for the thoroughgoing renewal of Catholic moral theology?" *FF*, 56-57; see also *MWC*, 33.

on conversion as a foundational perspective for Catholic moral theology and another titled "What can we Catholic moral theologians learn from Protestant and Orthodox Christians?" In 1954, his three-volume work *The Law of Christ* was published and enjoyed immediate success. Within a year, it was reprinted three times and in three years translated into fourteen languages.[15]

Häring retained a permanent position at the Academia Alfonsiana in 1953 and remained there until his retirement in 1988, when he moved back to his hometown of Gars, Germany, where he resided until his death in July 1998. He also served as professor of moral theology and professor of pastoral sociology at the Pastoral Institute of the Lateran in Rome. During the 1950s, while in Rome, he became active in the movement toward theological renewal prior to Vatican II (1962–1965).

During the Council, Häring served as a member of the preparatory theological commission and several subcommissions that reviewed the topic of the moral order—chastity, virginity, marriage, and the family; religious freedom; and the laity. He served as coordinating secretary for the editorial committee for *Gaudium et Spes* (for which he was called the "quasi-father"), the final editor for the sections on the laity in *Lumen Gentium,* editorial secretary for a special subcommission on *Dignitatis Humanae,* and was responsible for drafting the important wording on the role of Scripture in moral theology in *Optatam Totius.*[16] In addition, like many theologians at the time, Häring was able to influence a wide body of attendees through lectures and discussions.[17]

---

[15] The story about the publication of *The Law of Christ* by Dr. Erich Wewel, a Nazi prisoner of war, is illustrative of Fr. Häring's pastoral sensitivity (*MWC,* 29–30). Wewel owned a small publishing house before the war, and when he refused to work for the Nazis he lost the business and was imprisoned. After the war, through mutual acquaintances, he offered to publish Häring's first book. *The Law of Christ* was completed in 1953, but Häring agreed to wait until Wewel could secure a loan to begin his business again. When the book finally appeared in 1954, it was awarded "The Most Beautiful Book of the Year" by the Society of German Booksellers and its instant success secured the publishing business of Dr. Wewel.

[16] *FF,* 103. "Special attention needs to be given to the development of moral theology. Its scientific exposition should be more thoroughly nourished by scriptural teaching" (*Optatam Totius* 5.17). See *MWC,* 60, for Häring's original formulation of the statement.

[17] Häring recalls his own work at the Council (*MWC,* 59): "I actively collaborated by way of constructive criticism and concrete suggestions for improvement on all the documents which went through the Doctrinal Commission. . . . Various bishops took advantage of my services as a Latinist. In doing this the exact meaning and direction of the

Charles Curran, a prominent Catholic ethicist and student of Häring's, has noted that Häring's moral theology "epitomizes the Council with its many accomplishments and its shortcomings," which was "primarily pastoral in tone and scope—trying to make the Church more relevant in the contemporary world."[18] Häring was deeply committed to the teachings and reforms of Vatican II, and after the Council he traveled extensively, teaching and preaching to religious and lay groups in Europe, Asia, Africa, and North and South America.[19] Curran argues that this commitment meant that Häring would not continue to make scholarly contributions to moral theology:

> As the 1960s moved on and the postconciliar period of the Church opened, I was somewhat disappointed to realize that Häring's publications were no longer breaking new ground in a systematic way. We had a discussion about this while he was a visiting professor at Yale Divinity School in the 1966–67 school year. Häring pointed out that he was devoting much of his time and energy to bringing the idea of renewal in the Church to an even wider public, for he felt this was the most important need for the Church at the present. . . . One can say without fear of contradiction that no one has spoken to more people in more countries about contemporary Christian moral life than Bernard Häring. In the process it has been impossible for him to publish on a high, scholarly level, and thus he has not been able to continue charting the future course of moral theology.[20]

Despite Curran's criticism Häring was a prolific writer, publishing a new book nearly every year from 1963 to 1989, as well as a devoted preacher and teacher. Many of these books sought to explain the

---

various suggestions were discussed. During the four Council sessions as well as the in-between periods I was often invited by entire episcopacies to hold lectures and discussions concerning one or more conciliar texts." For a full discussion of Häring's involvement at the Council, see *MWC*, 40–89, and *FF*, 87–106.

[18] Charles E. Curran, *A New Look at Christian Morality* (Notre Dame, Ind.: Fides, 1968) 145. Häring also wrote a book about the Second Vatican Council: *The Johannine Council: Witness to Unity* (Dublin: Gill and Son, 1963) subsequently referred to as *JC*.

[19] See *FF*, 124–30, for a description of Häring's work in Africa and Asia.

[20] Charles E. Curran, *Ongoing Revision in Moral Theology* (Notre Dame, Ind.: Fides/Claretian, 1975) 265–66. As David Tracy describes, the work of the theologian is related to three publics: the society, the academy, and the Church. Häring is clearly a theologian who saw his work as located within the Church but not entirely at the exclusion of the society or the academy; rather, his purpose was to renew the life of the Church by means of the academy for the purpose of renewing the larger society. David Tracy, *The Analogical Imagination* (New York: Crossroad, 1981) 3–46.

teachings of Vatican II, some addressed specific moral questions, such as medical ethics, and others focused on sacramental and spiritual topics.[21] An important part of Häring's pastoral ministry since the 1960s has been his involvement in the House of Prayer movement, which aimed to encourage religious congregations of women, mainly in the U.S., to devote one household to continual prayer.[22]

Häring's writings on sexual and medical ethics were challenged by the Vatican's Doctrinal Congregation and he underwent a trial from 1975 to 1979, at the same time he was suffering from throat cancer. His conflicts with the Vatican commission began with his protest of *Humanae Vitae* (1967) and culminated with the publication of his book *Medical Ethics* in 1972.[23] Häring, well-known for his gentle and mild manner, sharply criticized church authorities after the trial for unnecessarily harsh treatment. In a letter to Cardinal Franjo Seper, prefect of the Doctrinal Congregation, he stated:

> During the Second World War I stood before a military court four times. Twice it was a case of life and death. At that time I felt honored because I was accused by enemies of God. The accusations then were to a very large extent true, because I was not submissive to that regime. Now I am accused by the Doctrinal Congregation in an extremely humiliating manner. The accusations are untrue. In addition, they come from a very high organ of the Church leadership, an organ of that Church which I in a long life have served with all my power and honesty and hope to serve still further with sacrifice. I would rather stand once again before a court of war of Hitler.[24]

Despite this difficult period, Häring published what he considered to be his main theological work, *Free and Faithful in Christ* (1978–81). Not considering this a restatement of *The Law of Christ*, Häring claimed that the new work represented the maturing of his own thought and

---

[21] For a complete bibliography of Häring's writings from 1953 to 1977, see Henri Boelaars and Real Tremblay, eds., "In Libertatem Vocai Estis," Festschrift Bernard Häring, *Studia Moralia* 15 (1977) 13–30. A bibliography of Häring's work in English is included in this book.

[22] See *FF*, 131–36; Häring also preached missions in congregations around the world, 153–54.

[23] See *MWC*, 90–180, and *FF*, 107–15, for a description of Häring's trial and his correspondence with the Vatican. See also Hamel, "Methodological and Substantive Development." In this work, Hamel argues that Häring made both significant methodological and substantive breakthroughs in the field of medical ethics drawing from both his theology of responsibility and freedom and his personalist philosophy.

[24] *MWC*, 132–33.

the changes within the Church since Vatican II.[25] During retirement Häring wrote several books on autobiographical and spiritual themes. Despite his anger at the Church throughout his trial and illness, and his more outspoken manner in recent years on several papal teachings, Häring remained a devoted servant of the Church.[26] The Church for Häring represents "an all embracing friendship gathered around Christ" for which he never lost his commitment.[27]

From his vocation as a Redemptorist priest, his training at Tübingen in moral theology, and his long experience in the war, Häring developed a deep commitment to changing moral theology from its legalistic approach to a more responsive, biblically based, dynamic understanding of the Christian moral life. Once Vatican II had authorized a view of the Christian life and Church that mirrored Häring's own theology, he committed himself to teaching, writing, and preaching so that the vision could become a reality.

[25] Häring states (*MWC*, 93): "Looking back I believe that I can nevertheless confirm that this was the most creative period of my life. The perspective of an imminent death gave me a great inner freedom from every form of external pressure. And the pressure which the Vatican offices wanted to place me under strengthened my alertness not to commit the sin of cowardice and dissemblance in the end. It was precisely in this period and under these circumstances that the major work of my theological effort, *Free and Faithful in Christ*, was written. . . . This book is not a new edition of *The Law of Christ*; for since 1954, the year of the first edition of that work, the situation in the world and the Church has changed drastically and so has my thinking, influenced so much by the Council and worldwide experiences." See also Bernard Häring, *Free and Faithful in Christ*, vol. 1 (New York: Seabury Press, 1978) 1–6, subsequently referred to as *FFC* 1. Most students and critics of Häring's work, however, see no major theological shifts in this book but rather an elaboration of his earlier theological positions and a more flexible and less strict approach to moral problems.

[26] Bernard Häring viewed *Veritatis Splendor*, released in 1993, as a significant set back and a return to an older, legalistic approach to moral acts. The encyclical was written because of what was perceived as a "new situation" in the Church in which "numerous doubts and objections" had arisen "with regard to the Church's moral teachings" which had become "an overall and systematic calling into question of traditional moral doctrine." (4) The encyclical places heavy emphasis on the moral law and commandments (12–15, 26), warns against the notion of fundamental option if separated from moral acts (65), and rejects the teleological ethical theories of proportionalism and consequentialism (75). See Richard A. McCormick, S.J., "Some Early Reactions to *Veritatis Splendor*," *Theological Studies* 55 (1994) 481–506, for a discussion of the reaction to the encyclical by the press, bishops, major Catholic periodicals, and Catholic moral theologians. Häring reacted strongly against what he saw as the main goal of the letter: "to endorse total assent and submission to all utterances of the Pope." Häring's response was part of a special issue of *The Tablet*, which contains eleven essays by well-known moral theologians, some of who agree with the encyclical's message and some who strongly dissent from it. Bernard Häring, "A Distrust That Wounds," *The Tablet* 247 (23 October 1993) 1378–79.

[27] Despite Häring's disagreement with Paul VI over *Humanae Vitae*, he preached retreats for the pope. *FF*, 159.

Häring's Contributions to Moral Theology

The Law of Christ was birthed into this theologically changing world. Its use of scripture, its pastoral orientation, its engagement with the intellectual currents of contemporary Europe, its emphasis on the imitation of Christ were likely to be seen as a wise and theologically responsible reading of and response to the "signs of the times."[28]

————————————————— John A. Gallagher, *Time Past, Time Future*

The Law of Christ is not the first of what John Gallagher calls the "alternative manuals" of moral theology that appeared in the mid-twentieth century.[29] As is described in more detail in the next chapter, several manualists were attempting to break from the neo-Thomist tradition in the 1930s and 40s; but Gallagher claims that Häring's work is "a watershed in the history of moral theology" that accelerated the decisive turn away from neo-Thomism in moral theology. As Gallagher observes "from the date of its publication (1954) a process was set in motion that would result in the gradual removal of the neo-Thomist manuals of moral theology from the seminaries of Europe and the United States."[30]

Häring's contributions to the renewal of moral theology have been noted by both Roman Catholic and Protestant scholars. For example, Charles Curran states that "for many, Häring's work stands as the most creative and important accomplishment in moral theology in this century, the most original and significant contribution in the recent history of the discipline of moral theology."[31] And Protestant ethicist James Gustafson has noted,

> For all its intellectual compromises, *The Law of Christ* has had an impact that no other book in moral theology can match in recent decades. On the whole the impact has been beneficial, if only in bringing to awareness the need for moral theology to begin to converse with biblical theology, ascetical theology, and fundamental theology as well as its ecclesiastical cousin, canon law.[32]

[28] John A. Gallagher, *Time Past, Time Future: An Historical Study of Catholic Moral Theology* (Mahwah, N.J.: Paulist Press, 1990) 169–70.

[29] J. Gallagher discusses four "alternative manuals" of moral theology written during the 1940s and 1950s by Fritz Tillmann, Bernard Häring, Dom Lodin, and Josef Fuchs.

[30] J. Gallagher, 169–70.

[31] Charles E. Curran, *Critical Concerns in Moral Theology* (Notre Dame, Ind.: University of Notre Dame Press, 1984) 3.

[32] James Gustafson, "Faith and Morality in the Secular Age," *Commonweal* 100 (April 12, 1974) 140.

Häring's accomplishments are numerous: he is credited with integrating Scripture into moral theology; developing a moral philosophy based on value, personhood, and personalism; emphasizing a pastoral approach to ethical issues rather than a legalistic one; and integrating dogmatic, historical, spiritual, and sacramental theology into moral theology.

Images from Scripture

One of the radical changes in Roman Catholic moral theology since Vatican II has been the attention given to Scripture as a primary source for the discipline. This turn to the Bible is, in many respects, due to the work of Bernard Häring and other "alternative manualists" from the middle part of the twentieth century. Häring's use of the Bible as the basic source for moral theology, a source used by the neo-Thomists primarily to support already-established norms, is one of his major contributions.

Häring does not look to Scripture for images and themes to fit his moral framework, nor does he look to the Bible initially for norms and principles to define moral and immoral behavior. Rather, he searches the Scriptures for the central themes, paradigms, and images of Israelite and Christian experience and builds a portrait of the Christian moral life from these.[33] He then identifies the norms and principles in the Decalogue and Sermon on the Mount, which he considers to be guides and signposts for persons in their response to the divine call.

In the foreword to *The Law of Christ*, Häring states that the Bible serves as the primary source for his moral theology.[34] He cites what he believes are the Bible's central concepts of the Christian moral life on the first page of *The Law of Christ:* it is rooted in the life of Christ, its motive is love (not merely the law), and its purpose the imitation of Christ that takes place in and through the sacraments.[35] The central

[33] For an analysis of Häring's use of Scripture, see Michael Clark, "The Uses of Sacred Scripture in the Moral Theology of Bernard Häring, C.Ss.R." (S.T.D. diss., Pontificia Universitas Gregoriana, 1979).

[34] *LC* 1:viii. Häring (*MWC*, 33) also stated later in an interview that he sought greater reliance on the Scriptures than earlier works in moral theology. "Already during my first stay in Rome in 1948, I worked on my manuscript of *The Law of Christ*. My various Roman experiences strengthened my determination to struggle against a legalism which is alienated from life, to work with greater fidelity to the Holy Scriptures and to address the problems of men and women of my time."

[35] "The principle, the norm, the center, and the goal of Christian Moral Theology is Christ. The law of the Christian is Christ Himself in Person. . . . Christian life may not

theme that Häring finds throughout the Scripture is the dynamic between God's gracious and freely offered initiative and invitation to human beings and the individual and communal response to God in worship and moral relations. This is the dynamic and dialogue that underlies both the covenant of the Old Testament and discipleship in the New Testament.[36] Häring uses the terms *responsibility* and *freedom* to capture this dynamic.[37] Responsibility draws together religion and morality: religion is expressed through adoration and worship, which is the community's response to God's gracious gift of creation and life; morality consists of a free and faithful response to God (through faithful obedience) and to the neighbor (through love and service).

Häring's moral theology is Christocentric. In Jesus, the Christian sees and experiences the perfect example of response to God in adoration, freedom, faithfulness, and love of neighbor. The Christian religious-moral life, according to Häring, consists of imitating Christ, through inner assimilation and outward action. Häring draws images of the Christian life from John's Gospel, St. Paul's let-

---

be viewed solely from the point of formal enactment of law and not even primarily from the standpoint of the imperative of the divine will. . . . In the love of Christ and through the love of Christ for us He invites our love in return, which is a life truly formed in Christ. The Christian life is following Christ, but not through mere external copying, even though it be in love and obedience. . . . The essential orientation in this moral theology . . . is toward 'the mysteries of the children of God.' It is a mystical identification of our whole being in Christ through the sacraments, a manifestation of the divine life in us." *LC* 1:vii.

[36] Häring's use of Scripture is not without limitations, however. In a recent study of the use of Scripture in Christian ethics, Jeffrey Siker notes that because Häring wants to replace the manualists' exclusive emphasis on the Decalogue and a legalistic morality, he makes the Sermon on the Mount and Jesus the center of his moral thought, but in doing so, at least in *The Law of Christ*, he accords the Hebrew Bible a secondary status. In Siker's opinion, "What becomes increasingly clear in *The Law of Christ* is that for Häring the Old Testament has no revelatory, and thus no authoritative capacity apart from its corroboration in the New Testament." Jeffrey S. Siker, *Scripture and Ethics: Twentieth-Century Portraits* (New York: Oxford University Press, 1977) 69. See *LC* 1:403 for an example.

[37] The choice of responsibility, for Häring, is not random. The term is central in the Bible and responds to the "signs of the times" in the modern world. "The choice of a leitmotif must not be an arbitrary decision. It should be made only after having carefully studied the biblical patterns and after discerning, in view of those patterns, the special signs of God's present action and call in history. . . . Since our life can be understood only in view of God's initiative, we exercise and develop our creative freedom and fidelity by listening and responding. It is therefore a distinctively Christian approach to emphasize responsibility as a leitmotif, but in a way that shows it as expression of creative freedom and fidelity." *FFC* 1:59. See Richard M. Gula, *What Are They Saying about Moral Norms?* (Mahwah, N.J.: Paulist Press, 1982) 29–30, for a discussion of biblical renewal in Häring's work as it relates to his response ethic. Gula also shows how Charles Curran continues this line of Häring's thought.

ters, and the Sermon on the Mount.[38] From these sources, he cites "freedom of the children of God" (Rom 8:21), "the law of the Spirit" and "the law of Christ" (Gal 6:2; Rom 2:14), and "being in Christ" repeatedly throughout his works. *The Law of Christ* is based upon Romans 8:2, "For the law of the Spirit of the life in Christ Jesus has delivered me from the law of sin and of death," and *Free and Faithful in Christ* is based on Galatians 5:1, "For freedom Christ has set us free." As James Gustafson points out, "this grounds central themes in Häring's work—Christian 'maturity' in the life of faith, life *in* Christ and the Spirit, love as a dynamism, imitation of Christ, and the concepts of the person, of response and responsibility, and of historicity."[39] These texts emphasize the transformation and conversion of the inner person—the attitudes, dispositions, and virtues—to the life of Christ. This inner assimilation takes place in and through the liturgy and sacraments and is essential for moral action.

The Bible is the primary source for Häring's moral theology, and his use of biblical themes is the first of his many departures from the manualist tradition. Häring initiated a dramatic change in the method and content of Catholic moral theology by his use of Scripture. According to James Gustafson, "Häring finds in the New Testament a basis for morality that is open, dynamic, positive, and personal; he finds in the New Testament the *theological* basis for overcoming the closed, static, negativistic, and impersonal moral theology of the manuals."[40]

Personalism and Value Theory

Häring's moral theology may be described as the wedding of Johannine and Pauline themes with the philosophies of personalism and value theory. In the same way that Scripture provides the theological foundation for the Christian moral life, personalism and value theory enable Häring to redefine moral anthropology and

---

[38] Another limitation of Häring's use of Scripture is an exclusive reliance on the Gospel of John, the Sermon on the Mount, and the letters of Paul that tends to exclude much of the synoptic tradition. Siker (61) notes that Häring does not change this emphasis in his later works, but does change the way he uses the Bible. For example, in *Free and Faithful in Christ*, Häring uses half the Scripture quotes found in *The Law of Christ*, because the book is shorter, he is not proof-texting as much, and there is a "sharp move away from the wisdom literature."

[39] James M. Gustafson, *Protestant and Roman Catholic Ethics: Prospects for Rapprochement* (Chicago: University of Chicago Press, 1978) 110.

[40] Ibid.

moral theory.[41] Häring employs personalism and value theory as a way of understanding and describing moral experience, although he never argues philosophically for this approach as opposed to that of neo-scholasticism. In large part, he uses personalism and value theory in much the same way as he uses the phenomenology of religion: value theory resonates with certain aspects of the Catholic and biblical tradition, it emphasizes experience over metaphysics, and it furnishes Häring with language to *describe* the primary moral experience for modern persons who reject the legalism of Catholic morality.

Häring, like other theologians at the time, turned to value theory and personalism in order to reflect on the human being, understood in existential terms, rather than on human nature, understood in metaphysical terms. Personalism, a philosophy portraying the person as a dynamic being who both creates culture and history and is shaped by it, offered Häring a philosophy of the human person that emphasized the mutually related aspects of body and soul, the individual and community, as well as the historicity of human life.[42] Personalism provides a dynamic understanding of human relationality, which coincides with Häring's notion that responsibility captures the essence of both religious and moral experience. As a relational being in time and history, the human person seeks to live and respond to others, as value-bearers, in an effort to maximize value in the created order. In this way, Häring was able to construct a theological anthropology quite distinct from the metaphysical categories of neo-Thomism.

Value theory also offers Häring a way to respond to individualistic approaches prevalent in both moral theology and liturgical practice. The manualists narrowly focus on discrete human acts, with little sense of the human person as living within a community of persons in history. Likewise, the manualists' theology of grace emphasized the metaphysical transformation of the natural to the supernatural,

---

[41] J. Gallagher argues that Häring's unique contribution is his moral theory rather than his theology, which he claims Häring borrowed from Fritz Tillmann. Certainly Häring's theology is dependent on Tillmann for some ideas but the sacramental theology that undergirds his system is his own synthesis.

[42] Häring anticipates contemporary conversations about the moral self and identity in such works as Charles Taylor, *Sources of the Self: The Making of Modern Identity* (Cambridge, Mass.: Harvard University Press, 1989). Taylor explores those aspects of moral agency which are prominent in the western tradition, but are to some extent unarticulated: a sense of inwardness, the spiritual and the moral, freedom and individuality, and embeddedness in nature.

so that the individual's experience of God is often eclipsed. This same understanding of grace informed sacramental theology, so that much of the emphasis focuses on the individual receiving grace necessary to live the Christian life, but does not focus on the community, or the experience. The liturgical reformers' emphasis on the communal and public nature of worship, and its ecclesiology of the Mystical Body of Christ, allows Häring a way to draw personalism into his theology of the sacraments.

Häring's use of Max Scheler's philosophy of values made an important contribution to moral theory. Through value theory Häring is able to place norms and principles in a broader existential context. Persons become aware of values through self-knowledge and relationships with significant persons ("value persons") and are able to know and choose the good because of these value-experiences, not because of their knowledge of abstract norms and principles. "The breakdown of moral knowledge is near if there is mere communication of concepts, laws and precepts formulated by an alien will, without sharing that self-giving word of wisdom and love that allows the person to interiorize the command and the value inherent in it. Values that appeal to freedom are those embodied in persons or understood as relevant to the growth of persons in their own identity and in healthy relationships with God, with fellowmen and the created universe."[43]

Norms and principles are still important for Häring, but not if they are perceived as being an external force imposed on the individual. The values inherent in norms and principles must be apparent for a free and faithful response to be made.[44] Häring adopts personalist categories but redefines them in theological terms. As discussed in chapter 3, Häring views the person as one who finds fullness and completion through listening and responding to the divine initiative

---

[43] *FFC* 1:111–12.

[44] J. Gallagher, 172–73. "The knowledge of value was the keystone of Häring's moral theory. Its function was similar to the role attributed to faith in *Die Idee Der Nachfolge Christi*. Such knowledge was the result of an apprehension of the divine image. As created in the 'image and likeness of God,' persons possessed a limited but real knowledge of the divine image. Such knowledge was an invitation, 'an appeal to us to choose God and His law.' The more comprehensive and profound one's understanding was, the greater one's responsibility before God. Knowledge of values was not just intellectual, but rather a dynamic awareness related to the will and emotions as well. It was an appeal to the whole person. Thus it was neither solely theoretical nor legalistic knowledge, but rather 'insight into value itself, which is the basis of obligation.'"

in creation, history, and community. Persons are unique as individuals, yet also social, and require community for the development of their full potential; they are endowed with personal freedom yet are shaped and conditioned by history.

A Pastoral Approach to Moral Theology

Häring should rightly be called a pastoral theologian because the primary motive and purpose for devoting his life to writing, teaching, and public speaking about the Christian moral life arises from his vocation as a Redemptorist priest. Shaped by the spirituality of the Redemptorist community, Häring's work embraces the pastoral sensitivity of St. Alphonsus Liguori by placing the rigors of moral thinking, casuistry, and problem-solving within a larger pastoral framework. Häring incorporates many of Alphonsus's themes in his work: the close presence of God's loving and merciful grace, the call to holiness of all baptized Christians, the primary place of the "law of the heart" and the secondary role of ecclesial norms and laws in morality, the freedom of the believer's conscience and its formation within the Church, and the idea of the confessor as spiritual and moral guide rather than judge.

The manualists have a narrower concern. They define moral theology as that discipline concerned with the proper administration of the sacrament of penance. But for Häring, the first, and most important role of the moral theologian, is to offer a complete portrait of the Christian moral life so that the duties and obligations that are a part of morality are incorporated into the religious and sacramental life of the believer and the community. He defines moral theology as a pastoral discipline intended to guide Christians toward a deeper understanding of what it means to imitate the life of Christ.[45] A moral theology that is pastoral has the broad aim of addressing the Christian life in its entirety—the full range of responses to God and neighbor.[46]

---

[45] For a study of Häring's pastoral approach to marriage, see Don Anthony Piraro, "A Program for Spiritual Growth for Married Couples, Utilizing Their Lived Experience and the Biblical Image of Marriage as Covenant of Conjugal Love" (D.Min. diss., Catholic University of America, 1985).

[46] J. Gallagher (204–5) claims that Häring rejects the manualists' moral legalism and creates a "healing" model for pastoral ministry: "Häring's introduction of concepts such as invitation and response, conversion, and the following of Christ provide a significantly different orientation in terms of the cure of souls."

In many ways Häring retains the earlier manualists' approach that moral theology aids ministry in the sense that it offers priests a way of understanding the moral life so that they can minister, preach, and teach effectively. Häring also reaches beyond the manualists by recognizing that moral theology also addresses itself to the lay Christian. In this manner his approach to moral theology overcomes the long-standing split between spiritual and moral theology—the former addressed to a spiritual elite and the latter addressed to those who need to know the minimum requirements necessary for salvation. In the spirit of the Vatican II, Häring presents his sacramental-moral theology as the path to holiness for all Christians, not only to priests. For example, Häring states in the introduction to *The Law of Christ* that the book is written in such a way as to "keep the technical terminology at a minimum and to provide a text within the grasp of the earnest layman and also suitable for ready use by preacher and confessor for whom it should lighten the burden of presenting the eternal truths in a manner befitting our times. The very fact that a moral theology has been adapted to the capacity of the interested non-theologian may prove to be its best recommendation to the theologian and director of souls."[47] He acknowledges that this influence comes from the nineteenth-century Tübingen theologian, J. M. Salier. But it also directly relates to the blind obedience to external law, both Nazi and church law, that convinced him of the need to move moral theology away from legalism and minimalism towards personal freedom and responsibility in relationship to God.[48]

In addition, his work as a medic during the war brought him into contact with wounded soldiers and poor peasants. Although forbidden by the Nazis to perform religious ceremonies, Häring recounts the many times he broke this law as he sought to serve the religious needs of soldiers and civilians. He faced situations in which both pastoral sensitivity and creative moral decision making were required, especially in the face of death. Pastoral work was the basis of his theology: "Theology has to be lived, above all, in its pastoral dimensions."[49]

---

[47] *LC* 1:ix; *FF*, 80.

[48] *MWC*, 33. See *EW*, 77, for a story about church legalism and Häring's struggle to overcome it.

[49] *FF*, 119. For a story about counseling soldiers during the war, see *EW*, 49–52.

Häring's pastoral approach to questions of abortion, divorce, and contraception has been noted many times by Richard A. McCormick, S.J. In "Notes on Moral Theology," which McCormick wrote in *Theological Studies* from 1965 to 1984, he discusses Häring's helpful distinction between moral theology, that operates with general rules applied to specific cases and pastoral prudence, which looks at the art of the possible. Häring rightly notes, according to McCormick, that "invincible ignorance" refers to the "existential wholeness of the person, the over-all inability to cope with a certain moral imperative. This inability can exist not only with regard to the highest ideals of the gospel, but also with regard to a particular prohibitive norm."[50]

Häring's pastoral sensitivity encourages a new tone and approach to moral problems. After Häring, moral theology was no longer solely concerned with the moral minimum or the sacrament of penance. Häring redefines the task of the moral theologian as that of guiding the Christian community to live the gospel as fully as possible. Häring's pastoral approach reminds moral theologians to consider how the discipline of moral theology serves as a guide for the Christian life and ministry. In that sense, it requires a solid biblical and dogmatic foundation in order to be fully integrated with other aspects of the Christian life.

The Integration of Dogmatic, Spiritual, and Sacramental Theology into Moral Theology

One of the major reforms of the Council of Trent (1545–63) was the creation of formal education for priests in order to combat liturgical abuses among the clergy. Courses of study were developed which covered different areas of theology—dogma, morals, canon law. Over time, these areas became distinct subdisciplines, each with its own specialists, authorities, and literature. Moral theology was created from the courses of study and a distinct body of literature for the training of priests as confessors emerged. On the one hand, the division between moral theology and dogmatic theology allowed deeper and more sys-

---

[50] Richard A. McCormick, s.j., *Notes on Moral Theology: 1965–80* (Lanham, Md.: University Press of American, Inc., 1981) 499. For a similar discussion of Häring's view on divorce and remarriage in response to the 1980 Vatican Synod, see Richard A. McCormick, s.j., *Notes on Moral Theology: 1981–84* (Lanham, Md.: University Press of America, Inc., 1984) 102–4.

tematic work on specific moral problems. On the other hand, it led to the isolation of moral theology from issues and topics in dogmatics.[51]

John Gallagher argues that after the Council of Trent moral theology separated Aquinas' moral thought from his dogmatic theology, with serious consequences.[52] Aquinas viewed theology as a complete system: according to his *exitus/reditus* schema, all things go out from and return to God. Aquinas did not consider these to be two separate, unrelated questions but rather two dimensions of human existence; one part could not be understood without the other. According to Gallagher the manualists divided the *Summae* into separate treatises that "may have been well-intentioned, it may have met a pedagogical need, but it undermined the unifying schema of the theological vision of Aquinas."[53] One of the outcomes of this split is a legalistic moral system in which law and grace are separated from other theological doctrines, particularly the doctrine of providence.[54] The result is a system of laws and obligations for Christians to fulfill in order that they may merit the rewards of eternal life. But Aquinas' nuanced theology of providence, according to Gallagher, was no longer considered within the framework of moral theology, and so God's relationship to human existence was not fully explicated.

[51] This isolation has been noted by several scholars. See John Mahoney, *The Making of Moral Theology: A Study of the Roman Catholic Tradition* (Oxford: Clarendon Press, 1987) 29, 45; Servais Pinckaers, "Revival of Moral Theology," *Cross Currents* 7 (1957) 60; and, on spiritual theology, Josef Fuchs, *Human Values and Christian Morality* (Dublin: Gill and Macmillan, 1967) 32–34.

[52] Karl Rahner argues that the split had serious consequences for dogmatic theology as well. The scholastic dogma textbooks were dry and lifeless and had failed to explicate the central paradigms of the Christian life. The consequence is that dogma becomes "esoteric" and moral theology "is in danger of becoming a peculiar mixture of philosophical ethics, natural law, a positivism based on canon law, and casuistry; in such a mixture the *theology* (both positive and speculative) in 'moral theology' is only a distant memory." Rahner, "The Prospects for Dogmatic Theology, *Theological Investigations 1* (Baltimore: Helicon Press, 1961) 1–18.

[53] J. Gallagher, 69–70.

[54] J. Gallagher (69) devotes a lengthy analysis to Aquinas' understanding of providence, a doctrine that holds a central place in all Aquinas' writings. Gallagher believes that this was a polemic against the Averoists who argued that divine providence did not reach the concerns of individuals. This doctrine explained how God sustains all things and moves them toward their goal. For humans, this plan existed in God's mind and directed each individual. The plan was carried out through "secondary causes," e.g., other persons. "As the law and grace were construed as external means by which God influenced human acts, so he also actively governed through the intrinsic principles of intellect and will. Every power of intelligence was derived from him as the primary intelligent being. The will was moved to good because it was sufficiently and effectively moved by God—only God could fulfill the will."

Moral theology, as it develops after Trent, had a specific purpose: to counsel priests who heard the confessions of ordinary Christians. The manualist tradition concentrates on problems of conscience (what was morally permissible or not) in order to ensure the right conduct to merit salvation; it uses casuistry to define acts as sinful according to a body of general principles and norms that are found in divine and natural law. Consequently moralists became concerned solely with the minimum requirements of salvation.

The creation of distinct theological disciplines had further consequences. Spiritual theology developed in the seventeenth century as the discipline, in contrast to moral theology, that focused on the elite few who went beyond these minimum requirements in order to lead a life of holiness and achieve perfection. Spiritual theology developed an understanding of the Christian pursuit of perfection and the methods for achieving mystical contemplation with God.

The sacraments are also treated separately from dogmatic theology. The rubrics for the correct administration and reception of the sacraments are defined within canon law and summarized at the end of moral theology manuals. Sacramental theology, from the Council of Trent until the liturgical movement of the late nineteenth century, which culminated in the vast changes of Vatican II, was reduced to the same kind of legalism found in moral theology. Both lacked a strong theological foundation. Thus spiritual, sacramental, and moral theology became distinct disciplines separate from each other and from dogmatic theology.

As theology was divided into discrete disciplines that addressed particular areas of the Christian life, the Christian moral and spiritual life were separated. The biblical and historical studies that flourished in the early twentieth century, however, showed that the patristic writers, as well as Aquinas, did not hold this distinction. The liturgical movement also revealed the close connection in the patristic period between the sacramental life of the community and the moral and spiritual development of the individual.

Häring broke from the manualist tradition by expanding his moral theology to include dogmatic, spiritual, and liturgical theology. Häring states at the outset of *The Law of Christ* that the "purpose is an integration and synthesis of various systems."[55] Curran credits Häring with drawing together various disciplines of theology into

[55] *LC* 1:viii.

his moral thought: "These newer approaches and vistas were epito-mized in Fr. Bernard Häring, who almost single-handedly pointed Catholic moral theology in new directions in the pre-Vatican II church. Häring's insistence on overcoming the dichotomy between moral theology and spiritual theology not only countered the legal-ism and minimalism of the manuals of theology but also gave moral theology a scriptural and liturgical dimension which it had previ-ously lacked."[56]

First, Häring's moral theology incorporates dogmatic theology; in-deed, it is established upon the central dogmas of Christian theology: creation, redemption, the Trinity, and Christology. Second, Häring re-jects the split between moral and spiritual theology and argues that every Christian is called to a life of holiness and perfection, antici-pating one of the central teachings of Vatican II.[57] Furthermore, his understanding of the relationship of religion to morality, and of the central role of the life of prayer and worship in the formation of dis-cipleship, draws together spiritual, liturgical, and moral theology. Third, Häring integrates the insights from the liturgical movement and creates a new way of understanding the relationship between the sacraments and the moral life.

Bernard Häring's early work initiated a significant change in Catholic moral theology. He overcame the juridical model predomi-nant in Catholic moral theology through his use of Scripture and of new philosophies emphasizing personhood and values, his broad understanding of the pastoral work of the moral theologian, and his

---

[56] Curran, *Ongoing Revision*, 264. Curran emphasizes this point again in *Transition and Tradition* (3–4): "Perhaps the most basic change in moral theology has been the orienta-tion of the discipline itself . . . . moral theology became separated from the other aspects of theology—especially scriptural, systematic and spiritual theology—and was character-ized by minimalism, legalism, extrinsicism and juridicism. The Tübingen School of moral theology and the Thomistic renewal in the twentieth century reacted against such an ap-proach, but Bernard Häring's *The Law of Christ* together with his other prolific writings and lectures has had the most influence in changing the orientation of moral theology." See also "Horizons," 102.

[57] "Häring boldly teaches that the universal vocation of all Christians to perfection is the fundamental consideration in moral theology. Conversion is not just a once for all time action, but rather a continual conversion is the law of life for the Christian. . . . Häring vigorously attacks the theory that only a few Christians are called to perfection. All those called to perfection do not leave the world and live in monasteries to follow the evangelical counsels while the majority of ordinary Christians are content to remain in the world and merely obey the ten commandments." Curran, *New Look*, 149–50. See also Curran's discussion of this in *Critical Concerns*, 9–11. See *Lumen Gentium*, 5 on the call to holiness.

dogmatic foundation for morality as well as the integration of spiritual and sacramental theology. His accomplishments have been significant and many recognize the way in which *The Law of Christ* served as an important bridge or transition between an old and a new world. Moving forward, however, was not without its limitations.

Common Criticisms of Häring's Thought

Häring could devote all his time to academic scholarship, but his primarily pastoral orientation shows through in the countless conferences, institutes, and retreats he has given all over the globe. Some of Häring's writings seem superficial and betray a rather hasty preparation. Häring would probably defend such books and articles, despite their obvious shortcomings, as another way of bringing the renewal in Catholic life and thinking to an ever wider audience.[58]

———————————— Charles Curran, *A New Look at Christian Morality*

Criticisms of Häring's scholarship have generally fallen into three categories. First, Häring's work is seen as an important transition between the legalistic approach of the moral theology manuals and the shift toward a more biblical and pastoral approach to moral issues after Vatican II, but it did not go beyond this initial contribution to the field. For example, Charles Curran states that, "*The Law of Christ* betrays its age and reveals its transitional character. Häring has taken the traditional moral theology with its strongly scholastic, philosophical underpinnings and put it in the larger context of a scripturally based, covenant relationship between God and man."[59] And in his review of Häring's *Faith and Morality in the Secular Age*, James Gustafson expresses a similar sentiment: "His many books since Vatican II have not broken new fertile soil. . . . There is little penetrating insight or scholarship to compensate for its datedness."[60]

Vatican II seemed to grant permission for new ways of thinking and moral theologians in the 1960s and 1970s pursued both philosophical issues and particular moral problems with great care and creativity. Häring did not make major contributions in either of these areas. In the case of value theory and personalism, for example, his use of these

———

[58] Curran, *New Look* (156) attributes Häring's "transitional" stature to his commitment to bring the teachings of Vatican II to the wider Church.

[59] Ibid.

[60] Gustafson, "Faith and Morality," 140.

theories lacks philosophical integration and coherence.[61] By placing such strong emphasis on the experiential in both religious and moral terms, Häring did not consider either metaphysical or philosophical claims as they pertain to moral discourse. In fact, he goes so far as to reject "all philosophical speculation primarily concerned with the metaphysical categories of being and beings."[62] His approach is largely descriptive, which again serves his pastoral emphasis, but many philosophical issues remain unexamined in his work.

A second criticism of Häring's work focuses on the role of norms and laws, particularly prohibitive norms, in Catholic moral theology. This is not to say that Häring does not consider laws and norms—he does so in relationship to value theory and "goal commandments"— but the problem remains, as Richard McCormick has stated, that moral claims require justification, particularly in searching to find the right behavior in difficult circumstances.[63] He fails to integrate value theory into discussions of specific moral problems, particularly in his early works.[64] For example, John Gallagher criticizes *The Law of Christ* because the explication of value theory which appears in volume 1 is not applied to specific moral issues in volume 2:

[61] Curran, *Critical Concerns*, 12, on *Free and Faithful in Christ*.

[62] *FFC*, 30.

[63] McCormick, *Notes on Moral Theology, 1981–1984*, 22. Hamel (77) makes a similar critique in terms of Häring's contribution to medical ethics. Häring helped frame Catholic medical ethics in terms of an ethics of disposition and virtue, but contributed little to the conversation about moral norms as they apply to decision-making in difficult situations.

[64] In *LC* 1:227–36 Häring defines moral norms according to value theory: "A norm of morals is not arbitrary restraint interfering with liberty, but the summons and invitation to the exercise of liberty arising from the value in the object, an invitation to man to preserve and nurture value in freedom. A norm which is not founded in a value and which does not present a duty through a relation to value has no moral force binding the will." Häring also considers the traditional categories of eternal, natural, and human laws (*LC* 1:236–52), but summarizes these categories in general terms. He also considers the New Law, the law of Christ, (*LC* 1:252–66) which does "not abolish the Law" but interiorizes it so that "obedience to the commandments of the law attains its fulfillment only in the imitation of Christ." Thus, Häring draws value theory and imitation into his discussion of law, but he does not specify norms of conduct, nor delineate prohibitive norms. A good example of Häring's generalizing of the categories can be found in *CRCW*, 44. In *FFC*, 24 Häring is even more suspicious of negative prohibitions: "In all these perspectives of the Old and especially of the New Testament, there is no place for a mere code morality or an allowance to confine oneself to static norms. . . . Doubtless there are norms in the sense of guidelines or 'goal commandments' and norms which indicate what opposes the kingdom of justice, peace and love, and therefore contradicts the new life in Christ; but the efficacy and clarity of these norms are in the salvation truth that makes us know God and know man in his dignity and his total vocation." See also the section on normative ethics, *FFC* 1:338–67.

Indeed at many points Häring attempted to discern particular moral values in relation to concrete moral issues. But when he turns to negative prohibitions, the mode of argument and language becomes quite traditional. . . . The point at issue here is not the moral rightness or wrongness of such actions, but rather that once a theologian has turned to the central role of value for theological ethics and to the centrality of person over nature, it becomes questionable whether such a presentation of specific moral topics remains consistent with or appropriate to the proposed moral theory.[65]

Joseph Omoregbe makes a similar point in his study of the evolution of Häring's thought. He argues that Häring applied an "axiological-personalistic" approach in his *General Moral Theology* but returned to the traditional deontological approach when he addressed questions of particular moral issues, for example, sexuality. Omoregbe explains this inconsistency in terms of "the weight of tradition and authoritarian conservatism that prevented him from applying these principles consistently to these issues from the beginning. Häring wanted to consistently apply his personalistic principles to the question of organ transplantation, and he came to the conclusion that there was nothing wrong with it, that it was morally justified. But (as he tells us) the Pope (Pius XII) condemned it as immoral, and Häring had to withdraw his view until after the Pope's death."[66] Omoregbe argues that Häring's later writings are more consistent: "the result was that he changed his views regarding these issues." Häring's pastoral focus, however, is limited in this respect: he does not help pastors and Christians in understanding the place of moral norms and laws, particularly prohibitive norms, in the sacramental-moral life.

Third, Häring's approach to moral decision making, especially in his early work, is cautious and hesitating, often when his own posi-

---

[65] J. Gallagher, 176. This same point is made by Raphael Gallagher and Charles E. Curran. R. Gallagher states: "If, at times, his synthesis is not fully coherent, or if the special part of *The Law of Christ* seems at odds with the basic principle of the first part, that is because of the pioneering nature of the work. The originality of *The Law of Christ* is not in its systematic-speculative thought but in the vision it ultimately implies." Raphael Gallagher, C.Ss.R., "The Manual System of Moral Theology Since the Death of Alphonsus," *Irish Theological Quarterly* 51/1 (1985) 12. See Curran's discussion of *Free and Faithful in Christ*, "Horizons," 104.

[66] Joseph Omoregbe, "Evolution in Bernard Häring's Ethical Thinking," *Louvain Studies* 7 (1978) 50.

tion differs from official Catholic teaching.[67] McCormick cites several examples of Häring's moral analysis which, when combined with his pastoral sensitivity and cautiousness regarding Vatican censorship, results in a confused argument. In a discussion on divorce, McCormick states, "His essay is vintage Häring, which is to say that it is characterized by obvious Christlike kindness and compassion, pastoral prudence, a shrewd sense of the direction of things, and a generous amount of haziness."[68] Häring can be seen as an equiprobabilist in the tradition of Alphonsus Liguori, but as many have noted his thinking on moral problems is at best wavering and a bit fuzzy.[69]

Häring's work has thus been seen as transitional, lacking integration between value theory and moral norms, and cautious to the point of being confusing.[70] Most scholars view Häring's writings as being important historically for understanding changes in Catholic moral theology but not as contributing to current discussions regarding moral problems and moral theory.[71]

An Overlooked Accomplishment: Morality and the Life of Worship

Since worship in its important moments is chiefly expressed by the liturgy and the sacraments, it is not surprising to find these taking the prime place in this [Häring's] moral synthesis. This is a new achievement. It is true that previous treatises on moral theology have dealt with the sacraments— and sometimes at considerable length—but they have done so in a totally

---

[67] See Mark Schoof, *A Survey of Catholic Theology, 1800–1970* (Paramus, N.J.: Paulist Press, 1970) 149–50, for a discussion of theologians of renewal in the 1950s who were cautious in regards to the magisterium.

[68] McCormick, *Notes, 1965–1980*, 340.

[69] *FFC* 1:288–89.

[70] Despite these criticisms, Gustafson ("Faith and Morality," 140) has defended Häring's work and his overall contribution to the field of moral theology: "It has become somewhat fashionable in theological circles to respond to the work of Bernard Häring in a somewhat condescending way. It is my judgment, however, that he will be seen to be a pivotal figure in the history of moral theology in the twentieth century both in the Catholic tradition, and in an ecumenical perspective. While *The Law of Christ* (3 vols.) clearly contains strains between the various strands that are brought together, it opened up many possibilities for further developments by theologians, by clergy and religious, and perhaps also by the laity."

[71] For example, William Spohn's book on Scripture and ethics makes no mention of Häring's work, even though it is very close to Häring's position on an ethics of the heart and affections. William C. Spohn, s.j., *What Are They Saying about Scripture and Ethics?* (Mahwah, N.J.: Paulist Press, 1984).

different spirit. They discuss them from the canonical standpoint of validity, or as new "duties" added to others, but not as an actual condition of all moral life. To place the sacraments "at the heart of life" is, in fact, to renounce the conception of morality as simply a perfecting of oneself through personal effort, and to place oneself in the sphere of influence of Christ dead and gloriously risen.[72]

————————— F. Bourdeau and A. Danet, *Introduction to The Law of Christ*

Häring's break from the neo-Thomist manualists and their understanding of the relationship between worship and the moral life was achieved in three ways:[73] by emphasizing the path of conversion, perfection, and holiness for all Christians, by establishing the sacraments as the foundation of the moral life rather than as obligations derived from morality, and by redefining the virtue of religion.[74] Some scholars have clearly missed this contribution. John Gallagher, for example, notes that Häring does not include a section dealing with the canon law of the sacraments, which allows him to create a less legal and juridical approach to moral theology in favor of a "healing" model. Gallagher misses a significant point: Häring drops the canonical approach to sacraments, but embraces a sacramental theology as his fundamental moral theology. In fact, *The Law of Christ* is the last manual that retains a connection between the sacraments and the moral life.

Häring overcomes the long-standing split between moral and spiritual theology. These disciplines, since Trent, were distinguished by their aim: moral theology defined the minimum requirements of the Christian life to ensure salvation, and spiritual theology defined

---

[72] F. Bourdeau and A. Danet, *Introduction to the Law of Christ* (Staten Island: Society of St. Paul, 1966) 237–38.

[73] J. Gallagher, 204.

[74] The terms worship, liturgy, and sacraments are used interchangeably in Häring's work and throughout this study. Worship is the broadest of the three terms and refers to any act of reverence, internal or external, private or communal, that is directed to God in acknowledgment of God's holiness, grace, and mercy. Liturgy, which comes from the Greek meaning "any work done for the people" was, by the fourth century, used to refer to the ritual celebration of the Lord's Supper—a work done by the bishop or priest for the people. Sacraments, in the Catholic community, have traditionally referred to seven ritual actions, instituted by Christ, to confer grace. The liturgical movement sought to redefine sacraments according to Augustine's formulation of "signs of faith" in order to emphasize a broader notion of sacramentality. Edward Schillebeeckx's ground-breaking work *Christ the Sacrament of the Encounter of God* (New York: Sheed and Ward, 1963) became the central treatise for this new understanding of sacrament as personal encounter with God.

what one was to do to go beyond these minimum requirements to achieve perfection through prayer, contemplation, and mystical union. Häring rejects this split by claiming that the life of perfection, holiness, and growth in God's grace is the call of all baptized Christians, and he demonstrates how the life of prayer, contemplation, and the interior and exterior acts of the virtue of religion are related to the moral life.

He also rejects the long-held position among spiritual theologians, particularly the neo-Thomist Jacques Maritain, that contemplation constitutes the highest form of "communion" with God. For Häring, contemplation has its proper place in the Christian life, but worship serves as the source and summit, the "warp and woof" of the Christian life, because it places the believer in dialogue and communion with both God and the neighbor.

Häring integrates sacramental and spiritual theology together with moral theology in ways not done previous to the publication of *The Law of Christ*, and he continued this pattern throughout his career. Moral theology today, however, does not encompass the sacraments, particularly reconciliation, within the scope of the discipline. Biblical and dogmatic theology has been incorporated into moral theology, but sacramental theology is considered a distinct discipline.

A second way in which Häring departs from the neo-Thomists is his rejection of the legalistic approach to the sacraments as well as their status as a subdivision of moral theology. In the moral theology manuals going back to the Council of Trent, the obligations concerning the valid administration and reception of the sacraments are treated in the third and final part of the manuals. Rather than defining worship and sacraments as moral obligations that bind the Christian, Häring places the sacraments and worship at the center of the Christian life by redefining them within the context of his theology of response and dialogue. Drawing upon the work of the liturgical movement, Häring seeks to place worship in right relationship to the life of moral action and spiritual growth.

In Häring's early works, particularly *The Law of Christ*, he redefines the relationship between worship and morality within the scholastic framework by reconceiving the role of the virtue of religion; in later writings he focuses on adoration. In these early works, Häring retains the structure of the manuals while radically altering the substance and content. For example, he retains sections on law, conscience, and special moral problems but adds sections on religion and morality, responsibility, value theory, and the virtue of religion. He also drops the third section on the sacraments, a standard part of the manuals. Rather than discussing each of the seven sacraments, Häring places worship at the center of the religious-moral life.[75]

Häring returns to Aquinas' understanding of the virtue of religion as the most important of the moral virtues but rejects Aquinas' (and the manualists') definition of religion as a moral virtue under the virtue of justice. According to the traditional understanding, the virtue of justice determines what is owed to another, and religion consists of determining what is owed to God. Häring rejects this juridical understanding of religion and argues that religion is a unique virtue because it stands between the theological and moral virtues, sharing characteristics of both types of virtue. Religion is similar to the theological virtues because it is directed toward God and similar to the moral virtues because it is directed toward external expression (signs, symbols, rituals). Its unique role means that religion is animated by and expresses faith, hope, and love but also provides the context for the conversion to and development of attitudes and dispositions that foster the moral virtues. While Häring maintains that religion and morality are philosophically distinct realities, for the Christian a religious morality means that persons' response to the divine initiative must find expression in both cult and service.

* * * *

The audience for my teaching. . . .was the adult Christian, that is, priests and lay people on their way to becoming adult Christians. . . . it no longer deals just with "saving souls," but with saving the world, with training adult Christians who feel and demonstrate a sense of responsibility for the Church and the world.[76]

———————————— Bernard Häring, *Free and Faithful in Christ*

Häring's use of the phrase "the law of Christ" as the title and theme of his first major work is provocative indeed. His radical departure from the legalism and minimalism of the manualists and his

---

[75] Häring discusses the seven sacraments in *A Sacramental Spirituality* (New York: Sheed and Ward, 1965) 44–278, subsequently referred to as *SS*; and *Sacraments and Your Everyday Life: A Vision in Depth of Sacramentality and Its Impact on Moral Life* (Slough, United Kingdom: St. Paul Publications, 1976) 181–244, subsequently referred to as *SEL*.

[76] *FF*, 81.

use of biblical images and disposition ethics places "the law of Christ" in Pauline rather than Thomistic terms. But Häring is also a German Catholic born at the beginning of the twentieth century, and his life spans the traumatic events of German history through two world wars as well as a period of turbulent change moving through the Catholic world. As a pastor and theologian he sought to guide Christians in making sense of a changing world where religious and political authoritarianism enslaved people to false concepts of self, God and community. The themes of his moral theology—freedom, responsibility, and existential choice—are reminiscent of other theologians from his generation. Within his system, these themes compose a particular theological and practical vision of the Christian life. Theologically, he uses the concepts of responsibility and dialogue to define the divine-human relationship made known in Christ. Practically, he explains worship not in terms of a moral obligation, but as the source of achieving the full imitation of the life of Christ. The imitation of Christ is motivated and sustained by a love for God; it is not a commandment or obligation that forces and binds the believer to a rigid set of cultic and moral laws. Rather, the imitation of Christ is achieved through the community's contact with Christian signs and symbols, its hearing and preaching of the Word, and its participation in the mysteries of the faith.

Chapter 2

Moral Theology
and Sacramental Practice

*Largely mechanical in nature, they [penitentials] placed an excessive stress
on sin and satisfaction for sin, disregarding the Christian ideal and many
fundamental moral principles. They are the first example of an unfortu-
nate tendency throughout the later history of moral theology, namely, the
categorizing or codifying of morality by stressing abstract cases and sins,
without due attention to their basis in moral principle.*[1]

———————————————— George Regan, *New Trends in Moral Theology*

From its beginnings Roman Catholic moral theology has been
closely linked to the sacrament of reconciliation. With the rise of private confession in the Middle Ages, a body of literature developed,
the penitentials and *Summae Confessorium,* that aimed at assisting
confessors in identifying the degree of sinfulness in human actions,
and the penance, or work to be performed that restored a Christian's
relationship to God. From the Council of Trent to the Second Vatican
Council, this literature took the form of manuals (*Institutiones Theologiae Moralis* and the neo-Thomist manuals) that defined the moral
acts, sins, and commandments regarding ethical behavior but also
treated the seven sacraments from the viewpoint of moral obligations and duties. The "theological genre" that shaped moral theology for nearly one hundred years prior to Vatican II has a distinctive
structure, style, and content.[2] From the earliest penitentials to the

---

[1] George Regan, *New Trends in Moral Theology: A Survey of Fundamental Moral Themes* (New
York: Newman Press, 1971) 24. Mahoney's study (7) places great emphasis on the overwhelmingly legalistic character of moral theology and the deficiencies of this approach.

[2] J. Gallagher (30) argues that these manuals were the "principal and frequently the
exclusive course" which prepared seminarians for the sacramental ministry.

twentieth-century neo-Thomist manuals this literature shared one aim: to guide priests in the proper administration of the sacrament of penance.

Bernard Häring's work emerges from two reform movements that began in the nineteenth century: the work of Catholic theologians from the University of Tübingen who were drawing new insights from biblical and historical studies into moral theology, and the liturgical movement, where similarly scholars were searching for the biblical foundations and historical development of the liturgy and sacraments. For many scholars in the late nineteenth and early twentieth century the Catholic Church's response to the modern world in the form of neo-scholasticism and neo-Thomism was insufficient. But what would Catholic theology look like outside of that traditional framework? Häring is one of many theologians who sought to make sense of the new discoveries and he did so in a most creative and perhaps singular way in the field of moral theology by drawing insights from the Tübingen tradition together with the sacramental theology emerging from the liturgical reformers.

Aids for Confessors: The Pastoral Focus of Moral Theology

The theologian, for his part, should be able to find in this moral theology— such is the earnest hope of the author—not only the essential materials for instruction in moral doctrine, but also what he may need as confessor and director of souls. For the confessor and director is not merely judge, but also pastor and guide of souls.[3]

—————————————————— Bernard Häring, *The Law of Christ,* vol. 1

The neo-Thomist manuals that constituted much of Catholic moral theology in the nineteenth and early twentieth century have their roots in a long history of pastoral guidance in the sacrament of penance. The history of this development, which can only be summarized here, falls into three general periods: the penitential books and *Summae Confessorium* that developed throughout the medieval period; the moral theology manuals that developed after the Council of Trent for the purpose of the training of priests, and a distinct kind of manual from the nineteenth century—the neo-Thomist manual.

[3] *LC* 1:x

Medieval Penitential Books and Summae Confessorium

The manuals of moral theology have their roots in monastic and Celtic Christianity of the sixth and seventh centuries. While public confession and penance had all but died by the sixth century, the monastic practice of seeking advice, guidance, and direction from a spiritual "father" began among the Celtic converts and became a central practice of medieval Christianity.[4] As private confession developed, monks needed assistance in defining sins and matching the offense with an appropriate penance. Books called "penitentials" were composed, consisting of lists of precise definitions of sins with penances matched to each offense. The penitentials served a practical purpose and did not aim at explicating a particular ethical or theological theory. As they became more widely used on the Continent, the penitentials became more detailed and specific in both their definition of sin and corresponding lists of penances.[5] And, as George Regan points out, this codification had a significant effect on the development of moral theology in terms of a nearly exclusive emphasis on law.

By the twelfth century several significant developments in the Church affected both moral theology and the practice of confession and penance: a theological renewal based upon the discovery of ancient Greek philosophy (primarily the work of Aristotle), the centralization of papal authority, the shift of ministerial responsibilities from monasteries to bishops and clergy, and, perhaps most importantly, the development of canon law. The elaborate and complicated scholastic theology of the sacraments became codified in the medieval summas and canon law. In 1140, Francis Gratian published *The Agreement of Disagreeing Canons*, popularly known as the *Decree*, the first comprehensive treatise on canon law, in which he sought to define the correct administration of the sacraments to insure their validity. Because the scholastics had taken up the question of causality,

---

[4] James Dallen, *The Reconciling Community: The Rite of Penance* (Collegeville: The Liturgical Press, 1991) 100–10. Albert R. Jonsen and Stephen Toulmin in *The Abuse of Casuistry: A History of Moral Reasoning* claim that the practice of examining cases regarding sinful behavior goes back to the patristic era (Berkeley, Calif.: University of California Press, 1988) 96. See Mahoney, chs. 1–4, and *LC* 1:5–10 for a discussion of the patristic period.

[5] See Jonsen and Toulmin, 98–100, for a more detailed discussion of the kinds of sins and penances defined by the penitentials. See Regan, *New Trends in Moral Theology*, 24, for a list of twenty varieties of murder, and Dallen, 110–18, for a description of the medieval sacramental rite.

the canonists sought to define the proper performance of the ritual in order to ensure its religious outcome. In effect, a minimalist approach to the sacraments developed. Canonists defined the minimum requirements for each sacrament according to the valid matter and form; they were not concerned with explaining the theological or experiential dimension of each sacrament. If the ritual was validly performed, the sacramental effect occurred *ex opere operato*.[6] Because the sacraments were the only path to salvation and because they worked on a supernatural level, Christians were obligated to receive them but not to experience their effects. As John Gallagher observes, "it produced the concept of sacraments as means to grace, mediated by the hierarchical church, which was controlled by a strong papacy and an increasingly powerful episcopacy."[7]

Regarding penance, the Fourth Lateran Council in 1215 called for all Christians who had committed a serious sin to make "an oral and secret annual confession" once a year and insisted upon the absolute secrecy of the confessor who was to "help the mostly uninstructed penitent to confess 'all his sins' and to enquire about their and his particular circumstances."[8] This requirement created a new kind of literature called the *Summae Confessorium* which, like the penitentials, had the purpose of guiding confessors in the sacrament of penance, but differed in regards to moral and legal theory—the authors attempted to assimilate and synthesize ideas from canon law and theology into one system.[9] During the thirteenth century, theologians began to compose treatises that systematized the patristic writings and conciliar and papal documents into one form. Häring calls this period the "Golden Age of the Penitential Books": "All these penitential summas have general tracts; most of them are arranged in alphabetical order; some are quite methodic, as is the

---

[6] Another issue was the question of "liceity," the legal requirements of sacraments. In many cases a sacrament could be illicit (some aspect may not conform to canon law) but still be valid.

[7] J. Gallagher, 19.

[8] Mahoney, 19. Canon 21 of the Fourth Council of the Lateran (DS, #812–14) states that the confessor is "to be discreet and careful in the manner of experienced physicians . . . diligently inquiring about the circumstances of the sin and the sinner, whereby he can learn what sort of advice to offer and what remedies to employ, making diverse attempts to heal the ailing person."

[9] J. Gallagher (18–19) points out the legal bias that encompassed the *Summa Confessorum*. Mahoney (19) points out that the *summas* were also a "product of a period in the Church obsessed by a desire to classify, digest, summarize and reconcile all possible data on any given subject."

Summa of Saint Antonine. But none can lay claim to be moral theology in the sense of the moral theological works of the seventeenth century. Nor are they manuals or texts of instruction in the sense of our current textbooks or handbooks of instruction, our *Institutiones Morales*. They are plain and simple *Lexica theologiae moralis,* a kind of dictionary of moral theology."[10]

A legal approach was applied to moral questions as well. The canonists, working with the newly discovered documents of Roman law, combined this legal tradition with patristic and conciliar texts to create a well-ordered juridical framework for the Church's belief and practice.[11] The framework fit easily with the penitential books and the *Summae Confessorum* and created an impressive organizational structure and rationalization of moral sin, but it meant that a legal model would dominate moral theology.[12]

Aquinas's theological achievement as well as the creative theological systems of the early scholastics had all but disappeared by the fifteenth century. The scholastics' question-and-answer method had given way to a deductive method that consisted of stating the answers absent the questions that formed Aquinas's inductive approach. Regarding morals, Charles Curran states that authors of the *summas* had "abandoned any attempt at a logical and speculative explanation of the material and just listed and explained the necessary items according to alphabetical order."[13] Canon law defined the valid matter and form of each sacrament with little attention to the theological foundation. Thus the long separation of dogmatic from moral and sacramental theology was underway.

By the late Middle Ages both sacramental and moral theology had undergone significant changes. The books used to aid priests in administering the sacrament of penance found theological support and

---

[10] *LC* 1:16.

[11] Jonsen and Toulmin (104–6) point out that medieval scholars wrongly believed that Justinian's code was a systematic and coherent whole.

[12] See Jonsen and Toulmin's explanation (115) of the fourfold impact of canon law upon the development of casuistry; Dallen, 156–62. Regan (25) notes: "Instead of viewing Christian morality as essentially an ethic of love as proposed by Jesus and the early Church, the canonists taught a morality of law. One searches in vain for stress on God's loving invitation to man, who is called to respond in love through Christ. Religion and morality are, on the contrary, seen as a rather impersonal adherence to a moral code imposed from without. Duty and obligation attain primary importance at the expense of loving response in union with and imitation of Christ."

[13] Charles E. Curran, ed., *Absolutes in Moral Theology?* (Washington, D.C.: Corpus Books, 1968) 12.

systematization in the work of Aquinas and other great theologians. But the impact of scholasticism and canon law introduced a legalistic approach into both areas of the Christian life that would only become stronger. A new kind of manual emerged in the sixteenth century in the wake of reforms defined by the Council of Trent and resurgence in scholasticism. The new manuals, which remained central to Catholic moral theology until the Second Vatican Council, were based on the tradition of defining sin and penance according to the penitential books and the *Summae Confessorum* with an even more elaborate approach to sin, conscience, and law.

Seminary Textbooks: Moral Theology Manuals (1540 to 1879)

John Gallagher divides the four-hundred-year history of moral theology manuals into three periods: (1) 1540–1650, which began with the revival of scholasticism and the publication of the *Ratio Studiorum* by the Jesuits;[14] (2) 1577–1879, during which the Jesuit manuals were refined and expanded to deal with probabilism; and (3) 1879–1960, when the neo-Thomist manuals provided the main content for seminary education. Gallagher's division helps in understanding the emergence of the neo-Thomist manuals in the nineteenth century.

In the first period, during the sixteenth century, the "second scholasticism" was initiated through the revival of Aquinas's theology by the Dominicans and Jesuits. Renewed interest in St. Thomas first spread throughout European Dominican houses of study, and the young Ignatius of Loyola, who founded the Jesuits in 1536, read Aquinas as a student and required that he be read by men joining his order.[15] New editions of Aquinas's works were printed and new commentaries written.[16] According to Häring, this period marks the "origin of moral theology" as it came to be known in the Catholic

---

[14] Jonsen and Toulmin (143) call the period from 1556 to 1656 the "century of maturity" for the method of casuistry.

[15] Gerald McCool, *Catholic Theology in the Nineteenth Century* (New York: Seabury Press, 1977) 1–35, defines three periods of scholasticism: the period immediately following Aquinas, the sixteenth-century revival of Aquinas among the Dominicans and Jesuits, and the rise of neo-Thomism and neo-scholasticism in the late nineteenth century. The sixteenth-century Dominican revival took place when Peter Crockaert required students at the University of Paris to read St. Thomas rather than Lombard's *Sentences*, which had been the standard textbook for centuries. Ibid., 17.

[16] McCool (17–20) discusses the differences that arose between the Jesuits and Dominicans in their interpretations of Aquinas. The Jesuit Francisco Saurez's (1548–1617) commentary became famous among his fellow Jesuits, and their approach became known as "Saurezianism." The Dominicans developed their own tradition, known as

tradition. But what began as a "splendid synthesis" of the speculative and practical gave way to the creation of a new manual and curriculum that defined moral theology as "an autonomous science with a practical orientation, leaving to dogmatic theology the entire area of the speculative."[17]

The development of the new manual was directly influenced by the Council of Trent (1545–1565). The Council recognized the need to reform abuses within the clergy, and it called for the establishment of seminary education in order to give rigorous and appropriate training to clergy who were expected to know Catholic theology and correct sacramental practice. In defining Roman Catholic beliefs, the Council adopted the revived scholastic approach and claimed, in opposition to the Protestant Reformers, no other theology as legitimate. The theology of penance did not undergo significant changes at the Council of Trent, and the practice was only slightly revised.[18] The Council affirmed the medieval practice that Catholics who had committed a serious sin were to receive the sacrament of penance once a year and, in addition were required to confess all serious sins according to circumstance, species, and number. Such precision in terms of knowledge about sin required a more educated priest who could determine both the nature of sin and the application of church law regarding penance.

In addition to clergy education, the Council demanded greater conformity to the prescribed rituals and published the Roman Missal in 1570 to insure uniform practice.[19] This uniformity was meant to guard against abuse and provide a universal foundation for the Church's practice; an unintended consequence, however, was a casuist approach to sacraments that also had its counterpart in morality.[20] The Roman Missal, and scholastic theology that supported the liturgical life of the Church, remained virtually unchanged until Vatican II.

Thomism. See Jonsen and Toulmin, 169–70. See *LC* 1:16–17 for a discussion of the main interpreters of Thomas Aquinas at this time.

[17] *LC* 1:17–18.

[18] Dallen, 176–80, on Trent's teaching on the sacrament of penance.

[19] The 1570 Missal declared the celebration of the private mass as normative. In the private Mass, developed in the 1200s, the priest took the role of deacon, lector, choir, and people.

[20] "But preoccupation with its exact observance came to absorb all energies; great thick volumes were written dealing casuistically with explanations of the rubrics of the Missal and Breviary. . . . It was the Age of Rubricism. Theodor Klauser has called this period of liturgical history 'The Epoch of Stagnation.'" Josef A. Jungmann, s.j., *Liturgical*

Moral theology took a similar turn to the method of casuistry after the Council of Trent. In 1586, the Society of Jesus responded to Trent's request that priests have a "more precise knowledge of Christian morality" by developing a curriculum for the seminaries. The *Ratio Studiorum,* a two-year course of study preparing priests to hear confessions, was designed to be both practical and pastoral. The curriculum consisted of two tracks. The first-year covered topics such as human acts, conscience, laws, sins, and the commandments, except the seventh. The second-year covered the seventh commandment, especially contracts, the sacraments, and the duties pertaining to married and religious life.[21]

Manuals developed—the *Institutiones Theologiae Moralis*—that soon became the central text for the training of all priests, not only the Jesuits.[22] The new manuals had both a positive and negative effect. Positively, they drew upon the revival of Aquinas's theology and developed a comprehensive analysis of moral problems and cases; negatively, they dropped Aquinas's central theological idea—man's last end—and, as Häring points out, this led to the further split between dogmatic and moral theology.

> The *Ratio Studiorum* (order of studies) of the Society of Jesus determined that in the houses of study the professors who were charged with lecturing on the *Summa* of Saint Thomas should limit their courses to the more basic principles of moral teaching. On the other hand, certain professors of moral doctrine were assigned the task of dealing professedly with 'cases of conscience' in moral matters. The theological activity of these latter professors of moral theology was different from that of the summas for confessors *(summae confessorum)* of the earlier period previously referred to. The goal of this present effort was to determine the doctrinal principles underlying the correct solution of cases. The result was the gradual development of an independent and self-sufficient moral discipline.[23]

Renewal in Retrospect and Prospect, trans., C. Howell (London: Burns and Oates, Challoner Books, 1965) 17.

[21] For an analysis of four Jesuit theologians from this period, see *LC* 1:19–20.

[22] According to J. Gallagher (24) the *ratio studiorum* became the standard for all clergy education. By 1600, the Jesuits had 372 colleges, and by 1669, 600 volumes of their textbooks had been published. Jonsen and Toulmin, 147–50.

[23] *LC* 1:18. See Jonsen and Toulmin, 149–55, for a discussion of the two tracks in Jesuit education and their impact on the development of casuistry. The Jesuits focused primarily on "how to choose a course of action prudently and virtuously, rather than how to ascend to a vision of eternal truth" (148).

The separation had serious consequences for moral theology. A legal approach to moral issues became even more central, and the theological foundation and substance all but vanished from the manuals. Moral theology became "an autonomous science with an exclusively practical orientation" that focused narrowly on cases of conscience. Häring notes that this exclusive emphasis on conscience accounts for the incorporation of canon law into moral theology at this time. "Certain tracts, in fact, are treated almost exclusively from the perspective of canon law, for example the treatise on matrimony and penance."[24]

This trend continued in the manuals published from 1577 to 1879. There was little innovation in method or content, and, as John Gallagher argues, the "casuistry of the canon law of the sacraments was being transferred to a casuistry of morals."[25] The manualists' legalistic approach to moral problems is exemplified in two ways. During the seventeenth and eighteenth centuries, the probabilism debate consumed moral theologians.[26] The controversy focused on two issues: to what extent a moral law was binding and the degree of certainty required for a law to be binding upon a person's conscience. As Jonsen and Toulmin point out probabilism was meant to "lighten the burden" of those with overly scrupulous consciences; however, its frequent use in the moral manuals led in an opposite direction—an "excessive laxism" for which casuistry became well known.[27] Second, a significant change regarding the structure of the manuals took place. Martin Azpilcueta, in 1556, published a handbook for confessors and penitents *(Enchiridion Confessariorum et Poenitentium)* that organized the material in a new way. The *summas* of the Middle Ages had been organized by topic and arranged alphabetically. Azpilcueta, however, arranged cases according to the Decalogue, "giving the

---

[24] *LC* 1:19. Regan (29–30) also notes: "Harmful casuistry prevailed, which reduced morality to a carefully constructed system of foreordained conclusions based on universally valid, abstract principles. . . . Such limited horizons soon left moral theology as a devitalized and insipid discipline of the obligatory and the minimal. A certain trend toward laxism followed as a natural consequence."

[25] J. Gallagher, 36–37. McCool (20–21) points to two reasons for this decline: the popular appeal of Enlightenment ideas that "led to contempt for scholasticism"; and the Jesuit suppression in 1772 which hampered theological developments.

[26] For a complete discussion of probabilism see Jonsen and Toulmin, 165–75, and Mahoney, 135–43.

[27] Jonsen and Toulmin, 168. See Mahoney, 91–94, for a discussion of the Jansenists' reaction against laxism in moral theology, and Jonsen and Toulmin, 231–49, for a discussion of Pascal's critique of the Jesuits.

work a logical sequence and stronger argument than the alphabetical style."[28] For the next few hundred years, most manuals used the Decalogue as a way to define sin, although a few followed Aquinas, who organized moral issues according to the moral virtues.[29]

One of the creative figures of this period, St. Alphonsus de Liguori (1696–1787), mediated between the extreme rigorists and laxists by developing a method called "equiprobabilism," which accepts a well-established probable opinion in matters of doubt and rejects the practice of allowing for a less probable opinion in light of a more probable one.[30] He developed this method in order to aid Redemptorist priests in their pastoral work. The Redemptorist Raphael Gallagher argues that Alphonsus's achievement centered upon three key ideas:

> (a) the general goal is a search for the truth, so that if the opinion in favour of the law is certainly more probable we must follow it; (b) in the life of the individual the dignity of conscience is paramount in that a person must not ultimately act merely according to external norms; rather the decision should be based interiorly on the goodness of the action; (c) at all levels of morality we must respect liberty: for instance, if the law is not properly promulgated it cannot be obligatory, since an uncertain law cannot impose a certain obligation.[31]

Between Alphonsus's death in 1787 and 1871, when he was declared a Doctor of the Church, moral theology went through a period of "questioning, doubt, and controversy."[32] The suppression of the Jesuits, the negative impact of Jansenism, and the growing influence

---

[28] Jonsen and Toulmin, 153. See p. 252 for a discussion of how the manualists moved from the general norm stated in the Decalogue to specific cases and then extreme examples.

[29] J. Gallagher (98) points out that whether the manualists used the commandments or the virtues to organize their material, the content of their moral theology was not affected.

[30] Jonsen and Toulmin, 175. See Frederick M. Jones, C.Ss.R. *Alphonsus de Liguori: Selected Writings* (New York: Paulist Press, 1999).

[31] R. Gallagher, "Manual System," 2. Mahoney (26) states, "The principal apostolate of the Order which he founded was to give popular missions, in which the hearing of confessions played a major part, and much of his effort went to the preparation of confessors who would be skilled moral theologians and would also have a mastery of casuistry." See *LC* 1:21–22, for a discussion of Alphonsus's influence on moral theology.

[32] Alphonsus was beatified in 1816, canonized in 1839, and declared a Doctor of the Church in 1871. In April 1950, Pope Pius XII, who began giving patron saints to professions, solemnly declared St. Alphonsus to be Patron of Confessors and of Moral Theologians. According to R. Gallagher, the debates during and after his lifetime were characterized by a general misunderstanding and misrepresentation of Alphonsus's views.

of Enlightenment philosophy led to a decline in theology. The moral theology manuals in particular were affected because they had little theological credibility and were not addressing the central social questions of the times.[33] In reaction to this weakened state greater papal control regarding faith and morals developed in the nineteenth century.[34]

From the Council of Trent until the late nineteenth century, moral theologians addressed moral issues according to the traditional scholastic method within the manualist tradition. These manuals were related to the penitentials and *summas* by their practical aim of assisting confessors in defining sins and penances. The manualists continued the long-standing emphasis on individual actions, sin, and law and listed sins according to the Ten Commandments. During this period, the specialization of moral theology and the incorporation of the sacraments meant that both disciplines became distinct from dogmatic theology. The "third scholasticism" that appeared in the second half of the nineteenth century reintroduced Aquinas's theological and philosophical method in Catholic theology and for moral theology this meant a further systemization of moral categories which now included Aristotelian scientific and metaphysical categories.[35]

Neo-Thomist Manuals of Moral Theology (1879–1960)

As Gerald McCool notes Catholic theology in the nineteenth century had two tasks: one defensive and another constructive. Theologians, first, sought to defend traditional Catholic categories against the Enlightenment's rationalism and religious skepticism, but they also sought to construct a positive system of Christian faith, like those of Fichte, Schelling, and Hegel, while maintaining both the transcendent and historical dimension of Christian revelation. The various attempts to reconcile faith and reason by engaging modern

---

[33] R. Gallagher, "Manual System," 3. See Jonsen and Toulmin, 270, for a discussion of casuistry after 1700.

[34] See Mahoney, 138, and ch. 4, "Teaching with Authority." See also Jonsen and Toulmin, 270.

[35] McCool states (29): "Nineteenth century scholastics were not necessarily neo-Thomists. The difference between a traditional scholastic and a neo-Thomist lay precisely in the neo-Thomist commitment to Thomism as a unified, Aristotelian science comprising philosophy and theology built upon an Aristotelian epistemology, anthropology, and metaphysics."

methods (e.g., Georg Hermes [1775–1831], Anton Günther [d. 1863], and the Tübingen School) were deemed by some to be a failure. Neo-Thomism emerges largely in response to the failure of these attempts to produce an "adequate and orthodox speculative system" and in recognition that one unified system of Catholic thought rather than a plurality of responses was needed. The neo-Thomists concluded that modern methods for dealing with rationalism were all dependent on a post-Kantian scientific method and that the only reliable epistemology and metaphysics for uniting faith and reason could be found in Thomas Aquinas. By the second half of the nineteenth century, the scholastic method had received papal approval, and the neo-Thomists were at the center of Roman Catholic thought.[36]

Leo XIII's encyclical *Aeterni Patris* (1879) called for the renewal of Thomism in all Catholic seminaries and colleges.[37] Leo XIII (1810–1903), considered to be the first modern pope, believed that Thomism offered the only alternative to the apparent weaknesses of modern philosophy. McCool summarizes Leo's argument in *Aeterni Patris*:

> The proper distinction between faith and reason which scholastic phi-
> losophy made possible, Leo wrote, could preserve the distinction be-
> tween philosophy and theology which modern systems of philosophy
> often blurred. By preserving that distinction, scholastic philosophy
> could mount strong philosophical arguments for the credibility of rev-
> elation without compromising the transcendence of Christianity's re-
> vealed mysteries. When employed by the theologian, it could organize
> the various parts of Catholic theology into an integrated, coherent
> whole; and it could provide the effective arguments needed for con-
> troversy with the Church's enemies. On its own strictly philosophical
> level, scholastic philosophy, which philosophized under the guidance
> of Christian revelation, could direct human reason more surely than
> the 'separated' systems of modern philosophy, which, on principle, ig-
> nored revelation.[38]

[36] McCool (17–20) argues that neo-Thomism won this battle in large part because other theologians could not solve these theological problems.

[37] See Gerald McCool, *The Neo-Thomists* (Milwaukee: Marquette University Press, 1994) 228–35, for a discussion of how Matteo Liberatore and Joseph Kleutgen, two early Thomists, began to assert that Aquinas's was the only philosophy and theology capable of countering the modern challenge. Both men had a great impact on Leo XIII, and so it is not surprising that when Leo became pope in 1878, he made Thomas's philosophy and the-ology the official methods of Catholicism the next year.

[38] McCool, *Neo-Thomists*, 35. Neoscholasticism, a "return to Catholic medieval thought in general" was another outcome of *Aeterni Patris*. See J. Gallagher, 49, for a discussion of

Moral theologians began to turn to neo-Thomism by the mid-1850s. The neo-Thomist moral theologians shared with their predecessors the goal of providing seminarians a "theological basis for a pastoral ministry focused on the sacraments" but departed from their "eclectic theological approach" and presented thorough summaries of Aquinas' moral theology.[39] This return to Aquinas meant that moral theologians expanded their treatment of cases to include a summary of Aquinas's treatise on man, with sections on human acts, conscience, and law. In addition, they added a third and final section on the sacraments, following Aquinas's three-part organization in the *Summa.*

The manualists were inspired by the neo-Thomist theologian Joseph Kleutgen (1811–1883), whose theological system McCool defines as "Catholic conclusion theology." Kleutgen's approach was "antisubjective and antihistorical," as was neo-Thomism in general, and this carried over into moral theology.[40] Conclusion theology was primarily deductive in its methodology, but its chief characteristic was the air of confidence that exuded even minor conclusions.

Although some of the better manualists began incorporating new historical and biblical information into their manuals, most ignored the scholarly breakthroughs in the late nineteenth and early twentieth century, particularly those from the liturgical movement. For example, a controversy among historians over the origins of penance took place in the 1880s but none of the ideas produced from this "enormous literature" had an impact whatsoever on moral theology. As Raphael Gallagher shows, the discipline turned in upon itself and became "vigorously conscious of its own proper methodology." He

---

neo-Thomism and neoscholasticism. McCool is critical of Gallagher's definitions of neoscholasticism and neo-Thomism; see Gerald A. McCool, s.j., review of *Time Past, Time Future*, by John A. Gallagher, in *Church History Review* 79 (July 1993) 499–501.

[39] J. Gallagher (48) argues that this first generation of neo-Thomists, particularly Kleutgen, directly influenced manualists in the twentieth century, while other forms of Thomism (e.g., traditional, historical, or transcendental Thomism associated with Gilson, Marchel, and Maritain) were largely ignored by moral theologians.

[40] "The syllogisms of an Aristotelian deductive science move from its self-evident first principles to its derived conclusions. In an Aristotelian 'science of faith' the Catholic theologian can proceed from his revealed first principles through his naturally known minor premises to his theologically certain conclusions. . . . Catholic speculative theology became a 'conclusion theology' whose aim was to derive an increasing number of theologically certain conclusions from its revealed first principles." McCool, *Catholic Theology*, 225. See, J. Gallagher, 49; McCool, *Catholic Theology*, 3–14, and chs. 7–8, for a discussion of Liberatore and Kleutgen, and *LC* 1:26–28.

calls the period after Vatican I the "age of specialization," in which moral theologians became absorbed with questions about the proper nature, object, and method of the manuals:

> Was it not legitimate therefore for moral theology to justify its own specialty as a study of what is of obligation and leave the other questions (e.g., of perfection) to others? The job of the confessor is after all a specialist one in that he is primarily a judge: why not a specialist science of moral theology to aid him? The manualist became more than ever convinced of the propriety of the casuistic method: if there were other questions there were other specialists to deal with them.[41]

The neo-Thomist manuals remained at the center of Catholic moral thought until the 1960s, when the manuals were replaced by new approaches to the discipline of moral theology and the sacrament of penance.

The strength of the neo-Thomist manuals is their common purpose, organizational structure, theology, and method. Their purpose remained that of the penitentials and *summas*—to help priests understand and utilize the Church's teachings regarding moral issues in order to ensure the proper administration and reception of the sacrament of penance. The seminary, which was the context for learning moral theology, tended to be isolated from external ideas and thus interpretation of moral questions remained internal to Church tradition and authority. Even though other areas of theology were engaging modern ideas, moral theologians were generally not open to new philosophical approaches, historical findings, or biblical insights. Their chief weakness emerged from this closed method. As R. Gallagher notes the manuals became consolidated into a tight narrow system in which the "only task was a perfection of its own unquestioned method. The agenda of the manuals was the manuals themselves."[42]

The neo-Thomist manuals are divided into three parts, following Aquinas's organization of moral theology. The first section, general moral theology, examines human acts, conscience, law, and sin. The second part, special moral theology, defines moral behavior accord-

---

[41] R. Gallagher, "Manual System," 8–9.

[42] Ibid., 9. J. Gallagher (41) makes a similar point: "These manuals were once again seminary texts intended for the preparation of young men for a sacramental ministry and especially as ministers of the sacrament of penance. They did not intend to give rise to speculation; they were not interested in assimilating the learning of the wider culture. To learn from these texts meant to learn their dogmatic positions. They were not university texts."

ing to the Ten Commandments or the virtues. The final section outlines the licit and valid administration and reception of the seven
sacraments as determined by canon law. As will be discussed in
chapters 5 and 6, moralists who used the schema of the commandments treated religion under the first three commandments. Those
who followed the virtues treated religion under the virtue of justice.
Both approaches define religion according to interior and exterior
acts, for example, adoration, prayer, sacrifice. In addition, they go to
great length to define sins against religion, for example, blasphemy,
irreligion, and superstition. Generally, there is little relationship between this section on religion and the third part on the sacraments,
although both address religious acts from a legal point of view.

The neo-Thomist manualists cite three sources to support their
teachings—the Bible, reason, and tradition. For the manualists, the
Bible is God's direct revelation to humanity and the source for
knowledge of the divine law, which is in turn interpreted by the
Church.[43] Reason consists of the human person's ability to discern
from the natural law (creation and nature) and the divine law the
moral principles for conduct. Tradition represents authorities from
the past, and for the neo-Thomist these include Augustine, Aquinas,
Alphonsus Liguori, conciliar and papal documents, and current
manualists. An interesting feature of the manuals is their authorship—a manual may have multiple authors and could be written
over several generations. A new author added his name to the list of
previous authors and updated the text.[44]

The manualists used two methods: scholasticism and casuistry. The
scholastic method consists of identifying a system of universal principles from the divine and natural law which can be further defined
into particular moral norms. As J. Gallagher points out the scholastic
system "presumes the existence of a whole which stands in need only
of clarification from within and defense against external opposition."[45] Because moral theology retained a practical approach to moral

[43] Many scholars, notably Curran and Gustafson, claim that the manualists use the
Scriptures as proof-texts. J. Gallagher (52) disagrees with this claim, arguing that the
manualists view Scripture and patristic commentaries on Scripture, as positive sources of
theology.

[44] "The authority of these writings was not the product of the talents or insights of a
particular author, but rather the authority of a self-authenticating tradition. The manuals
retain a medieval notion of authority residing in the text and the tradition, rather than in
the authority of the author" (J. Gallagher, 51).

[45] Ibid., 53.

problems, casuistry remained the primary method of defining the rightness or wrongness of Christian moral behavior. For the casuists, the general moral principles are given and must be applied to concrete particular circumstances, with special attention to the variety and exceptions within cases.[46]

From 1910 to 1940 moral theologians were consumed by a second period of questioning, doubt, and controversy in moral theology, according to Raphael Gallagher. Even though the manualists appeared entrenched in their own intellectual world, which was reinforced by the publication of the *Codex Juris Canonici* in 1918, and even though they showed little awareness of biblical, liturgical, or historical developments, challenges to the neo-Thomist system slowly began to appear. Three issues in particular arose: scholars recognized that casuistry "was not an end in itself" but needed "theological coherence"; the return to Thomas's original writings demanded a reexamination of the role of conscience; and Thomas's use of the virtues challenged the predominant schema of the commandments.

The neo-Thomist manuals stood at the center of Catholic moral theology for nearly one hundred years. They were cautious documents, neither incorporating new ideas nor questioning Church law, but they stood as faithful inheritors of a tradition of moral thinking that saw the moral life in terms of moral and sacramental action guided by the traditions of divine and natural law and moral reasoning. But change was slowly creeping into moral theology as moralists in the twentieth century began to see that neo-Thomism could not respond adequately to contemporary social and political issues. Further, questions of historical development and change challenged more static presentations of faith and morals, communal and biblical ecclesiologies challenged the individualist approach to moral and sacramental practice and the role of the laity vis-à-vis Christian faith and practice.

Seeds of Change:
Reform Movements in Liturgy and Moral Theology

Another reason for the demise of vigorous casuistry within the Roman Catholic tradition was the application of the technique to matters of ritual and ec-

---

[46] The theology of the neo-Thomists will be discussed in chs. 5 and 6. See J. Gallagher, 50–71, for a thorough discussion of neo-Thomist philosophy and theology.

clesiastical discipline. Proper performance of ceremonial ritual was required for the validity of the sacraments; thus questions about the appropriate manner of wearing vestments and correct gestures became important. Similarly, church discipline required attendance at Sunday Mass, fasting during Lent, abstaining from meat on Friday. Problems were posed about how late one could arrive at Mass in order to fulfill one's Sunday duty, how much food constituted a permitted meal, whether frogs' legs were meat or fish.[47]

————————— Albert Jonsen and Stephen Toulmin, *The Abuse of Casuistry*

The Liturgical Movement

There were no dramatic changes in the official theology and practice of the sacraments between the Council of Trent and Vatican II. Sacramental practice was defined according to the moral and legal obligations that were summarized in the third part of moral theology manuals, according to the rubrics of canon law. As moral theology became more consumed by casuistical disputes, Toulmin and Jonsen note, sacramental theology followed close behind. Even though the Church's liturgy became subjected to the same kind of legalism as moral theology, changes were beginning to emerge in both France and Germany as early as the eighteenth century.[48]

Historians mark the beginning of the liturgical movement in France when Prosper Louis Pascal Guéranger (1805–1875) in 1833, along with several priests, moved to St. Peter's Abbey at Solesmes in order that they might live the Rule of St. Benedict and celebrate the Divine Office according to its original and most authentic form.[49] In

[47] Jonsen and Toulmin, 272. The authors note that Henry Davis's moral theology manual, published in 1952, is dominated by these kinds of rules regarding the sacraments. 281 pages of the 474-page book address the valid administration of the sacraments.

[48] For a discussion of liturgical reforms in eighteenth-century France, which include the use of the vernacular, celebration at one altar, community Masses on Sunday, the use of the offertory procession, Communion under both species, and greater reception of Communion by the laity, see R. W. Franklin, "Guéranger and Variety in Unity," *Worship* 51 (September 1977) 378–99, and Kathleen Hughes, ed., *How Firm a Foundation: Voices of the Early Liturgical Movement* (Chicago: Liturgy Training Publications, 1990) 10. Also, see Hughes for a discussion of German reform that stressed communal masses, the singing of parts of the Mass by the laity, and the reform of the breviary. For a discussion of German liturgical reforms in the eighteenth century and those under Joseph II in the early nineteenth century, see Dom Olivier Rousseau, o.s.b., *The Progress of the Liturgy: An Historical Sketch* (Westminster, Md.: Newman Press, 1951) 51–55.

[49] Franklin argues that the liturgical movement arose from three simultaneous events in 1833: Guéranger's move to Solesmes; the beginning of the Oxford movement in England

order to do so, they undertook a comprehensive study of the liturgy in order to restore the French church to a pure form of liturgy that Guéranger believed was found in the Roman rite.[50] Guéranger was motivated by more than a desire for pure liturgy. He believed that liturgical renewal, based on a spirit of communal participation, would challenge the Enlightenment's emphasis on individualism and rationalism as well as extirpate the individualism fostered by popular devotions in the Church. According to Guéranger, the liturgy is the communal prayer of the Church and should be the center of the Church's life and activity. He abhorred the fact that the laity rarely attended the liturgy, and when they did they did not understand what was happening, had no role to play in the liturgy, or carried on with extra-liturgical devotions. Guéranger's concerns regarding the historical foundations of the liturgy, individual piety countering the communal aspect of the liturgy, and the passive role of the laity became the foundation of the liturgical movement.

The liturgical movement spans roughly 150 years, from Guéranger's initial work in the 1830s to Vatican II and the subsequent reforms of each sacrament up to the 1980s. The movement, which embraces a range of practices and thinkers in both Europe and North America, has three phases: monastic, parish and academic, and official.[51] The monastic phase begins with Guéranger and continues to the end of the nineteenth century and is primarily a

---

led by E. B. Pusey, and the publication of Johann Adam Möhler's *Symbolik* in Germany. Most scholars agree that Guéranger's work initiated the liturgical movement and Möhler's ecclesiology became its theological foundation.

[50] Benedictine monks at Solesmes spent more than sixty years exploring the history of non-Roman and medieval liturgical practices. This exploration was unraveling a long-held assumption that the liturgy had been handed down from the earliest Christians and celebrated in the same manner since the time of Christ. Trent had called for the reform of the liturgy by returning to the "ancient rite and norms of the Holy Fathers," and it was commonly believed that the 1570 missal was as close to the early Church's tradition as possible. But historical studies began to show that the missal was not the ancient rite but was based on a 1474 missal and reflected the traditions of thirteenth-century Christianity. In addition, scholars discovered that the Tridentine Mass was a composite of prayers, readings, and gestures from different times throughout history and that the liturgical and sacramental practices of Christianity had not always been consistent. Guéranger's desire to celebrate the liturgy in its purest form actually led to the undoing of the Tridentine model.

[51] I have identified these three phases for purposes of summarizing the liturgical movement. See Franklin (49:327) for a different arrangement of this same period. See Robert Tuzik, ed. *How Firm a Foundation: Leaders of the Liturgical Movement* (Chicago: Liturgy Training Publications, 1990) 6–13, for a chronology of activities from 1833 to 1989, which shows the relationship between European and American reformers.

Benedictine revival that begins at Solesmes and moves on to French and German abbeys at Beuron, Maredsous, Mont-César, and Maria Laach.[52] The monastic phase did not focus solely on monastic liturgy, but sought to spread reform through publications and people's personal experience and education at Solesmes. The monastic reforms came to Germany in the late nineteenth century; Maria Laach became the center of German liturgical reforms up to the 1950s.[53]

In the early phase, Johann Adam Möhler (1796–1838), stands out as central to the liturgical movement, particularly as it developed in Germany, although he never wrote directly about the liturgy. A leading member of the Catholic Tübingen School in the early nineteenth century, Möhler drew upon patristic texts to develop the notion of the Church as the Mystical Body of Christ. His idea that the Church and the sacraments are united through the mystery of the Incarnation became the central theological idea of the nineteenth-century liturgical movement. Möhler understood the Church to be "a visible, divinely constituted society which is the sacramental manifestation of God's saving mercy." The Romantic concept of organism helped Möhler describe the theological reality that draws together all the aspects of the institutional church into one. According to R.W. Franklin, his ecclesiology of the Mystical Body of Christ came to "stand behind the thinking of almost all French and German liturgists."[54]

During the second phase from 1903–1950 the liturgical movement expanded beyond the monastery into parishes and universities. In 1903 Pius X's *motu proprio* on sacred music called for "active participation in the sacred mysteries and the public and solemn prayer of the Church" by "all the faithful." The call for more active participation laid the foundation for the two landmarks of the liturgical movement in the early twentieth century: Lambert Beaudin's manifesto to Belgian workers (1909) and Romano Guardini's *The*

---

[52] Franklin 50:146. Also, see R. W. Franklin, "Nineteenth Century Liturgical Movement," *Worship* 53 (January 1979) 12–39, for a discussion of the decline of Solesmes after Guéranger's death in 1875. The liturgical movement spread from Solesmes to German monasteries, where it remained central in the early half of the twentieth century. See Rousseau, 21–35, for a discussion of nineteenth-century French liturgical reforms.

[53] See Franklin (53:29–38) for a discussion of these German monastic centers.

[54] R. W. Franklin, "Response: Humanism and Transcendence in the Nineteenth Century Liturgical Movement," *Worship* 59 (July 1985) 348. Franklin also notes that the work of Guéranger and Möhler came together at Beuron in the late nineteenth century and from Beuron inspired liturgical renewal in other Benedictine monasteries, and Protestant communities and spread to the United States. Möhler's authored two major works, *Die Einheit in der kirche* (1825) and *Symbolik* (1832).

Spirit of the Liturgy (1918). In 1909 Dom Lambert Beaudin called upon workers to make the liturgy the great weekly meeting of Christian unity and "the most powerful antidote against individualism."[55] Beaudin's commitment to the liturgical movement in the midst of social renewal grew into the Young Christian Workers movement in Belgium and the Catholic Youth Movement in Germany, of which Romano Guardini (1885–1968) played a key role in the 1930s.[56] Both movements defined baptism as active membership in the church and encouraged full lay participation in the liturgy. For the first time the sacraments were linked not only to fraternity within the Church but to social and economic transformation. In addition to his pastoral work as director of the Quickborn Association of Catholic Youth, Guardini held teaching posts at the University of Bonn (1920–1922), where he was coeditor with Odo Casel of the *Handbuch für Liturgiesewissenschaft* from 1921 to 1941, the University of Berlin (1923–1939), and after the war at Tübingen and then Munich.[57] His small book *Spirit of the Liturgy*, published in 1915, became the first volume of the series *Ecclesial Orans,* a journal published at Maria Laach. The book soon became "the bible of the movement as it moved out from the Benedictines."[58]

By the 1940s and 1950s, the liturgical movement was well under way—journals were being published, and institutes and conferences were held in Europe and North America.[59] In the third phase,

---

[55] Franklin 53:37. Beaudin's *The Piety of the Church* (1914) expresses this same sentiment: "by means of living the liturgy wholeheartedly, Christians become more and more conscious of their supernatural fraternity." Quoted in Franklin, 59:349. See Tuzik, 23–28, for biographical information on Beaudin.

[56] Romano Guardini, in 1927, became director of Quickborn, which was housed at Burg Rothenfels, a castle near the Main River, until the Nazis confiscated the building in 1939. Guardini and a group of young people lived in community centered on the sacraments. Guardini, through preaching and teaching in the community, had an enormous impact on German intellectuals. He considered himself a teacher of teachers. Tuzik, 42–46.

[57] See Robert A. Krieg, c.s.c., ed., *Romano Guardini: Proclaiming the Sacred in the Modern World* (Chicago: Liturgical Training Publications, 1995), and *Romano Guardini: A Precursor of Vatican II*; Heinz R. Kuehn, *The Essential Guardini: An Anthology of the Writings of Romano Guardini* (Chicago: Liturgical Training Publications, 1997).

[58] Franklin 53:37; Tuzik, 36–49. Karl Rahner said of Guardini, "It is a widely known fact that the Rothenfels experience was the immediate model for the liturgical reforms of Vatican II. Seldom was the origin of a spiritual movement of worldwide dimensions, a movement of immeasurable depth of soul and spirit, as historically traceable to almost one single person as in the case of Guardini." Quoted in Tuzik, 48.

[59] See Josef Jungmann, *Liturgical Renewal in Retrospect and Prospect* (London: Burns and Oates, 1965) 10–36 for a discussion of the liturgical movement in France, Ireland, and

1943–1980, liturgical reforms receive official sanction and implementation. Pius XII's publication of *Mystici Corporis* and *Divino Afflante Spiritu* in 1943 and *Mediator Dei* in 1947 began the move toward renewal of liturgical practice and acceptance of modern biblical scholarship.[60] The official work of the Church culminated in the first document published by Vatican II, the *Constitution on the Sacred Liturgy*, in 1963. The Council called for the reform of all seven sacraments, which took place between 1969 and 1989, and effectively ended the prevailing scholastic approach to the sacraments.

Over the course of 150 years the liturgical reformers emphasized several basic concepts: Möhler's Mystical Body of Christ ecclesiology, encouragement for greater lay understanding and participation, the Eucharist as the center of the Church's life along with a social understanding of liturgy as the answer to modernity's prevailing individualism. Through historical and biblical research, the search for reforms brought Catholic sacramental theology and practice closer to biblical and patristic sources that challenged the institutional or juridical terms by which neo-Thomism defined these realities. Neo-Thomist moral theologians did not consider the ramifications of the liturgical movement for their own system; changes did not begin to occur in moral theology until a generation of moral theologians, mostly from the Tübingen School, began incorporating a new understanding of liturgy and sacraments into moral theology.

The Decline of Neo-Thomism:
The Tübingen School and Alternative Manuals of Moral Theology

Even though neo-Thomism was the center of Roman Catholic theology for nearly one hundred years, movements such as modernism and *nouvelle théologie* began challenging its dominance in the first part of the twentieth century.[61] Both movements were eclipsed

---

Great Britain. See Koenker, 15–27, for a discussion of the movement in Europe. Rousseau (97–112) discusses reforms in England, 82–96, and Belgium.

[60] Gerald Ellard, "The Liturgical Movement in Catholic Circles," *Religion in Life* 18 (Summer 1948) 370–81. Ellard discusses papal documents on liturgy and the Eucharist from Pius X through Pius XII.

[61] Modernism was not in fact a movement at all but a name given to a few theologians who, early in the twentieth century, began drawing from new insights in biblical scholarship and challenging neo-Thomism. Pius X's encyclical, *Pascendi Dominum Gregis* (1907), ended the modernist era, brief though it was, by reasserting neo-Thomism as *the* theology of the Church. See J. Gallagher, 124, and Schoof, 45–68. The *nouvelle théologie*, associated

by papal encyclicals that warned of the dangers of modern thought to traditional Catholic authority. Although these movements did not affect moral theology, each began opening new avenues for Catholic theologians.[62] The movement away from neo-Thomism in moral theology began with the work of scholars at the University of Tübingen in the early nineteenth century and was continued by several moral theologians up to and including Bernard Häring. His accomplishment of renewing moral theology stems largely from his place within this tradition.

Early in the nineteenth century a Catholic theological school opened in Ellwangen, Germany, and five years later was joined with the Protestant faculty at Tübingen. Johann Michael Sailer (1751–1832) and Johann Baptist von Hirscher (1788–1865), considered the first phase of the "Catholic Tübingen School," laid important foundations for future moral theologians even though they were not effective in altering the discipline in the early nineteenth century.[63]

The encounter with Protestant scholarship opened up to Catholic scholars the world of historical and biblical criticism and the philosophical challenges to the Enlightenment, particularly in romanticism.[64] Rather than reacting defensively to these new insights, Sailer and Hirscher attempted to integrate new ideas into Catholic theology,

---

with the French theologians Jean Danielou, Jacques Leclerq, Marie-Dominique Chenu, Henri de Lubac, and Yves Congar, began after World War II and ended with papal condemnation in 1950 (*Humani Generis*).

[62] Another movement called transcendental Thomism emerged in the work of Karl Rahner and Bernard Lonergan; it was more successful than modernism and *nouvelle théologie* in its reconciliation between Aquinas and modern philosophy. J. Gallagher, 151–58.

[63] For the complete story, see W. Fehr, *The Birth of the Catholic Tübingen School: The Dogmatics of John Sebastian Drey* (Chico, Calif.: AAR Scholars Press, 1981) 12. See also Schoof, 23–28. Fehr (3) states that this term can be somewhat misleading because "there was not a complete uniformity of thought, nor did Drey's students follow closely in all respects the master's teaching . . . the theologians of this tradition were strikingly original and independent." R. Gallagher ("Manual System," 10) claims that neither the manualists nor the Tübingen scholars addressed the social, political, and economic issues of the day and therefore were irrelevant to many.

[64] According to Horton Harris, "The Tübingen School was based on a definite theological principle, namely, the purely historical, non-supernatural, and non-miraculous interpretation of Christianity. . . . It was therefore clear that this involved a radically new approach to the investigation of the early Church and the authorship of the New Testament writings." Horton Harris, *The Tübingen School* (Oxford: Clarendon Press, 1975) 246. Schoof, 24–25. See Thomas F. O'Meara, *Romantic Idealism and Roman Catholicism: Schelling and the Theologians* (Notre Dame, Ind.: University of Notre Dame Press, 1982).

not in order to contradict the past but to find new ways of expressing its essence. The Church, they advocated, is a dynamic, historical reality, the earthly forerunner to Jesus' proclamation of the Kingdom of God. Sailer and Hirscher rejected scholastic categories in favor of biblical themes and emphasized a more positive, less legalistic understanding of morality.[65]

Sailer, considered the first to break with scholasticism, stressed the inner subjective experience of faith and the experience of "a grasping of being grasped" by the divine.[66] His *A Handbook of Christian Morality* stresses the virtues and the attainment of Christian perfection through conversion and growth. As Häring states, "The strange notion that moral theology should busy itself only with delineating the minimal requirements or obligations of the Christian, while leaving the doctrine of full perfection of Christian virtue in conformity with the Sermon on the Mount to ascetic theology, was simply incomprehensible to Sailer."[67] Hirscher published treatises on moral theology, homiletics, catechetics, and liturgy but is most well known for being the first moral theologian to bring New Testament scholarship to bear on the moral life.[68] Hirscher rejected the cold legalism of the manuals and emphasized the moral life as realizing the fullness of the Kingdom of God as found in the gospels.

The achievements of the Catholic Tübingen School were not integrated into moral theology because of the rise of neo-Thomism. With the advent of neoscholasticism and neo-Thomism, the openness of the Tübingen School ceased, and a suspicion of such concepts as change, development, and history stood in stark contrast to scholastic

---

[65] Jonsen and Toulmin (271) point out that the earliest challenges to casuistry began with Sailer and Hirscher: "Within the world of Catholic moral theology, a serious theological critique of casuistry appeared. Initially put forward by the faculty of the University of Tübingen in the first half of the nineteenth century, it criticized casuistry as diverting attention from the moral teaching of the Gospels; as stressing sin rather than perfection; and as viewing the moral life as a matter of observing lower limits rather than of aspiring to the higher ideals of love and sacrifice. In ironic contrast to the Jansenist charge of laxism, this later critique accused casuistry of legalism. Though repeated many times, this critique did little to impede the work of the casuists." See *LC* 1:22–33 for a description of Sailer, Hirscher, and the tradition of moral theology at Tübingen.

[66] Dru, 43. J. M. Sailer, *Handbuch der Christlichen Moral* (Munich, 1817).

[67] *LC* 1:24.

[68] Johann M. Hirscher, *Die Christlichen Moral als Lehre von der Verwirklichung des gottlichen Reiches in der Menschheit* (Tübingen, 1835). Interestingly, his earliest work was on the liturgy; there he called for the end of private masses, the use of the vernacular, and communion under both species. His book was placed on the Index in 1823, and Hirscher did not pursue the issues further.

notions of metaphysics and tradition.[69] Even though the early work of the Tübingen scholars remained outside the main theological currents, several moralists continued the tradition begun by Sailer and Hirscher. The renewal in moral theology in the 1940s and 1950s, Häring argues, can be traced to such Tübingen scholars as Francis Xavier Linsenmann (1835–1898), Otto Schilling (d. 1956), Fritz Tillmann (d. 1953), and Theodore Steinbüchel (1888–1949), each of who carried the fundamental historical and biblical direction of the school into the mid-twentieth century. They rejected the legalism and minimalism of the manualists and pursued biblical ideas of conversion, perfection, and holiness as the center of the moral life.[70]

Häring stands squarely within the Tübingen tradition and its approach to moral theology. *The Law of Christ* can be seen as the culmination of many of the themes in this long tradition. The Tübingen scholars, as well as Häring, view moral theology as an introduction to the Christian life rather than exclusively as a priest's manual for the sacrament of penance. Moral theology, they believe, should focus on the dynamics of grace and conversion rather than exclusively on sin, law, and obligations. It should have a strong theological and biblical foundation, focused on the central theme of the New Testament, the Kingdom of God.

Several of Sailer's main insights can be found in Häring's work: the need for ongoing conversion within the Christian life, the central place of the virtues (rather than the commandments), and the idea of growth in the Spirit. Häring notes that the subtitle to *The Law of Christ*, "moral theology for priests and laity," is taken from Sailer, who criticized the minimalism of the manualist tradition and argued that all Christians are called to the same life of holiness.[71]

---

[69] Schoof (27–28) comments that already by 1850 the chance for Tübingen's achievements to be brought into the Church had passed. Fehr (6) argues that "it was in Tübingen more than a century and a half ago that Catholic theology for the first time took seriously the modern understanding of history and allowed history to become a constitutive dimension of theological method. If this orientation of the Tübingen School had prevailed in the Catholic Church, the crisis of modernism would undoubtedly have been experienced differently, if not averted. In fact, the promising confrontation of Catholic theology with history was broken off around the middle of the nineteenth century."

[70] Häring (*LC* 1:29–30) also discusses those moral theologians of the late nineteenth and early twentieth centuries who carried on the neo-Thomist tradition with its strong emphasis on legalism. Schoof (72–90) concludes that German theology between 1920 and 1945 was not affected by the modernist debates but that a "Catholic revival" began among various Catholic movements.

[71] *LC* 1:ix.

Hirscher's biblical approach to moral theology influenced Häring primarily through Fritz Tillmann, who drew extensively on Hirscher's work.[72] Häring borrowed several important themes from Tillmann: personhood, conversion away from sin and rebirth in the Spirit, the I-Thou model of encounter with God, the "religious-moral character" of human response, and the imitation of Christ.[73] Häring did, however, reject Tillmann's legalistic understanding of the role of the sacraments.[74]

The Tübingen tradition also influenced Häring's dogmatic theology through the works of Johann Adam Möhler from the nineteenth century and Romano Guardini and Karl Adam (1876–1966) in the mid-twentieth century. Möhler's ideas were kept alive by liturgical reformers who gained widespread attention in the 1920s, particularly in the works of Guardini and Adam. Both taught Häring at Tübingen, and several of their theological ideas about liturgy made their way into Häring's dogmatic theology: the conception of the Church as the Mystical Body of Christ, an emphasis on the incarnation of Christ, and the liturgy as the central act of the Church.

Moral theologians began to break with neo-Thomism in the 1940s, although several manuals appeared earlier in the century that hinted at this eventual divorce.[75] By the 1940s and into the 1950s, several "alternative manuals of moral theology" began to appear,

---

[72] J. Gallagher, 163.

[73] It should be noted that Häring (*LC* 1:5) finds these themes in patristic writings as well. J. Gallagher (171) argues that Häring did not emphasize rebirth to the same extent that Tillmann did but gives little evidence for this claim.

[74] Häring states (*LC* 1:32): "It is a matter of some surprise that sacramental unity with Christ is not brought out in strong relief as one of the constructive elements in the imitation of Christ. Likewise, we are somewhat shocked to note the treatment of the sacraments under the title: *Duties toward Oneself in the Religious Sphere*. For a manual or handbook of doctrine, casuistry is dismissed somewhat too cavalierly. Yet in defense of Tillmann it should be noted that he limited the sphere of his work in this matter of set purpose and design."

[75] John C. Ford and Gerald Kelly summarize the main challenges to moral theology during this period in *Contemporary Moral Theology,* vol. 1 (Westminster, Md.: Newman Press, 1958) 42–59. Thomas Bouquillon argued in his manual of moral theology written at the turn of the century that moral theology had cut itself off from dogmatic theology and did not address social questions of the times. Arthur Vermeersch, in 1929, also argued that moral theology was not attending to the philosophical and social issues of the day. He argued for a more positive approach to the Christian life and for the need to integrate the theological virtues into the moral life. In 1940 Gustav Thils radically redefined the Christian moral life in relationship to Christ, the sacraments, and personal values, all areas he claimed were overlooked by the manualists. See Ford and Kelly, 1:61–63, for a discussion of Vermeersch, and J. Gallagher, 142, for a discussion of Thils.

which retained the external look of the manuals but were based on different philosophical and moral theories and advanced alternative moral theologies. Each author in his own way called for a more positive, relevant, and biblical moral theology that could meet the challenges of modern life.[76] John Gallagher identifies four alternative manualists—Fritz Tillmann, Dom Odon Lottin, Bernard Häring, and Josef Fuchs—who began engaging different philosophical and theological methods and ideas, while remaining within the neo-Thomist framework. Eventually their distinctive styles, as well as moral theories, meant that moral theology would take on a different character, leading to the eventual decline of neo-Thomism.

The alternative manualists' called for the renewal of moral theology in regards to five basic issues. First, moral theology needs to be fully integrated with Scripture and dogmatic theology. Second, the end of human existence is defined according to the New Testament image of the Kingdom of God rather than in scholastic metaphysical terms. Third, the dynamics of human personhood are more central than human nature, requiring a shift away from the metaphysical to historical and social categories. Fourth, is a biblical understanding of grace that defines grace as God's free self-giving offer to persons in history and community in contrast to the neo-Thomist understanding in which grace moved the will which in turn moved the intellect to God. Finally, as had been suggested by the work of J. M. Sailer, a virtue ethic was needed to replace the legalism of the neo-Thomists, without abandoning the tradition of norms and principles. For example, the alternative manualists' attempt to construct a more biblical and positive understanding of the moral life, the virtues became the primary center of moral personhood, and norms and laws are considered secondary.[77]

[76] Calls for renewal in moral theology were given papal support in 1926 by Pius XI, who encouraged moral theology to be the "school of the Charity of Christ." Quoted in Ford and Kelly, 1:65. One of the most significant works of the era is Gérard Gilleman's *The Primacy of Charity in Moral Theology* (Westminster, Md.: Newman Press, 1961). Gilleman's work had a significant impact on moral theology by correcting, what the author termed to be a fundamental mistake of the manualists: the absence of charity as the center of Christian morality.

[77] Philip J. Murnion, "The Renewal of Moral Theology: Review and Prospect," *Dunwoodie Review* 3 (1963) 54; and Dom P. Gregory Stevens, o.s.b., "Current Trends in Moral Theology," *Catholic Educational Review* 58 (1960) 6.

When Häring's *The Law of Christ* was published in 1954, however, it was seen as the most significant, comprehensive attempt to bring these five insights into moral theology.[78] The alternative manualists, and in particular Häring, launched a new era of moral theology. The neo-Thomist manuals eventually fell out of use in seminary education largely because of the movement toward change in both theology and liturgy that was solidified at Vatican II.

* * * *

In like manner the other theological subjects should be renewed through a more vivid contact with the Mystery of Christ and the history of salvation. Special care should be given to the perfecting of moral theology. Its scientific presentation should draw more fully on the teaching of holy Scripture and should throw light upon the exalted vocation of the faithful in Christ and their obligation to bring forth fruit in charity for the life of the world.[79]

———————————————————— *Optatam Totius,* October 1965

Vatican II (1962–1965) brought significant changes to Roman Catholic life and thought. In moral theology the Council muted the voice of scholasticism and neo-Thomism and affirmed the movement toward a biblical ethic rooted in charity. The conciliar documents emphasize biblical themes of covenant, discipleship, and conversion, and the theological model of divine invitation and human response.[80] The major reforms of Vatican II concentrated on the liturgy and its revolutionary ecclesiology. The first document issued in 1963, *Sacrosanctum Concilium* calls for the "reform and pro-

---

[78] R. Gallagher ("Manual System," 12) claims: "The mood for change and for a substantial alternative to the manual system found its most popular and influential symbol in Bernard Häring whose *The Law of Christ*, published in 1954, was to become the major reference point in the debate about the inadequacies of the manualist system." Not all viewed these changes as positive, however. See Ford and Kelly, 62–63, for criticisms of the changes in moral theology. Some moral theologians, while recognizing the need for moral theology to be concerned about modern issues and to incorporate new ideas from other theological disciplines and the social sciences, still argued that moral theology should return to Thomas Aquinas for its method. See Murnion, 55, and Pinckaers, 66. For a discussion of the positive aspects of the manuals, see Regan, 32.

[79] *Optatam Totius* (Decree on the Training of Priests, October 1965) 16.

[80] Several scholars regard the Tübingen tradition of moral theology to be the significant impetus to the changes at Vatican II; see Jonsen and Toulmin, 273, and J. Gallagher, 204. The invitation and response model is a central motif in Catholic moral thought after Vatican II and is evident in conciliar documents such as *Dei Verbum* (November 1965). See

motion of the liturgy" which "daily builds up those who are in the Church" for apostolic mission in the world.

The changes instituted by Vatican II had a dramatic impact on the relationship between moral theology and sacramental practice. The end of neo-Thomism and the manualist approach meant that moral theology turned away from a predominantly legalistic approach to moral questions and eliminated the sacraments as an area of major concern.[81] In turn, sacramental theologians began grappling with the reforms of Vatican II and the major revisions of each sacrament. The renewal of both disciplines along biblical and historical lines meant that they became integrated with dogmatic theology once again. But because moral theology was no longer solely concerned with defining the parameters of the sacrament of penance, moral theology and sacramental practice became two separate areas of theological specialty. But the history of the one cannot be understood apart from the other. In the 1950s Bernard Häring could not imagine a separation either. He envisioned a reform of moral theology that looked toward a new way of defining the relationship between the sacraments and the moral life.

Richard M. Gula, *What Are They Saying about Moral Norms?* (Mahwah, N.J.: Paulist Press, 1982) 29–30, and Regan, 4.

[81] See R. Gallagher, "Fundamental," 149, for a discussion of the problems facing moral theology after Vatican II.

Part II

The Dogmatic Foundations of Häring's Sacramental-Moral Theology

Chapter 3

Word and Response:
The Theological Foundation
of the Religious-Moral Life

It is not at all my intention to present a comprehensive moral theology as a rigid system . . . flowing from a single idea. . . . This does not, however, prevent us from looking for a leitmotif and for key concepts that would help today's Christians to understand what it means to live one's moral life as witness to Christ. The choice of a leitmotif must not be an arbitrary decision. It should be made only after having carefully studied the biblical patterns and after discerning, in view of those patterns, the special signs of God's present action and call in history. Since our life can be understood only in view of God's initiative, we exercise and develop our creative freedom and fidelity by listening and responding. It is therefore a distinctively Christian approach to emphasize responsibility as a leitmotif, but in a way that shows it as expression of creative freedom and fidelity.[1]

——————————— Bernard Häring, *Free and Faithful in Christ,* vol. 1

Häring is not the first moral theologian to employ the term *responsibility* as a theme for Christian morality, but he is the first to introduce it into Catholic moral thought.[2] For Häring *responsibility* serves as a leitmotif for the Christian religious-moral life for several

———————

[1] *FFC* 1:59–60.

[2] Albert Jonsen's study of the use of responsibility in Christian ethics gives a brief overview of the term as it has emerged in Western philosophy, beginning with the work of David Hume, and in Christian theology, beginning with Emil Brunner. Albert Jonsen, *Responsibility in Modern Religious Ethics* (Washington, D.C.: Corpus Books, 1968) 3–7. Jonsen analyzes the work of four twentieth-century theologians who use responsibility as the center of their ethical system, including Bernard Häring, Dietrich Bonhoeffer, H. Richard Niebuhr, and Robert O. Johann. Jonsen distinguishes between philosophical and theological uses of responsibility in regard to both attribution and appropriation. For example, moral philosophers speak of "holding" a person responsible for certain actions under certain conditions; theological ethicists speak of a person being "made" responsible by God

reasons. First, responsibility most adequately explains the inner dynamics of religion as dialogue between God and humanity, a dialogue that begins with God's initiation and is followed by the human person's response. Responsibility also captures the inner dynamics of morality as response to value as manifested through the moral virtues and expressed within the created order. Moral responsibility consists of responding to God (ultimate value) through the created order by listening to and discerning God's word spoken through creation, Scripture, the Church, especially the sacraments, and other persons. Most importantly, however, responsibility captures what Häring calls the "interpenetration" of religion and morality in such a way that the moral life arises from its foundation in the religious response to God: "From this it is evident that the term responsibility is best suited to express the interpenetration and formation of the moral through the religious, and also the distinction of the two."[3]

Second, responsibility is a key leitmotif of the Bible. According to Häring, a leitmotif must be drawn from an analysis of "biblical patterns" and the "special signs of God's present action and call in history." A leitmotif, in other words, is not the center of the Christian life, but most accurately points to the center—Jesus Christ. Häring observes: "An abstract concept, even if well chosen, cannot inspire action . . . people are more effectively influenced and brought to common action by symbols rather than by abstract concepts. Neither the word 'freedom,' nor 'responsibility,' of itself, nor all of them to-

---

so that a person's total life, not only specific actions, is before God. "Only because man is *made* responsible by God's acts of creation and redemption, can he be given duties and enabled to fulfill them. It is in this sense that Christian ethics has recognized that an indicative precedes an imperative: you are made God's beloved children: therefore act as such." (Ibid., 85) Appropriation, those conditions that define an action as the agent's, is defined by theological ethicists according to the actions that God sets forth as right and true. See 88–107 for an analysis of Häring's use of the term "responsibility."

[3] *LC* 1:47. In a recent work William Schweiker critiques the dialogical model of Christian ethics put forth by Karl Barth, H. R. Niebuhr, and Bernard Häring. According to Schweiker, two problems emerge from this model. First, "any moral concepts which did not fit within a call-response model or could not be reformulated in terms of that model" are dropped, such as virtue, happiness, and moral perfection. The second problem is that the I-Thou model is too simplistic for the challenges facing contemporary Christian ethics. Schweiker argues that any constructive theological ethic today must take into account the problem of moral pluralism and the rapid extension of human power. See William Schweiker, *Responsibility and Christian Ethics* (Cambridge: Cambridge University Press, 1995) 40–47. It should be noted that Häring did in fact retain the category of virtue within his dialogical system.

gether would be a sufficiently unifying symbol. They receive, in this moral theology, their basic force and dynamics in Christ. . . . While we choose as paradigms or symbols those perspectives and key concepts that respond to the passionate interests of today's world, we bring them into the all-inclusive vision of our central and real symbol, Christ."[4] In addition to its Christocentric focus, responsibility is the dynamic that under girds the story of God's covenant with the Israelites and the New Testament themes of incarnation, discipleship, and redemption through the cross and resurrection of Christ.[5]

Third, responsibility serves as a heuristic device that can assist modern Christians in understanding the nature of discipleship. Häring recognized that existentialism, as well as socialism, provided powerful alternatives to the Church's morality, largely because Christian morality had become overly legalistic and authoritarian in contrast to movements that accented personal freedom and responsibility. He recognized that existentialism, with its emphasis on the unique individuality of each person and the person's responsibility for shaping her existence through choice, had much in common with Christian discipleship, although he rejected the extreme individualism of existentialist thinkers.[6] He also recognized that traditional categories of Catholic morality, terms such as *salvation of the soul, commandment,* and *law,* failed to grasp the historically dynamic character of moral living. And, in this sense, he argues that *responsibility* is closer to the center of Catholic morality because it emphasizes the dynamic, interpersonal, and social dimension of human personhood: "To our mind the term *responsibility* understood in its religious sense is the most apt; even from the mere standpoint of etymology the word designates the personal-essential characteristic of religion. This is the relation of dialogue, word and response, in a community. It apparently is the most apposite to express the personal relation between God and man—which is the I and Thou relation—of word and response—specifically God's word calling and inviting man and the human decision in response of acceptance."[7] Häring further states

---

[4] Ibid., 1:59ff.

[5] See *LC* 2:xxi–xxxviii, and *FFC* 1:7–15, for a discussion of the word-and-response motif in the Hebrew Scripture and New Testament.

[6] *FFC* 1:74. *JC,* 52. See *MP*, 3–33, for a discussion of existentialism and personalism, a critique of legalism in Catholic sacramental and moral theology, and a critique of Jean Sartre, Albert Camus, and Martin Heidegger.

[7] *LC* 1:46.

that responsibility is the basis for a "normative pattern" that "permeates and elucidates all our norms, ideals, and goals."[8]

Albert Jonsen identifies a fourth reason for Häring's introduction of the term *responsibility* into Catholic ethics. According to Jonsen, it affords Häring a way to overcome the long-standing split in Catholic moral thought between dogma and morals, and the natural and supernatural. Häring recognized that the manuals failed to ground moral norms in central Christian dogmas. For example, Häring criticizes the manualist Anthony Koch for dividing the work of dogmatics and moral theology in such a way that dogmatics is concerned with the "nature of God" and moral theology primarily concerned with "happiness," as though "the living friendship with God was only an essential means for the full attainment of the moral purpose." He sought to overcome this gap by basing his moral theology on themes such as the Father's call to repentance and acceptance of the sinner through grace, the imitation of Christ, and fellowship in the divine life through the gift of the Holy Spirit.[9] The separation between the supernatural life of grace (received from God in the form of the theological virtues) and the natural state (the created order, particularly reason) effectively reduced morality to obedience to norms, leaving little room for an experience of grace.[10] Häring's definition of religion and morality as word and response overcomes this dichotomy by emphasizing the experiential side of both religion and morality through the I-Thou encounter and the experience of value, an encounter between persons in relationship. In both cases, the person's response is grounded in the apprehension of the ultimate value, God, to whom all action, both religious and moral, is aimed.

Section Two examines the leitmotif of *responsibility* and the theme of word-and-response as the foundational concept of Häring's sacramental-moral theology. For Häring the ongoing, dynamic, historically-grounded relationship between God and persons begins in God's continuing invitation (word) spoken to persons and the human word "spoken" to God through cult and morality (response). Word-and-response shapes Häring's understanding of religion and morality, his Christology, theological anthropology, and sacramental theology as

---

[8] *FFC* 1:82–85. Häring also discusses how the leitmotif of responsibility is related to deontological and teleological ethical theories.

[9] See, for example, *LC* 1:41–42. Jonsen, 86–88, 101–7.

[10] Häring so adamantly rejects legalistic morality that he claims the Church itself is in need of confession. See *JC*, 121 and *SS*, 110–19.

well as each category of moral theology (e.g., law, conscience, sin, and virtue). Many of his ideas about religion are influenced by Max Scheler, Rudolf Otto, and Martin Buber, all of whom shared the phenomenological search to understand religion's distinctive character. But Häring is not a philosopher of religion and his purpose in highlighting religion as encounter and dialogue was to return to Catholic moral thought an experiential and relational foundation for the religious-moral life.

Once he had this point established, he moved quickly forward to define how religion and morality are related, this being the central intellectual task of his early works. The dialogical understanding of the sacred and humanity forms the basis for his Christology and theological anthropology; these ideas are largely influenced by Karl Adam and Romano Guardini, both of whom share with Häring an indebtedness to the German phenomenologists. Chapter 3 examines the themes of religion and morality, and Christology and anthropology; chapter 4 turns to Häring's sacramental theology and examines how he draws together the word-and-response theme with the sacramental theology of the liturgical reformers.

In summary, Häring's portrait of the religious-moral life is built upon the following claims: Religion and morality share the features of dialogue and response-ability through word and response; Jesus Christ as Word of God and High Priest is the responder *par excellence* to God's initiative; the imitation of Jesus is the central religious and moral response of persons to God; and formation in the life of imitation takes place in and through the sacramental life of the Mystical Body of Christ, the Church.

The Dialogical Character of Religion and Morality

On the contrary, true morality may be said to accept all earthly tasks only in their relation to God. If the religious in the narrow sense of the term is response directed immediately to God, then the moral is response-ability as to the spatial-temporal before God and toward God. For the religious man morality is a summons issuing from the immediate encounter with God. It is a call for action in the world. It is not merely a task commanded by God but a task which must be ordered to the glory of God.[11]

——————————————— Bernard Häring, *The Law of Christ*, vol. 2

———

[11] *LC* 2:123.

Early in his intellectual development Häring identifies a common problem shared by both secular and Catholic ethics: the divorce between religion and morality. Moral philosophers since the Enlightenment, particularly Immanuel Kant and Karl Marx, reject religious ethics as heteronomous and untenable, producing ethical systems that place autonomous persons at the center of existence with no ultimate or transcendent referent. According to Häring the ethics of Aristotle and the Stoics also share this fundamental flaw: "But the ultimate meaning and goal is always man and his own development and perfection. . . . The value of all values for him is his own soul, the preservation and development of the worth of his own person. The center of all these ethical systems is man himself. His moral obligation is self-perfection."[12]

Häring's position echoes Max Scheler's idea that the goal of religion and metaphysics are distinct. Metaphysics seeks to make claims about absolute being, whereas the goal of religion is relationship with the living God, that comes through faith and love primarily, but not through reason.[13]

Häring recognizes a similar problem in religious ethical systems, particularly the neo-Thomist manualist tradition in Catholic moral theology, which also split apart religion and morality. The manualists separate moral acts from their dogmatic foundations and define the moral life largely in metaphysical and legal terms, resulting in a distorted view of the Christian life. Hence, not unlike secular ethics, Catholic ethics lost its transcendent referent. In much the same way, Christian morality could be viewed from the perspective of self-perfection: a set of rules guiding the person toward salvation.[14]

But the problem of secularism and legalism is not only an intellectual issue; it is also personal, existential, and pastoral. Häring, like many in his generation, recognizes that modern forms of seculariza-

---

[12] *LC* 1:39. For Häring's critique of Kant, see *DHG*, 111–135; *LC* 1:42–46; *LC* 2:121–25. For Häring's discussion of religion and morality see *LC* 1:35–49; *LC* 2:111-21; *CE*, 33–49; *FFC* 1:62–65; *ET*, 66–67. For an analysis of Häring's work on religion and morality, see Hamel, 13–42, and Jonsen, 87–92. Häring takes up an argument advanced by Max Scheler regarding the influence of Greek philosophy on Christian theology. Scheler was particularly critical of Greek philosophical concepts in theology and rejected neo-Thomism for precisely this reason: metaphysical categories of forms, existence, and essence could not express the essential Christian message of God as "love-directed person." See *On the Eternal in Man*, 130–34.

[13] Ibid., 334–35.

[14] *LC* 1:40–41.

tion, industrialization and technology create multiple kinds of alienation, thwarting the authentic drive for true human encounter in community. Likewise, the Catholic propensity toward legalism in both morals and liturgy leads to alienation from God and the Christian community precisely because it does not emphasize religious encounter and fellowship.[15] According to Häring these factors contribute to modernity's confusion and rejection about the true meaning of the religious-moral life: persons stood, falsely, at the center, while legalistic moral and liturgical practice had all but stripped people of a relationship with the sacred. The modern person comes to reject religion and religious morality precisely because it was impossible to accept; or they decide for a religious morality but precisely for the wrong reasons, out of passive or blind obedience.

Through personalism Häring develops an understanding of the religious-moral life that seeks to reclaim the proper relationship between religion and morality and challenges the claims of secular ethics. Most importantly it provides a lively option for Christians seeking a deeper religious and moral self-understanding.[16] Personalism, according to Häring, could appeal to modern persons because it emphasizes the unique individuality of persons as well as their social and religious character. His response to Kantian-dominated secular ethics is to demonstrate that religion and morality are distinct but share a common bond: "Ultimately morality and religion must have the same center: community and fellowship with God." Secular ethical systems are incomplete because they reject the true end of persons—communion with God—in favor of an ethics based on self-fulfillment.[17] He also rejects religious ethics that make this same mistake.[18] In making his case for the Christian moral life to complacent Christians and atheists, Häring embraces the term *responsibility* in order to demonstrate the dynamic basis of the Christian religion as personal response to an inviting and saving God.[19] Christianity counters the depersonalization of modern life because the individual finds the true self only in communion with God and

[15] Bernard Häring, *Morality Is for Persons: The Ethics of Christian Personalism* (New York: Farrar, Straus, & Giroux, 1971) 3–4, 21, subsequently referred to as *MP*.

[16] For Häring's discussion of personalism see *CE*, 1–30, *MP*, 3–25, 33–42, 50–58. For an analysis of this concept see O'Keefe, 22–25, and Hamel, 55–59.

[17] *LC* 1:39–42.

[18] See Häring's criticism of Anthony Koch's moral theology, *LC* 1:41–42.

[19] Bernard Häring, *Faith and Morality in the Secular Age* (Garden City, N.Y.: Doubleday, 1973) 176.

other persons. "Viewed in the perspective of religion, the human person can be understood only from the standpoint of personal community and fellowship with God."[20]

As demonstrated throughout this study Häring departs from the neo-Thomist manuals at several important junctures; but he also retains, certainly in *The Law of Christ*, much of the basic structure and terms of traditional Roman Catholic moral theology. An important exception, however, is the first volume that begins with an historical overview of moral theology, followed by an analysis of religion and morality, and the human person. This all precedes what traditionally is the starting point for the neo-Thomist manuals: an analysis of the human act. Häring shifts the context of human action to the category of response: in the realm of religion, response is directed to the divine initiative, and in the realm of moral action, response is to value. The next two sections examine each of these areas of Häring's thought and address the question, how does Häring understand the relationship between religion and morality and how is moral response, finally, a response to the divine initiative?

Religion as Word and Response

Häring does not develop a sophisticated philosophy of religion. He derives ideas mainly from Max Scheler's, *On the Eternal in Man*, Rudolf Otto's, *The Idea of the Holy*, and Martin Buber's, *I and Thou*, all of whom employ Husserl's phenomenonology in search of understanding religious experience.[21] While there are important differences between Scheler, Otto, and Buber, Häring draws upon a common set of ideas from their work: a non-reductionistic *a priori* understanding of religion; the experiential basis of the person-to-person encounter (including the divine Person), the "given-ness" of the divine encounter as well as its social character (i.e., the I-Thou encounter understood within the larger dynamic of I-Thou-We). Though Häring's ideas are largely derivative, he synthesizes them in a creative way that also distinguishes him from his intellectual forebearers. These ideas are developed in Häring's two early works, *Das*

---

[20] *LC* 1:40. See also *CE*, 36; *MP*, 3–6; *SEL*, 3–13.

[21] See Edmund Husserl, *Logical Investigations*. 1900/09 and *Ideas*, 1913. Rudolf Otto, *The Idea of the Holy* (London: Oxford University Press, 1923). Max Scheler, *On the Eternal in Man*, trans. Bernard Noble (London: SCM Press, 1960). Martin Buber, *I and Thou*, trans. Walter Kaufmann (New York: Charles Scribners' Sons, 1970).

Heilege und das Gute and *The Law of Christ;* later he relies primarily on a biblical understanding of the divine-human dialogue.

Häring begins *The Law of Christ* by highlighting three essential features of religion: religion is constituted by dialogue, first initiated by God, followed by a person's response; it is personal, that is, the individual is grasped by God, the divine Person (and through the person of Jesus Christ) who addresses the individual as a unique person; and religion is experienced and lived out within the fellowship of community.[22]

The essence of religion is dialogue that takes place between two poles: the divine initiative and the human response. Häring states, "Religion truly lived must have as essential characteristic the element of response. Response, responsibility, dialogue belong to religion essentially. We have religion only if man conceives of the Holy as a Power which advances toward him and to whom he can turn in dialogue." Religion, the human response, is often associated with motivations to "save one's soul" or "seek eternal happiness," but for Häring the essence of religion is "fellowship with the living God" and "the point of encounter between the word of God and the response of man."[23] In this encounter persons experience God as "the infinite personal God" who "in the glory of His love" advances toward man "taking man seriously." There is a note of tension within this encounter because of the "infinite distance" experienced between God in his "transcendent holiness" and the human person.

Häring cites the German Lutheran systematic theologian Rudolf Otto (1869–1937), as the greatest influence on the idea that dialogue is the essence of religion. Otto's 1917 classic *The Idea of the Holy* identifies a fundamental category of religious experience, the "numinous," that highlights the nonrational dimension of religious experience, as distinct from the rational and moral. In numinous experience the human person apprehends the sacred as the "holy," a quality of divine being that evokes two responses: *mysterium tremendum et fascinas*, the sense of "creature feeling" before the holy that produces a sense of fear and repulsion as well as attraction and

---

[22] In later writings, Häring (*MP*, 153) states that there is no way to be certain which comes first: religion or morality. For an analysis and summary of his position see Hamel, 13–42, and Jonsen, 87–92. In my personal correspondence with Häring, he mentions that he regards Otto as the one "whom I prefer to all the others" (July 27, 1993).

[23] *LC* 1:35.

fascination. Häring accepts many of Otto's basic claims about religious experience. Both hold that religion is fundamentally a nonrational experience of the divine, an encounter between the infinite, holy One and the finite human person, which is prior to any conception of the moral law or demands eliciting from such a relationship. For Häring it is the encounter with God as all holy and divine that initiates and sustains the religious life of the believer, and Otto's description of religion helps him reclaim the relational character of this encounter.

Häring expands the concept in Christian spiritual terms: the experience of the holy or sacred as a nonrational experience is felt as a "conviction of the heart."[24] The sacred manifestation is uninitiated and experienced as gift that is beyond human control or manipulation. According to Häring, the experience must be grasped and held in faith, which consists of opening the heart, will, and intellect to accept God as the origin and fulfillment of the self. He writes:

> salvific faith, through which religion becomes life, is the grateful, joyful acceptance of the living Word of God and a trusting self-communion of man's whole intellect, heart, and will. Faith is the reply from the depths of the person, looking to the Person, Who is messenger and message. Faith is the fundamental event between the Thou of God and I of man. Through it, man becomes an "I-self," because he is addressed by God as thou. In faith, man emerges from himself and enters into the most intimate communion with God.[25]

---

[24] Otto, 1–4. Hamel (19) points out that this experience is central to Häring's thought but that he fails to elaborate the concept: "The type of knowledge operative here is most significant not only for our present concern, but especially for Häring's methodology in general. It is characteristic of the *Gesinnung* school of German philosophy which stresses affective knowledge or what is more technically called, the 'intentionality of feeling.' Again, the influence of Otto and Scheler is evident. As central as this mode of knowledge is to Häring's theology, he does not elaborate on the meaning of the term, perhaps expecting the reader to understand it in the sense of Scheler. On this point, Häring is also walking in the footsteps of Augustine, Ambrose, Bonaventure, and Pascal." Krieg (*Guardini*, 17) makes a similar point regarding Guardini's method. He uses both a deductive neo-scholastic method alongside the inductive approach of Augustine, Anselm, and Bonaventure. Guardini acknowledged the tension between these methods but argued for their use in dialectical tension with one another.

[25] *CE*, 36. Hamel distinguishes between Häring's use of the terms "faith" and "religion." *Faith* refers to God's gracious self-communication, opening the person's intellect and heart, and the cooperative acceptance by the person. *Religion* refers to the "state of existing in a faith relationship," expressed by adoration and worship. Häring does not always hold to these as strict definitions and often uses *religion* to refer to both. See Hamel, 15–16, and *LC* 2:16–23, 119–20.

Häring emphasizes this-worldly religion as opposed to other-worldly salvation, which had become the overriding motivation of much Roman Catholic moral theology.

Häring connects Otto's concept of religious experience with the Christian category of *imago dei.* The encounter between persons and God allows persons to know their true self as known by God, and the emergence of the self derives from the *imago dei,* the bond of fellowship and dialogue between God and persons: "We can realize the true meaning of human personality only in the light of man's likeness to God. The more intimate the bond between man and God, the word-response relation, so much the more is the personality enriched and perfected as 'image and likeness of God,' who imparts in word and in love the glory of the intimate life of the Trinity."[26] Häring's description of the divine reality emphasizes the Logos character of the divine self, God as Word, communicating through the Word, speaking to persons in "words comprehensible to us." The Logos character of God speaks urgently to persons, summoning them to response.

Like Otto, Häring wants to maintain the radical distinction within this encounter, but he does not as readily adopt Otto's categories of *mysterium tremendum and fascinas.* Otto emphasizes God as "wholly other," one who provokes fear, terror, dread, and awe. The numinous experience expresses the initial sacred encounter, but goes no further. Häring does not reject the *mysterium tremendum* aspect of the numinous experience, though he is more inclined to accent the concept of *fascinans*—the positive side of the divine encounter. He describes the experience of *fascinans:* "As soon as the soul really encounters God, it reflects the splendor of His holiness. It has worth before God, a value which indeed is intimately entwined with this fellowship with God. The soul exults before the majesty of the all-holy God, not only in adoration, but also in astonishment at the glance of the divine love resting upon it."[27] Häring departs from Otto in other significant ways. For example, Otto largely excludes morality

---

[26] Ibid.

[27] *LC* 1:36. Häring, unlike Protestant theologians such as Karl Barth and Rudolf Bultman who attacked Otto's universal understanding of religion, seems to accept this broad theory of religion, though he immediately applies it to Christianity. Häring was not so much interested in applying his theory to other religions and he accepts Otto's affinity and argument that Christianity is the highest, most complete and true path to God. See Otto, *The Idea of the Holy,* 56, 72, 75.

from his theory of religion in order to highlight the nonrational prior to any rational construction in religious forms. Häring, on the other hand, begins with the nonrational encounter and moves to describe how religion and morality form a twofold response to God. Otto's theory of religion also focuses on individual encounter, which is primarily ahistorical.[28] In contrast, Häring understands religious encounter in social and historical terms.

The second theme of Häring's understanding of religion is personalism. The Logos character of God is not a static, other-worldly cosmic structure, but a Divine Person. The individual person encounters the Holy as person, as one who can be known, named, and loved, not as an impersonal object or idea. "To be pierced by the word of the divine love obviously means to be liberated from the masses, from the namelessness and anonymity of the flux of life. For in truth God calls us personally, each by his own name."[29] God advances toward the person in love, and in turn, by faith, the person responds to God in love. This dialogue-in-love binds the sacred and human together because it is deeply personal. The individual person is grasped in his unique essence, known by name and loved.[30] In the *imago dei* exists the capacity for dialogue and free response to the divine initiative:

> We can realize the true meaning of human personality only in the light of man's likeness to God. The more intimate the bond between man and God, the word-response relation, so much the more is the personality enriched and perfected as "image and likeness of God;" God imparts in word and in love the glory of the intimate life of the Trinity. Religion as community with God is also the foundation of the human community, the genuine fellowship with other persons.[31]

Experience of and dialogue with God creates conditions for true personhood; that is, the true self is found only in relation to and dialogue with God. Häring states:

> Personalism that is related to vitalized religion essentially emphasizes the truth that *man exists only through the Word*. He is a person by reason

---

[28] Alles, 34. See "Otto's humanistic critics," 26–38.

[29] *LC* 1:38.

[30] See *CRCW*, 108–10, *CE*, 2, and *MP*, 3, for a discussion of personalism and its rejection of viewing persons as objects.

[31] *LC* 1:37–38. Häring gives lengthy consideration to *imago dei* as participation in divine freedom and knowledge of value. *LC* 1:99–135; *FFC* 1:110–14.

of God Who calls and appeals to him. Hence, man's only road to self-realization is that of total surrender of himself to the call, thereby emerging from himself and advancing to the One to Whom he simply owes himself, because the calling is not something additional to man's reality. The person rather becomes a self precisely through the call. Everything in him and about him is call, response to the call, or a warping of self through an imperfect surrender to the call.[32]

Häring's personalist interpretation of the divine Person and the human person are influenced by both Martin Buber (1878–1965) and Max Scheler. In *I and Thou* (1923) Buber makes a distinction between two types of encounter: the I-Thou and the I-It. The I-It emerges when persons treat others as instruments and means, reducing them to the same level of usefulness or disuse as material objects in technology and science. Häring agrees with Buber that this de-valuing of the human person is the central problem of modern alienation. The true authentic self emerges in the I-Thou encounter, in which the unique, non-reducible other is met as an end, not as a means. Häring uses Buber's concept of the uniqueness of persons and the quality of the dynamic inter-relationship between persons that actualize the full potentiality of each other. The I-Thou encounter is an encounter with one's whole being, an essential concept in Häring's anthropology.[33]

Two other ideas from *I and Thou* find their way into Häring's work. The first is the Logos character of the encounter—the whole person is a word spoken and encountered and the I-Thou relationship takes place within this logos structure. For Buber, "The basic word I-You can be spoken only with one's whole being" and "When I confront a human being as my You and speak the basic word I-You to him, then he is no thing among things nor does he consist of things."[34] Second, Häring draws on Buber's idea that all I-Thou encounters involve response to the Eternal Thou. Buber describes three spheres of encounter: life with nature, where the relation "remains below language," life with men, where the relation is "manifest and enters language" and life with spiritual beings: "Here the relation is wrapped in a cloud but reveals itself, it lacks but creates language.

---

[32] *CE*, 13–14. For a similar discussion see *CE*, 35; *FFC* 1:62, 74, 86. On the relationship between the individual "I" and the "Thou" see *LC* 1:73–76; on the individual and community, *LC* 1:77–87.

[33] Buber (54) states: "The basic word I-You can only be spoken with one's whole being."

[34] Buber, 62, 59; see also 151.

We hear no You and yet feel addressed; we answer—creating, thinking, acting: with our being we speak the basic word, unable to say You with our mouth." Buber goes on to claim that in and through every I-You encounter we address the Eternal you: "In every sphere, through everything that becomes present to us, we gaze toward the train of the Eternal You; in each we perceive a breath of it; in every You we address the eternal you, in every sphere acceptable to its manner."[35]

Häring is closer to Buber's understanding of God as both "wholly other" and "wholly present" than he is to Otto's concept of the "holy." Buber takes exception to Otto's one-sided emphasis of the wholly other, but for Buber, and likewise for Häring, God is both *"mysterium tremendum* that appears and overwhelms; but he is also mystery of the obvious that is closer to me than my own I." Similarly Buber departs from Otto's conception of "creature feeling" and highlights the quality of dependence on both sides of the I-Thou encounter with the Eternal You.[36]

Häring's theory of religion is also deeply indebted to the German philosopher Max Scheler's work *On the Eternal in Man*; his moral philosophy builds upon Scheler's value theory in *Formalism and Nonformalism in Ethics.*[37] Häring, like many religious thinkers who are indebted to Scheler, rely on Scheler's middle period, a time he took up the task of "applied phenomenology" and was a believing Catholic.[38] Häring draws primarily from Scheler's personalism—the philosophy of the person as a dynamic, ontic sphere in man. Religious acts for Scheler are distinct from all other kinds of acts because they respond to the divine as Person. Häring is interested to show, however, that all acts, religious and moral, are grounded in the religious response to God, and all share this same basic character.

[35] Buber, 56–57; see also 123ff. and 150ff. "Extended, the lines of relationships intersect in the Eternal You. Every single You is a glimpse of that. Through every single You the basic word addresses the eternal You."

[36] Ibid., 129–30.

[37] No one has yet to take up a full-scale analysis of Scheler's influence on Häring, and it is beyond the scope of this work to do so. Jonsen and Hamel detail Häring's main ideas about religion and morality and his use of value theory, but do not analyze in detail Scheler's influence on Häring's system.

[38] Häring criticized Scheler for his rejection of religion and the Catholic faith, *LC* 1:566, n. 51. See also, Manfred S. Frings, *Max Scheler: A Concise Introduction into the World of a Great Thinker* (Pittsburgh, Pa.: Duquesne University Press, 1965) 21–30, and Alfons Deeken, *Process and Permanence in Ethics: Max Scheler's Moral Philosophy* (Paramus, N.J.: Paulist Press, 1974).

According to Scheler God is "person of persons," a personal being, not an object, who can be known only in relationship, and not through metaphysics. God's existence cannot be an object of reasoning or logical analysis because He is the Person of persons. The basis of the divine-human relationship for Scheler is the eternal *in* man because there exists in all persons a "sphere of the absolute," which can be suppressed or rejected in favor of other sensible objects.[39] Persons can falsely fill this sphere with earthly goods, creating idols of money, nation, or love—material or philosophical objects rather than true religion. Because persons, in addition to the sphere of the absolute, have, consciously or unconsciously, a metaphysical idea or feeling that life is wholly dependent on something greater.

For Scheler true religion is found in religious acts such as prayer, giving thanks, fearing, repenting, and worshiping. Such acts share three characteristics: (1) they transcend the world; (2) they offer an experience of possible fulfillment by the divine *only*, and negatively a sense that all finite things cannot fulfill one; (3) the fulfillment of a religious act is only possible by a Being which "bends down" to man and opens Himself to man. Hence, a religious act always implies an act of *response*. The existence of God can only be given in a religious act through God giving Himself *in* such an act. "A religious act is, paradoxically, a receiving act, in which man at the same time intends the divine correlate and unfolds himself for divine fulfillment, revelation, and ultimately response" (157). These three human characteristics correlate with Scheler's understanding of the divine Person as beyond contingent being, who's power is of an infinite nature, and it must be the only kind of response that can ever be received in terms of fulfillment. Through Scheler's religious anthropology Häring discovers a way of interpreting the *imago dei*.

The third dimension of Häring's theory of religion is the social character of religion. Häring's personalism, which uses Buber's I-Thou-We pattern, highlights the essentially social character of persons.[40] The individual, a free and unique being, enters into relationship with other persons, so that the I-Thou relationship participates in a larger network of social relationships. Persons are open not only to divine initiative but also to encounters with other persons and the community of persons.

[39] See Frings (145–48) on the concept of "sphere."
[40] *CE*, 8–150, and *MP*, 1–5, 35.

Religion is fellowship because it constitutes the ongoing dynamic communication between God and persons within the context of community. The individual's encounter is never in isolation from the community of followers. God's invitation comes to the individual through the community, and response to God is lived out in loving service of the neighbor.[41] Häring writes:

> Religion as community with God is also the foundation of the human community, the genuine fellowship of persons. True community of men rests on word and love, and perfects itself in the dialogue of love. The capacity for word and love, which centers in the very heart of the Thou, is fulfilled in us, however, only in so far as we are caught up by the word and love of God and give to God our response and love in return. Fellowship with God in word and love develops and fulfills our individual personality (the image of God in us) and at the same time reveals our essentially social nature. Therefore religious living, if it develops its own sound dynamic, places us necessarily in the human community—the word-love fellowship with our fellow man.

Community allows the individual to become fully human and fully religious, and for Häring, the individual-social dynamic models the inner relationship of the Trinity: "God is an absolute Self in ultimate community, and in this community, which is the Trinity, all true community of persons is rooted."[42]

Häring draws the phenomenology of religion into his virtue theory. The primary dialogue and encounter of the person with God is through prayer and likewise within the community is through worship, communal prayer. Häring retains the category of virtue to describe the human capacity to respond to divine initiative. Religion consists of two responses by human persons: the interior response constituted by faith, hope, and love (the theological virtues) and the exterior response constituted by worship (the virtue of religion).[43] Häring asserts that "Religion is the bond with God mutually joining together in the community of faith and worship all those who are thus united with God and acknowledge their union with Him and with one another. Nothing manifests and sustains this common

---

[41] *FFC* 1:63–64.

[42] *CE*, 14.

[43] The relationship between the theological virtues, the virtue of religion, and the moral virtues will be discussed in the following chapters.

bond more perfectly than community of cult."[44] Worship is the formal ongoing dialogue between the community and God. Religion is social because this bond is shared with those who have the same relationship with the sacred. In worship, human persons place themselves in relation to the divine, opening their intellects, hearts, and wills to the sacred person, manifest in word and symbol. For Häring, "worship is the fullest 'yes' to God's majesty and dignity, but by its very nature it includes the belief that God intends to enter into communion with man."[45]

Even though Häring's discussion of religion comprises only a few pages at the beginning of *The Law of Christ* it constitutes a dramatic departure from the neo-Thomist manuals that place the divine-human relationship almost exclusively in terms of law (e.g., God as divine Lawgiver and Judge; human persons as law-abiding, salvation-seeking creatures). Häring's purpose at the beginning of his own manual is to remind the reader that there is something prior to obligation, more fundamental than the religious and moral "ought." As noted at the outset, Häring was not interested in developing a full-scale theory of religion. For example, he shows little interest in myth, mysticism, or other religions. Rather, he is content to integrate certain basic concepts and categories from the German phenomenologists in order to highlight a very basic biblical idea: God has created human persons to be in fellowship with God and with each other, and this fellowship forms the basis of all human life and action.

Morality as Response to Value

Häring's phenomenological analysis of religion demonstrates that religion is distinctly defined in terms of dialogue through the dynamics of invitation, response, and worship. Just as religion is constituted by dialogue, initiated by the Thou which advances toward human persons, so morality is response to value within the created order. Häring again turns to the philosophy of Max Scheler's value theory as his main source.[46] Moral response involves several important aspects: freedom, knowledge of and response to values (including

---

[44] *LC* 2:120.

[45] *CE*, 37.

[46] *LC* 1:47–48. See Jonsen's analysis (92–99) of response to value in Häring's moral theology. Jonsen (94) points out that Häring's value theory is closest to Scheler, "for whom value is Person offering and accepting love."

knowledge of norms and laws), inner dispositions, and conscience, each of which is given extensive treatment in Häring's work.[47] In this section the discussion will be limited to value theory and the concept of responsibility.[48]

Häring's special indebtedness to Max Scheler should be noted. Scheler's philosophical ethics rests on three important ideas: the development of personalism, that is the human person understood as a concrete, social, historical being; "a philosophy of plentitude" that emphasizes the rich variety of moral values available to human persons; and, the moral life as a historically conditioned search for the realization of values, growth and development through the realization of values in history. Scheler's value theory, like his theory of religion, also utilizes a phenomenological approach to moral experience.

Value theory allows Häring to move beyond the strict and formal legalism of Catholic moral thought by emphasizing the values beneath norms and laws and the deep motives and attachments to value that are experienced through love. Persons can know value through norms, but real attachment to and love of value comes through experience of value. Within moral experience, persons perceive value "in its clarity and splendor and its concrete worth and claim to our acceptance."[49] This fundamental perception of value, then, has two aspects: the objective worth of value in and of itself (and not according to its utility) and the obligation imposed which requires a response corresponding to the nature of the value.[50]

Value experience is grounded in the person's basic potentiality for openness to the other. Value experience consists of a "spiritual affectivity" *(Gesinnung)*, an act that involves the whole person (combining yet transcending the intellect and will) and consists of the free offer and acceptance of love.[51] The human heart (Gemut) is not a total chaos of feeling-states, but an ordered whole, that is both a counter-

---

[47] For Häring's discussion of freedom, see *LC* 1:99–120; *CRCW*, 50–90; *FFC* 1:67–74; on disposition see *LC* 1:195–213; *CRCW*, 141–73; *FFC* 1:88–93; on conscience, see *LC* 1:135–89; *CRCW*, 91–140; *FFC* 1:224–96.

[48] For Häring's discussion of value, see *DHG*, 60–65; *LC* 1:120–35, 227–36; *FFC* 1:110–13; *MP*, 136–45. For analysis of his position, see O'Keefe, 24–25; Hamel, 23–26; and Jonsen, 92–99.

[49] *LC* 1:125.

[50] Jonsen, 93.

[51] See *LC* 1:120–24 for a discussion of knowledge and will and 124–26 for a discussion of different levels of perception, knowledge, and experience of value. See *FFC* 1:90–93 for a discussion of *Gesinnung*.

part to the cosmos, and a microcosm of the gradual order of values. Thus, intuition, knowledge, and acceptance of value are the basic dynamic movement of persons toward value, which is based on "our affinity for the good," a "kind of second nature *(connaturalitas)*."[52] Because persons are bearers of value, they encounter value most directly through other persons, the "Value-Person." For Häring, the value encountered in the other is the realization that they also embody the *imago dei*.[53] Häring states: "In fact, the sense of value attains perfection only in the total response to its word of love, only when the attitude of the one who perceives it measures up to the essential attraction of the good, in so far as this is possible. For ultimately the essence of the good is its appeal to love."[54]

In addition to the experience of value in the other, Häring identifies two other kinds of value experience: experience of moral values (interior to the subject), which consist of virtues, dispositions, and motives that allow one to be open to and responsive to value; and experience of objective values (exterior to the subject), which consists of the realm of values within society that support institutional and cultural practices toward encouragement of value.[55] Through all these value experiences, human persons intuit that no particular value is ultimate, but rather that all value rests on the ultimate value, "the Person of God offering himself and summoning unto himself."[56] The experience of value, rooted in communion and love with the other, draws the person more deeply into the knowledge and experience of the ground of all value as sacred and rooted in God. In addition to experience, knowledge of value comes through the "realm of values," or a hierarchy of value, which is determined by divine revelation, the community (particularly the Church), and natural law.[57]

---

[52] *LC* 1:133–34.

[53] *FFC* 1:64; see also 90–96. See *CE*, 15, for a discussion of Christ as the ultimate Value Person. Häring draws on Scheler's understanding of value-persons in *Formalism in Ethics and Non-Formal Ethics of Values* (Evanston: Northwestern University Press, 1973) 27ff., 85ff.

[54] *LC* 1:125.

[55] Jonsen, 96.

[56] Ibid., 94.

[57] Häring calls the former the "subjective source of moral knowledge, which for the Christian includes submission to God's will and prayer" (*LC* 1:133–35). Hamel (25) discusses how the personal freedom of the individual accepts an impersonal value as obligatory, which according to Häring is a "logic of the heart." Although this explanation does

The community generalizes and formulates values into universal statements which are meant to guide action in order to promote value. Value, according to Häring, "dictates norm" because it is the foundation of norms and laws. He states: "A norm of morals is not arbitrary restraint interfering with liberty, but the summons and invitation to the exercise of liberty arising from the value in the object, an invitation to man to preserve and nurture value in freedom. A norm which is not founded in a value and which does not present a duty through relation to value has no moral force binding the will."[58] The hierarchy of values, and the norms and laws that guide them, are determined in two ways. Norms derived from the created order are based on a hierarchy of values, ranked according to what promotes and enhances human freedom to realize value in the communion of love. Häring observes that "Insofar as love rightly perceives value, it will perceive not single values in isolation but the order of value: things subservient to and for the service of persons, dispositions as expressions of persons, persons in their uniqueness and inviolability yet ordained to communion. Love recognizes and realizes the order of values."[59] In addition to values in the natural order are values and norms known through divine revelation. The ultimate norm for Christians is the will of God, which is most completely and visibly manifested in Jesus Christ.

Value theories, along with theories of encounter, provide Häring with a means for describing what is distinct about religion and morality, but also how they are united. Religion and morality are united because they are deeply personal and demand a response. They are distinct because the immediate response of religion is worship, and for morality it is the increase of value in the created order. But the moral life is never completely distinct from religion, according to Häring. True morality recognizes its ultimate source and makes of all moral response a response to God. Religious morality is true morality because it understands its source and aim, whereas secular ethical systems, because they fall short of this realization, are incomplete. According to Häring, this union between religion and morality is most completely manifested in Christianity, and within

---

not resolve the question, Häring is attempting to show that morality consists of two poles—freedom and obligation—which are both incomplete if not grounded in the religious. He calls the latter the "objective source" of morality (*LC* 1:131–33).

[58] Ibid., 227.
[59] Jonsen, 98.

Christianity it is best exemplified in the John's Farewell Discourse (John 14–17). Häring states, "The fundamental invitation expresses the essence of religion ('abide in me and I in you') and the mystery of oneness with Christ, who is one with God, finds fruitfulness in brotherly love."[60]

Häring uses the idea of responsibility to draw together several key ideas in religion and ethics. As a central anthropological idea, responsibility explains the human person's capacity for free response to divine initiative and value. As a biblical motif, it captures the essence of the story of God's relationship to the people of Israel and the New Testament understanding of discipleship. It also appeals to modern persons struggling to understand religious faith and morality because it expresses personal choice and freedom in relation to divine life. Finally, responsibility serves as a thematic link between central dogmas and the moral life. Because Häring defines the human person as "responder," the moral and religious are united in the quest for dynamic interrelationship with God and neighbor. God calls persons through the community, and human persons respond to God through love for the other.[61] This dialogue-in-love is manifested most fully through the divine person, Jesus Christ, and the Christian life is most fully and completely expressed in the imitation of Christ.

Christ and Humanity

So deep is our conviction that the doctrine about man in moral theology (anthropology) must be studied in the light of Christology that it seems to us to be in a measure an actual part of Christology. Let us note that if we are to understand man who is called by Christ, this is possible only in the light of Him who calls. Our study of man is not just man, but man as created in the Word of the Father, who is Christ.[62]

———————————————— Bernard Häring, *The Law of Christ*, vol. 1

Jesus Christ: Word of God and High Priest

Jesus is the center of the Christian religious-moral life and therefore "the principle, the norm, the center, and the goal of Christian Moral

---

[60] *CE*, 47; *MP*, 34.
[61] *CE*, 10, 15.
[62] *LC* 1:61. This idea is repeated several times in *FFC* 1:2, 14, 120.

Theology."[63] Häring's Christology is drawn largely from Karl Adam's dogmatic theology, but his unique contribution consists of uniting Christology with his word-and-response model that allows a synthesis of major dogmatic themes with moral categories. For example, Häring weaves the invitation-response theme throughout several major christological dogmas in *The Law of Christ* in order to demonstrate how God's invitation through Christ extends from creation through the Incarnation to the Second Coming.[64] He also explicates how Jesus Christ forms the foundation and essence of each aspect of the moral life such as conscience, disposition, virtue, norm and law, and conversion.[65]

Karl Adam, Häring's professor at Tübingen in the 1940s, influenced a generation of Catholic theologians through his Christology and ecclesiology. He was influenced by both Romano Guardini and Josef Jungmann, who each published important books in the 1920s that gave the liturgical movement a more solid theological foundation. Guardini's, *The Spirit of the Liturgy*, emphasizes Jesus as a human person, "entirely one of us," who walked the streets and lived among ordinary people. In terms of Jesus' divinity, Guardini retrieves the idea of Jesus as mediator, High Priest, and Incarnate Word.[66] Jungmann's study, *The Place of Christ in the Liturgy*, took Guardini's idea of mediator and High Priest and traced it to early Roman liturgical practice and theology.[67] A strong emphasis on the humanity of Jesus, supported by growing historical work on the New Testament, countered the prevailing "Christology from above" of the neo-Thomists.

---

[63] *LC* 1:vii. Häring continues to make Jesus Christ the center of his moral theology. See *FFC* 1:1.

[64] *LC* 2:xxi–xxxviii.

[65] For a discussion of conscience and the imitation of Christ, see *LC* 1:135–39; norms and Christ, 232–35, 252–53; the new Law and Christ, 257–63; human laws and the imitation of Christ, 267–70; Christ and sin, 339–40; imitation of Christ and sin, 340–42; and Christ and conversion, 387–96. In fact, each section of Häring's moral theology, which follows much the same outline as the manuals of moral theology, begins with a discussion of Jesus Christ and includes a section on the imitation of Christ and the sacraments.

[66] Jesus is "sovereign mediator between God and man, the eternal High Priest, the divine Teacher and Judge of the living and of the dead; in His body, hidden in the Eucharist, He mystically united all the faithful in the great society that is the Church; He is the God-Man, the Word that was made flesh." Romano Guardini, *The Spirit of the Liturgy* (New York: Sheed and Ward, 1935) 155–56.

[67] Jungmann argued that early Christians prayed with Jesus, but that the anti-Arian mood of the Church shifted the emphasis away from the humanity of Jesus as mediator between God and persons, to Jesus as the Second Person of the Trinity, one worthy of direct prayer and worship. Josef Jungmann, *The Place of Christ in the Liturgy* (Staten Island: Alba House, 1965).

Karl Adam draws upon and expands Guardini and Jungmann's Christology in *Christ Our Brother*. He argues that the humanity of Jesus had all but been forgotten in Catholic theology and piety.[68] Adam places the incarnation at the center of his Christology and portrays Jesus as true God and true man, fully united with both God and humanity. Through the incarnation, Jesus bridges the divide between God and human persons, raising humanity up to a new kind of relationship with God: "not because we leave behind our human nature, but because in Jesus Christ God has entered totally into our humanity."[69] Adam's Christology is also influenced by Max Scheler's idea that human persons are essentially relational beings and find the "true self" only in community. Adam applies this idea to Christ, arguing that Jesus, as the "true man," unites human persons with God in true community. Adam is also responsible, along with Guardini, for retrieving Möhler's concept of the Church as the Mystical Body of Christ and integrating this idea into his Christology.[70] For Adam Christ is the head of the Mystical Body uniting all believers in one community of faith.[71]

Häring's Christology draws from Adam's focus on the central role of the Incarnation and his interpretation of Jesus as the Word of God and High Priest, and interprets each within his word-response theology. As the Word of God, Jesus embodies God's invitation to humankind and is the supreme example of the perfect response to God. Häring writes, "Jesus Christ is the ultimate and definitive Word of God's love to us, and also the sole worthy response of man to God's love. In Him alone we have a response of infinite and ultimate value

---

[68] Karl Adam, *Christ Our Brother* (London: Sheed and Ward, 1931) 38–57. See Krieg, 57–78, for an analysis of Adam's Christology "from below."

[69] Adam, 131.

[70] Karl Adam, *The Spirit of Catholicism* (Garden City, N.Y.: Doubleday, 1935) 13–15. See Krieg's discussion (17–55) of the impact of this book on Paul VI and *Lumen Gentium*. See Josef Jungmann, *Liturgical Worship* (New York: Frederick Pustet, 1941) 31–46, for a discussion of the Church as the Mystical Body of Christ.

[71] Adam (*Christ*, 40–52) was concerned with Christology's relationship to liturgy and how the liturgy fostered a relationship with Christ. He was critical of the scholastics' ahistorical Christology "from above" because it promoted a one-sided view of Jesus. Rather than viewing themselves as members of the Mystical Body and praying in union with Christ, most Catholics saw themselves as individuals before God, whose salvation depended on private devotions. Adam explained that Jesus, as head of the Mystical Body, is where the Christian community meets God. Thus for Adam, as well as Jungmann, all liturgical prayer should be joined to prayer with Jesus as mediator and High Priest. See Jungmann, *Liturgical Worship*, 34.

to Infinite Love."[72] Jesus is the "prototype of religion" because he comes from God and is the "most complete reply of love to God." In this way, Jesus is the perfect example of the unity of religion and morality.

Häring argues that the biblical metaphor of High Priest, drawn from the book of Hebrews, most aptly demonstrates this union between religion and morality.[73] According to Häring, Jesus is the ideal and norm of religion and worship. As High Priest, Jesus' response to the Father consists of adoring love and obedience the essence of religion. God's invitation to human persons begins in creation and continues throughout Israelite history but finds its most complete and fullest expression in the incarnation of Jesus Christ.[74] The incarnation is the anointing of Jesus by the Holy Spirit as High Priest. As the Anointed One, Jesus lives in the world, bearing God's invitation to humankind through his teaching and actions. He is also perfect man, completely open to God's will, freely responding to God's invitation, and obedient to God's call in adoring love.[75] If the incarnation is the anointing of Jesus as High Priest, then the cross is the supreme sacrifice, an act of perfect obedience and love. Häring writes: "If the Incarnation was priestly consecration of Christ through the anointing of the Holy Spirit, then His sacrificial death was the supreme act of priesthood and the preparation for the consecration of the Church as a whole, as well as of the individual man for priestly activity with Him."[76] By his death, Jesus gives his life to

---

[72] *LC* 2:xxx. Häring's is primarily a Logos Christology. See *LC* 1:52, 61, 89; *LC* 2:xxi–xxxv; *FFC* 1:20, 60–62, 106–7.

[73] In later works, Häring departs from the priesthood Christology and includes several images of Jesus from Scripture. For example, Christ as the New Covenant (*FFC* 1:15–17), the Prophet (*FFC* 1:17–18, *SEL*, 27, and *A Theology of Protest* [New York: Farrar, Straus, and Giroux, 1970] 21–38); Liberator (*FFC* 1:18–19), Alpha and Omega (*FFC* 1:19), Word (*FFC* 1:20), Truth (Ibid.), and Lord (*FFC* 1:21–22). These various images are united in the theme of freedom and faithfulness, which Christ embodies perfectly and which Christians are called to imitate: "fidelity to Christ, the Faithful One, who is Liberty incarnate and our Liberator" (*FFC* 1: 3). For a discussion of Christ as Truth and man as searcher for truth see *FFC* 2:7–20. Häring also made Christ the center of his spiritual writings. For a meditation on the images and names of Christ, see *Prayer: The Integration of Faith and Life* (Notre Dame, Ind.: Fides, 1975) 1–49. For a meditation on Christ as the hope of the world, see *Hope is the Remedy* (Garden City, N.Y.: Doubleday and Co., 1972) 21–29.

[74] *LC* 2:xxx.

[75] *LC* 1:72; *FFC* 1:20. This is a central thesis in Adam's *Christ Our Brother*. He (20–30) emphasizes Jesus' complete surrender to God's will and the personal dialogue between Jesus and his Father through prayer.

[76] *LC* 1:93.

God in order that humankind's priestly vocation may be restored and that all may share in the priestly vocation of Christ. Häring states that "our union with Christ, the High Priest, is effected in the sacraments, in which the Holy Spirit continues the work He initiated in the anointing of the Messiah. . . . As a result, all the activity of sacramental man, even the fulfillment of his mission in the world, bears the seal of the divine cult in the most exalted sense of the word. It partakes of his worship of God. For to be anointed by the Holy Spirit ultimately means nothing less than to be made to share the inner divine jubilation with which the Father and the Son eternally rejoice in the Holy Spirit (the jubilee of divine love).[77] By placing the metaphor of High Priest at the center of his Christology, Häring situates Jesus' teaching, actions, and death within the realm of religion, arguing that all of Jesus' responses to God's initiative are acts of worship.

Jesus as God's Word and High Priest is the perfect model for the Christian life, and the central act of the Christian life consists of imitating Christ. But the imitation of Christ is never merely an external act for Häring. The Christian life consists of inner assimilation into the life of Christ, which takes place through the sacraments and shapes all inner dispositions in conformity to Christ. In this sense, Häring's word-and-response model forms the basis of his Christology and anthropology, thereby linking Christ and humanity. In this sense he follows Karl Rahner's famous dictum, "Christology is the end and beginning of anthropology."[78]

Humankind: Created as Word for a Priestly Vocation

Häring's Christology and theological anthropology are linked by the two main themes of Word of God and High Priest. Human persons, as part of the divine creation, are word, spoken by God with the capacity to respond to God.[79] Häring states, "*Man is a word* and he can find the Word who calls him, and thus understand himself as an embodied word spoken by God and as a calling to respond in freedom

---

[77] Ibid.

[78] Karl Rahner, *Theological Investigations*, vol. 4 (New York: Crossroad, 1982) 117.

[79] Häring's theological anthropology in *The Law of Christ* consists of four parts: man as body-soul totality, man as individual and social being, the historical dimension of man, and man as "devoted to prayer and cult." See *LC* 1:61–97; *FFC* 1:85–101; *CE*, 23–26; *MP*, 43–49.

and gratitude."[80] According to Häring, the purpose of creation is to give glory to God; therefore human persons' essential nature is priestly. "It was the first intention of the Creator that man should be by nature a creature of prayer."[81] This priestly vocation was lost through Adam's sin of disobedience, which Häring defines as the refusal to offer God glory and praise. If through Adam this priestly vocation is lost, then through Christ it is fully restored by the power of the Holy Spirit. As Christ is anointed High Priest through the incarnation and makes the ultimate priestly sacrifice on the cross, so Christians enter into their priestly vocation through the sacrament of baptism, which anoints them as adopted children of God.

Baptism bears the gift of consecration and imposes the obligation of response. The baptized person is consecrated as the adopted child of God and thereby enters into communion with God and neighbor. Through consecration she shares in the priesthood of Christ, and this priestly vocation also demands a response in accordance with the actions of Jesus. Like Christ, human persons are called to share divine life with the Triune God, which is accomplished through imitation of Christ's obedience, freedom, love, and sacrifice. The priestly vocation of the Christian is fulfilled through the imitation of Christ.[82]

In Häring's moral theology, *Nachfolge Christi* combines several aspects of the Christian religious-moral life.[83] First, imitation of Christ is based on responsibility, which unites religion and morality and makes all action a response to God.[84] The moral response is a personal response to God through love of neighbor which arises from

[80] *FFC* 1:106. Häring also notes, "Our nature as individuals and the place of each of us in the creation rests on the fact that we are called by God in this way . . . we can answer him" (*SS*, 22).

[81] Ibid.

[82] *LC* 1:92–93. Jungmann's research demonstrated that the notion of priesthood in the early Church applied first to "Christ himself" and secondly "to the whole Christ, which is the totality of those who compose His Mystical Body and therefore share His life and also His priestly dignity" (*Liturgical Worship*, 38).

[83] Häring uses the German term *Nachfolge*, meaning both "imitation" and "following" in order to emphasize the life in Christ which the Christian strives to achieve. According to Jonsen (90–91), this imitation and following has taken on a variety of expressions in Christianity, and Häring has emphasized the sacramental and mystical union with Christ over other models that stress external poverty or suffering. "Haering indicates that the response of loving obedience grows out of and deepens the mystical and sacramental union. The moral life does not simply effect fellowship with God; it springs from fellowship with him."

[84] Häring (*LC* 1:51) states: "In a moral teaching based on the imitation of Christ, the essential characteristics of religion as fellowship with God, and morality as responsibility before God, are entirely in the foreground."

the religious encounter. Second, the imitation of Christ also combines two seemingly contradictory aspects of Christian anthropology: freedom and obedience. According to Häring, obedience is the
most free of all acts.[85] Christ is the one who exemplifies the perfect
obedient religious response to God as well as moral response to his
neighbor. But this obedience is not a cold and static response, based
solely on commandment; rather it is obedience based on love, which
are both gift of the Holy Spirit and the free response of the individual. Because human persons are created in the divine image and
recreated by the Holy Spirit through baptism, they possess the inner
capacity to respond to God in and through Christ. He states that:

> The foundation for the imitation of Christ is the incorporation of the
> disciple in Christ through grace. Imitation of Christ in our lives is ac-
> complished through activity of love and obedience in objective union
> with Christ. Imitation binds us to the word of Christ: in His grace, in
> the gift of love, Christ binds us to Himself. In love we unite ourselves
> with His person, the Incarnate Word. Our obedience unites us with
> Him through the following of His example eloquently inviting us to
> imitate Him.[86]

Third, imitation of Christ involves imitation of his priestly role
which grounds all moral actions in the religious. The imitation of
Christ, Häring repeatedly points out, is not "mere external copying"
but an "inner assimilation" into the life of Christ.[87] This inner assimilation means that one is open to receive God's grace, which enables one to live more fully the life of Christ. Häring writes that:

> The core of moral decision is the spirit of loving obedience to
> God. . . . Because of his love for God, man makes a personal and
> communal effort to discover the proper response that should be made
> to God through human relationships and activities. The moral deci-
> sion requires humble attention to the Will of God and hence to one's
> own possibilities, to the needs of one's neighbor, to the needs of the
> true brotherhood of men in all fields of life. Man has to make his own

---

[85] *FFC* 1:118–19.

[86] *LC* 1:51; for a similar quotation see *FFC* 1:20. Häring places great emphasis on the
relationship between obedience and love, stressing that obedience is to the person of
Christ, not to an impersonal law. For his discussion of law and imitation of Christ, see *LC*
1:52.

[87] Jonsen, 90. As Jonsen states, the term *Nachfolge* captures what is essential to Christianity: "the person, word, and act of Jesus Christ lays claim on the decision, deeds, and
manner of life of men in order to exemplify and carry on in them his work."

decision. Often it may be a bold choice among several possibilities, but it should never be an arbitrary choice. Responsibility means the effort to make a choice that can be offered to God as a response to His love as Creator and Redeemer, a choice that builds up the brotherhood of free persons to the glory of God.[88]

The core of the religious-moral response is obedience to God's will: "Responsibility, seen in a distinctively Christian way, is our God-given capacity to make all of our moral aspirations and decisions, indeed, all of our conscious life, a response to God, and thus to integrate it within the obedience of faith."[89]

* * * *

Häring's anthropology, like his Christology, rests upon his understanding of religion and morality, word and response, and the priestly vocation of all Christians. In his moral system the indicative is the imperative. As a child of God, sharing in the priesthood of Christ, the Christian who is grasped by God's saving grace experiences the divine presence, demanding a response. The invitation may be refused. But if accepted, Häring argues, the only possible response is the religious. In other words, the experience of God's grace elicits a particular knowledge of God (that this is an all-powerful, saving, loving God) to whom there is only one adequate response (adoring love and obedience). Even though this response rests on free choice, it is, according to Häring, the only possible choice to make.

The primary avenue of this experience of God and knowledge of God's gifts and demands is expressed in and through Christian worship, most particularly the sacraments. The encounter of God through

---

[88] CE, 49.

[89] FFC 1:65. Häring defined obedience in terms of love in The Law of Christ and expanded this notion to include "creative fidelity" in Free and Faithful in Christ. Obedience, for Häring, does not mean a cold, static observance of the law; static obedience is grounded in love and cannot be reduced to a "simple yes or no." Obedience consists of searching for faithful ways to respond to God's invitation: "The core of moral decision is the spirit of loving obedience to God. . . . Because of his love for God, man makes a personal and communal effort to discover the proper response that should be made to God through human relationships and activities. The moral decision requires humble attention to the Will of God and hence to one's own possibilities, to the needs of one's neighbor, to the needs of the true brotherhood of men in all fields of life" (CE, 49). Häring states that responsible action for the Christian consists of giving a "fitting reply" to God, a phrase adopted from H. R. Niebuhr, The Responsible Self: An Essay in Christian Moral Philosophy (New York: Harper and Row, 1963).

the sacraments is personal. Each sacramental encounter elicits a sense of one's sin, the need for God's grace, and the hope of salvation.[90] A person experiences God's word spoken to him; he hears a call of conversion and the demand for response. Häring links his Christology and anthropology to his sacramental theology through the word-and-response model: God invites the Christian community to accept his divine grace and to this invitation Christians respond through adoring love and obedience. This invitation and response is the foundation of all response to God in the world. Thus moral response to God and neighbor arises from the sacramental encounter.

Drawing upon history, the phenomenology of religion, value theory and the liturgical movement's sacramental theology, Häring is able to expand the sources of moral theology beyond those of the manualists and create alternative approaches to commonly accepted theological categories. It is obvious, however, that questions of theological method did not drive Häring's interests. If *The Law of Christ* is viewed as a transitional work and as an alternative manual of moral theology the assessment is based largely on the fact that the three volumes display an eclectic use of sources and methods, which include neoscholasticism and neo-Thomism as well as value theory, existentialism, personalism, phenomenology, biblical studies, liturgical studies, and the social sciences, particularly the sociology of religion and psychology. The unity of the book resides in its major themes; the methods to achieve a broad portrait of the Christian life are only a secondary concern to Häring and the extent to which these methods concur with one another is of little concern whatsoever.[91] In other words, he utilizes those methods that best explicate a theme within a given category but does not take up the task of arguing for particular methods over against the neo-Thomism of the manuals. He generally retains the structure of the neo-Thomist manuals, although he also departs from it at times, and he generally replaces the metaphysical explanations with biblical themes and

[90] "The awareness of God's abundant grace intensifies one's sense of sin and need for God" (*SEL*, 98). "They are signs which arouse hope in us . . . they arouse in us a longing for the fulfillment of all that is promised to us" (*SS*, 8). "The good news of the Kingdom of God and rule of his love is announced to us every time we participate in the sacraments" (*SS*, 9).

[91] R. Gallagher (12) notes, "The originality of *The Law of Christ* is not in its systematic-speculative thought but in the vision it ultimately implies." Also, see J. Gallagher (204–5) for a discussion of Häring's method. Robert Krieg (19) notes a similar approach to method in his study of Romano Guardini.

images, although he sometimes blends the two. His focus is primarily pastoral that combines both a concern about what people *know* regarding the religious life and what people *experience* in terms of the dialogical character of God's relationship to humanity.

Chapter 4

Sacraments as Word and Response

Jesus willed that even after His ascension His truth, His salvific will, His love should remain visible and perceptible on earth in the mystery of His Church. The Church is the visible sign of the continuing love of Christ in the world.[1]

_____ Bernard Häring, *The Law of Christ*, vol. 2

Häring dramatically altered his alternative moral theology manual by explicating the dogmatic foundations of the Christian life. Christology, anthropology, and ecclesiology are interpreted through his two main influences: a phenomenological understanding of religion and morality and the liturgical reformers' sacramental theology. Häring does not develop a separate sacramental theology to accompany his moral theology; rather, his system is a sacramental-moral theology and is shaped by four central elements. First are the categories of scholastic theology. Häring does not entirely reject scholastic categories of sacramental character, grace, and causality, but rather retains and reworks them within his word-and-response model, emphasizing their biblical and personalist dimensions. Second, Häring accepts the phenomenologists' understanding of religious experience and encounter as the basis of the religious life. The dynamic interplay between divine initiative and human response shapes his understanding of religion as worship and morality as religious-moral action. Third, he discovers synergies between these ideas and those of the liturgical reformers. Häring incorporates both

[1] *LC* 2:8.

the sacramentally-focused Christology and ecclesiology into his dogmatic framework, and he highlights participatory and social aspects of liturgy that were central to liturgical reforms of the times. Finally, Häring uses the theme of conversion to describe and explicate the sacraments of baptism, Eucharist, and penance in order to overcome the juridical emphasis of the manuals and emphasize a more biblical, dynamic understanding of the sacraments. In each of these illustrations, Häring's invitation-response model forms the background for his sacramental theology.

One of Häring's important departures from the neo-Thomist manualists' treatment of sacraments is that he does not define the rubrics of each sacrament in *The Law of Christ*, but rather identifies the sacramental theology under girding the seven sacraments and ties this to a vision of the moral life. Penance is an interesting case in point. As chapter 2 demonstrates, moral theology grew out of the sacrament of penance, developed and refined itself as the practice became more institutionalized, and served as the handbook for the confessor, until the decline of the neo-Thomists manual after Vatican II.

Häring's treatment of penance in *The Law of Christ* demonstrates his attempt to integrate the insights of the liturgical movement into his modified manual and to apply the concepts to this particular sacrament. He does not treat penance as a single sacrament, rather he considers three sacraments—baptism, Eucharist, and confession—as the "sacraments of conversion." His discussion of the sacraments of conversion follows the same pattern as the other categories of moral theology: he reinterprets the sacraments within this invitation and response model. Throughout his writings he continues to include this sacramental focus, especially in several books he authored on the sacraments, thereby retaining the moral theologian's concern for sacramental practice.

Refashioning Scholastic Sacramental Theology

It is most essential for the Christian not to view the reception of the sacraments and particularly the great sacrament of divine love, primarily in the light of obligation. He must see them as invitations and gifts of love and approach them in the spirit of loving and grateful response.[2]

———————————————— Bernard Häring, *The Law of Christ*, vol. 2

---

[2] *LC* 2:185.

The Catholic sacraments were systematized by medieval scholastic theologians and institutionalized by the Council of Trent, although the form of scholastic thought endorsed by Trent had shifted by the late sixteenth century. Trent's scholastic formulation of the seven sacraments endured for four hundred years with only minor changes until the Second Vatican Council. During this period, sacramental theology became a subdivision of moral theology. The manualists summarized and reduced sacramental treatises found in canon law and sacramental theology textbooks into guidelines that would assist priests in determining valid and licit reception of the sacrament, with particular attention to extreme cases.[3] Thus, the theological and philosophical background for the Catholic sacramental system was largely assumed and not fully explicated in moral theology manuals. It remained unchallenged and essentially unchanged despite the reforms initiated by the liturgical movement.

Early in his career Häring rejects a legalistic and individualistic approach to both morality and worship and recognizes that the renewal of moral theology is related to liturgical reform. The liturgical movement, first, sought to recover the "realism of symbols" and the "sacramental kerygma" of the words and rites, which the manualists considered only in terms of validity.[4] Liturgical reformers emphasize a more personal, dynamic, and experiential approach to

---

[3] A *valid* sacrament is defined according to the minimum requirements of the rite regarding the proper minister, matter, form, and intention. A *licit* sacrament is administered according to canon law; if one or more violations occur the sacrament is illicit, but not necessary invalid. *Fruitful* refers to acceptance of the grace by the recipient. *Reviviscence* refers to reviving the grace that was not received in a sacrament because of a state of sin. Upon repentance, it was understood that the grace was granted. Bernard Leeming, *Principles of Sacramental Theology* (Westminster, Md.: Newman Press, 1956) 267–69. On sacramental casuistry, see Jonsen and Toulmin, 272.

[4] Häring summarizes the manualists' approach: "The traditional manuals . . . presented Christian life by taking the decalogue as starting point; the written law was integrated with the natural law which was subsequently set forth almost like a moral code written once and for all. Then were added all the Church laws, without any clear distinction between the permanent values of the law written in men's hearts and the norms of moral codes reflecting past historical conditions. Only after this were the sacraments mentioned, with countless reminders of the vast aggregate of regulations, laws and rubrics formulated by Church authorities in view of a becoming celebration. The moralists detailed which rules obliged under pain of mortal sin and which under venial sin, all the while placing the greatest importance on sacred things: stones, places, vestments, and the like. 'Validity' became a function of eternal forms. Little was said relating moral life to the sacraments; a brief hint here and there was about all one could expect. Supposedly, the sacraments conferred grace to observe the norms regulating the moral life as expressed in the various legal formulations" (*SEL*, 3). For similar remarks, see *SS*, 23–24.

worship. Their recovery of biblical and patristic interpretations of the sacraments extends beyond scholasticism and opens up new ways of interpreting the Christian life. These approaches, Häring found, were more consistent with the New Testament, more appealing to modern Christians, and they move the moral and sacramental life beyond a legal minimalism.

Second, Häring recognizes that this shift defines the moral life as flowing from the sacraments rather than the sacraments construed as moral obligations.[5] The liturgical movement retrieves the notion of Christ as the sacrament of God and the Church as the sacrament of Christ and, according to Häring, this broader understanding of sacrament emphasizes the many "tangible signs of God's loving, creative and redeeming presence" which would "bear the fruit of love and justice for the life of the world."[6] The renewal of the liturgy would eventually lead to the renewal of the Christian life because without a more dynamic religious encounter in the Church's liturgy modern Christians would not be able to face modernity's challenges.

Häring's sacramental theology in *The Law of Christ* exemplifies the transition between the manualists' neoscholasticism and the new approaches emerging from the liturgical movement as well as other alternative manualists. But unlike other alternative manualists, he does not entirely reject the scholastic categories of sacramental character, grace, and causality; in fact, they are quite central to his sacramental-moral theology. Häring reinterprets each of these in accordance with his word-and-response theology, drawing from the Bible and patristic theologians rather than scholasticism. He emphasizes how each of these aspects of the sacraments combines the radical, free offer of the gift of divine life and the demand, and duty that arises from the individual's free acceptance of this gift. As in his moral theology, he retains the structure and terms of scholastic sacramental theology but expands the categories by including a dogmatic and biblical foundation. Before turning to the influence of the liturgical movement on Häring's sacramental theology, a brief examination of sacramental character, grace, and causality will demonstrate this point.

---

[5] *SEL*, 13.
[6] *SEL*, 2, 3.

Sacramental Character

In explaining the rituals and symbols of the early Christian community, patristic theologians drew from both biblical and cultural sources. For example, explanations for how baptism brings a person from an old to a new life drew upon the biblical image "marked with the seal of the promised Holy Spirit" (Eph 1:13). Patristic theologians viewed the seal as imprinting Christ's image on the Christian's soul in order both to protect him against temptation and evil and to enable him to live a Christian life.[7] Augustine argued in his treatise *On Baptism Against the Donatists* that baptism and ordination could be received once because they granted the sacramental seal, an indelible mark on the soul that constituted an ontological change that could never be removed; the two sacraments also granted grace, which could be lost through serious sin. Apostates had lost the grace of baptism or ordination but effectively were still Christians because they retained the seal. In seeking reentry into the Church, an apostate was not required to be rebaptized or reordained; rather, if he was contrite, his relationship with God was restored.

The scholastics accepted Augustine's position, but they could not decide which aspect the seal, the grace, or the ritual constitutes the sacrament. Through an elaborate philosophical explanation that cannot be discussed here, they came to regard the seal (the "character," as they called it) as the sacrament. The sacramental character elevated the soul from its natural to its supernatural level, thereby permanently transforming the person. The scholastics determined that three sacraments confer a character: baptism, confirmation, and ordination; and proceeding logically from this idea determined that the other four sacraments must also confer a *sacrament* and *grace,* that is, something both permanent and able to be lost because of sin.[8]

---

[7] The patristic authors drew from several sources for their understanding of the seal: the Hebrew Scriptures (Exod 9:4, 28:36); New Testament (John 6:27; Eph 1:13, 4:30; 2 Cor 1:21-22; 1 John 2:27; Rom 4:11, 6; Col 2:11); and secular images such as the branding of animals, military brands and tattoos, and imprints used on documents, letters, and coins. Leeming, 162–83.

[8] See Leeming, 263–66. Throughout the Middle Ages, scholastic theologians determined a threefold distinction that eventually became church law: the outward rite or sign, bread and wine in the case of the Eucharist, is the *sacramentum tantum*; the body and blood, under the appearance of the bread and wine, is the *res et sacramentum,* the reality and the sign; the body and blood also point to something beyond the sign, that is, spiritual union with Christ and the Church, the *res tantum*. By the time of Thomas Aquinas, the *res et sacramentum* was generally accepted as the sacrament. Scholastic theologians applied this threefold definition to all seven sacraments.

Häring retains the interpretation of the seal as corresponding to the priesthood of Christ (a point stressed by Cyril of Jerusalem, Thomas Aquinas, and the Council of Trent) and adds to it the theme of word-and-response. Häring argues that the sacramental character is Christ's priestly image that is lost through the Fall and restored in baptism. The sacramental character is both gift and demand. First, it restores the priestly dignity of the Christian so that he or she may now participate in the divine cult: "The sacramental character disposes the recipient of the sacrament for the celebration or for participation in the celebration of the divine mysteries and for the cultal orientation of his whole life."[9] Through baptism, the person is consecrated to a priestly role, assimilated into Christ, and shares in the life of sacrificial service.

The sacramental character also imposes a duty and imperative. The character imprints the priestly vocation of Christ so that the individual is to follow Christ's life as her own. The character imposes the obligation to live as an "adopted child of God." Häring explains:

> Through him we are incorporated into the Anointed One from whom we receive our tasks assigned through the sacred signs of cult, the holy sacraments. Particularly, the privileges and duties flowing from baptism, confirmation, and holy order can be understood only in the light of the priesthood of Christ and His Church. God's gifts to earthly pilgrims are pressing *imperatives*. Hence the power and grace of the sacraments bear with them a sacred obligation. Clearly the sacramental character is a sign and consecration to sacred duty; it is assignment to the most intimate partnership in the priestly activity and priestly spirit of Christ and the Church.[10]

Even though baptism, confirmation, and holy orders were traditionally defined as granting a special character or seal, Häring argues that each of the other sacraments, while not imparting a seal, nonetheless orders the Christian to divine cult and places them under the obligation of giving glory to God through all their actions: penance (second baptism) restores one to full cultal participation; Eucharist joins Christians together as a community of priestly sacrifice; anointing of the sick is a "cultal union of man's final illness and death to the passion and death of Christ"; marriage is an image of the union of Christ and the Church and therefore bears the mark of

---

[9] *LC* 2:146.
[10] Ibid., 2:147.

sacrificial love.[11] The sacramental character, according to Häring, is God's gracious and free gift of divine life to the believer that promises the presence of the Holy Spirit in order that the Christian, through acceptance of God's grace, becomes fully assimilated into the life of Christ.

Sacramental Grace

Each sacrament, according to scholasticism, confers both a sacrament, which is permanent, and grace, which can be lost because of sin. Generally, grace is seen as a divine power that brings about a metaphysical transformation of the soul, elevating it to a supernatural level and thereby removing original sin and restoring capacities for divine communion. According to scholastic theologians there are three types of grace: habitual (sanctifying), actual, and sacramental. Habitual grace refers to God's power to elevate the soul to a new, supernatural level, commensurate with one's supernatural end, the Beatific Vision. Relying on Aristotelian categories used by Aquinas, the neoscholastics explained habitual grace as an "accidental modification" of human nature; grace restored what was lost in the Fall, namely the human person's capacity to attain a supernatural end.[12] Of course, no person could achieve this end on his own, and so habitual grace was completely unmerited. It created a new habitual orientation with new powers known as the theological virtues.[13]

In addition to taking on this new orientation, a person's actions required they be consistent with the "new man," and so each action needed particular assistance from God. Actual grace was understood to be granted according to the aid required for performing good works. Good works in turn merited more grace, and so cooperating with actual grace initiated further growth in holiness. It was never

[11] Ibid., 2:147–49.

[12] J. Gallagher, 63. See McCool, *Nineteenth Century Scholasticism*, 196–201, for how Kleutgen understands grace and his critique of Hirscher.

[13] J. Gallagher (55–56) discusses the manualists' understanding of grace in relation to moral acts and notes that they did not make "elaborate distinctions with regard to categories of grace." In regard to moral acts, they emphasized the supernatural principle (that power which made natural acts supernatural) as habitual grace, which cooperated with the human will so that the will was moved toward an ultimate end (God) and not merely a proximate end. They also understood habitual grace as the theological virtue of charity, which was also defined as the infusion of grace, a gift freely given by God, which transformed their acts into supernatural efforts. (A fuller discussion of theological virtues follows in the next chapter.)

entirely determined among scholastic theologians whether sacramental grace was a separate form of grace or a type of habitual or actual grace, and this conundrum led to centuries of heated debate.[14]

Häring turns to a biblical understanding of grace and bypasses the problem regarding sacramental grace as habitual or actual. In *The Law of Christ* he simply states that there is no absolute distinction between habitual and actual grace and the sacramental character; rather, these are different ways of describing the same reality. Häring retains the scholastic notion that the sacramental character "disposes" the Christian to receive the grace necessary for living the Christian life but goes no further in defining the various forms of grace. He elaborates:

> To fulfill the cultal duty we stand in need not only of abundant actual graces as aids in the task imposed by the sacramental character. If our worship is to be truly pleasing to God we must reflect in our souls the celestial glory of God and Christ. This is to say that we must be endowed with the life of grace. This sanctifying grace of the sacraments should not be looked upon as something separated from actual grace and the sacramental character. The three are not disjointed and independent realities, but rather diverse forms or phases of the real initiation on our part into the radiant splendor of the divine glory, the *dóxa* of that divine mystery which merits all our honor and praise. The three—habitual grace, actual grace, sacramental character—in their totality and unity give us the capacity and impose the duty of honoring God worthily in Christ.[15]

Häring defines grace according to the biblical understanding of God's holiness and glory; grace "radiates" from God's "majesty and holiness." Sacramental grace is God effectively sharing divine holiness, through the sacraments, in order that each person may in turn respond to God in holiness. (This is the same divine life shared through creation, Incarnation, and salvation history.) According to Häring, by entering into God's holiness, persons are made worthy to enter into the divine cult: "the sanctifying action of God upon man, with its center and most manifest expression in the holy sacraments and its goal primarily in the glory of God."[16] The sacraments are the

---

[14] In this debate some theologians sided with Aquinas, who argued that sacramental grace is like an infused habit that flows from sanctifying grace but is distinct from it. Others argued that sacramental grace is the actual grace needed for living a Christian life. For a summary of this debate, see Leeming, 268–74.

[15] *LC* 2:146.

[16] Ibid., 2:141–42; *SS*, 77; see 1 Pet 1:2; 2 Thess 2:13.

privileged locus of divine activity through which God speaks the divine word to humanity.[17] Sacramental grace, according to Häring, is not made up of discrete gifts from God but is the outpouring of divine life that enables persons to respond and accept this gift. In this sense, sacramental grace is both relational and experiential.[18] Häring states:

> All the imperatives for the baptized, for the confirmed, for those joining Christ at the sacrificial Banquet are imperatives of grace. They are commands flowing from God's love for us to be transformed into our love for God, flowing from the majesty of God to lead to the glorification of God. Not that it is we who begin to honor God; for it is God who invests us with His own glory. Not that we begin to sanctify our lives; God sanctifies us. The result for the one sanctified is the great imperative, the imperative demanding the Christian life, the life of discipleship. This imperative is the *Law of Grace*.[19]

Sanctification, according to Häring, is both "our grace and our task," a "commitment and promise."[20] Through the sacraments, persons encounter the divine initiative and the demand for response, and God's invitation and gift demands a response that is both cultal and moral.

Sacramental Causality

The idea of sacramental causality expressed in the scholastic teaching *ex opere operato* ("by the work worked") also has roots in Augustine's debate with the Donatists. Augustine argues that the change brought about by the sacrament cannot be dependent upon the minister or the recipient because God is the ultimate cause of the sacrament. If the sacramental change is dependent on the spiritual or moral state of the minister, any sacrament he or she conducts if they are in a state of sin would be invalid. The scholastics accept this idea but recognize an inherent danger if the participants have no role whatsoever. They determine that the minister and recipient need to have the proper intention for the sacrament to be effective.

---

[17] For Häring's comments on sacrament as privileged but not sole signs of grace, see *SEL*, 94, and *SS*, 16. In these later works he argues that sacraments are like sources of heat and light; they lead one to recognize God's word and grace beyond the sacraments and Church in the world.

[18] *SEL*, 98.

[19] *LC* 2:141.

[20] Ibid.

The participants in a sacrament must intend what the Church intends, they reason, otherwise there is no sacramental effect. According to Aquinas grace is always granted in a sacrament, but is not always received if the person is not properly disposed.[21] A serious and unintended outcome of the scholastic understanding of sacramental causality was a weakening of the experiential dimension of the Church's sacraments, especially as canonists focused exclusively on the minimum standards for valid and licit administration and reception.

Häring places the traditional concept of *opus operatum* within his word-and-response theology. Once again he emphasizes God's offer of grace, through the sacraments, that is unmerited and freely given. Häring states that God is the ultimate cause of sacramental transformation, inviting persons to respond to the offer of divine life. "The Church's doctrine on sacramental causality *(opus operatum)* with its priority over the work of the recipient brings to the fore the gratuitous efficacy of God's presence and the primacy of His grace."[22] In this sense, Häring defines the sacraments as "effective and causative signs of grace" because God acts through them to invite persons into the divine life and transform them so they may in turn respond.[23] In this sense, the sacraments are consistent with God's activity in the world from the creation to the present: God's grace is operative throughout salvation history, and the sacraments are a continuation of God's active presence in history. God's grace is a gift that effects a transformation within the person according to God's will.

Rather than drawing upon traditional metaphysical language to explain this change, Häring draws on Pauline and Johannine images to *describe* the change. He selects the biblical motif of conversion to emphasize God's radical, free offer of grace that effects a change described in John's gospel as "rebirth from God" and "darkness to light" and in Paul's letters as "a new creature," the "new freedom of the children of God," and "justification through grace by faith."[24] Equally important to Häring is the free response to God's initiative. He states:

---

[21] *ST,* I-I.112.1.

[22] *LC* 2:154. Häring later rejects the Aristotelian notion of causality that informed scholastic sacramental theology (*SEL*, 98). See Adam, *The Spirit of Catholicism*, 26, for a similar interpretation.

[23] Häring argues (*SEL*, 97) that if the Church speaks of sacramental causality, it will fail to grasp the modern person's search for meaning. It must stress divine initiative coming to man.

[24] *LC* 1:399–402.

Both must be fully stressed: the creative, sanctifying, and healing work of God and the personal response and responsibility under the impulse of grace. The Catholic concept stresses the personal no less than does the Protestant notion. Precisely because we place clearly in the foreground the creative bounty of the divine action and derive from it the moral-responsive endeavor of man, our concept of sacrament is unsurpassably dynamic, religious-moral, and personal in the sense of the *I-Thou* personalism of the inspired pages.[25]

Häring argues that valid and fruitful reception of the sacrament constitutes far more than merely following the rules defined in the rubrics. He is concerned with the interior disposition of the recipient: "From the standpoint of the person receiving the sacrament we must be concerned with the relation toward God in Christ, with the work of Christ in the Holy Spirit, and with the form of words and the efficacy of the sacred encounter itself."[26] Häring expands the scholastic notion of the recipient's disposition to include seven dispositions necessary for reception: right intention, faith, hope, charity, docility, willingness to participate in divine cult and to fulfill special sacramental obligations, and gratitude. He places these in a pastoral, rather than legal, context.[27]

According to Häring, then, the sacraments have a "threefold significance and efficacy: they are *cultal, salutary, social*."[28] First, as defined above, the sacramental character consecrates the person into a priestly vocation. The response to God's initiative to share divine holiness demands the immediate response of cult. Second, sacramental grace enables the Christian to live out this priestly vocation. Häring argues that sacraments do not "cause" a person's salvation; rather, sacraments, in the Pauline sense, are the means through which God's word and grace come to the individual, open her heart, and invite her to live a sanctified life. Through accepting God's holiness

[25] *LC* 2:155. This is most clearly spelled out in Häring's discussion of conversion in *LC* 1:399–404.

[26] Ibid., 2:159–60.

[27] Ibid., 2:159–66. Häring discusses validity in the administration of the sacrament within the context of defining the sacraments as personal encounters with Christ. He emphasizes that the minister is responsible to make the liturgy an experience of God's grace through full expression of the symbols. He argues that even though the Church has changed the matter and form throughout its history, the individual priest has no right to do so. In regard to Latin, it is a "pressing duty" of the ministry to explain the rich meaning of the symbols and the sacraments. He also takes a pastoral approach to issues of validity that previous moralists considered with "increasing severity."

[28] Ibid., 2:143.

and becoming "an adopted child of God," a Christian lives the life of holiness to which she is called. In this sense, the life of sanctification participates in salvation history.[29] Third, the sacraments unite the individual to the "saving bond in the Mystical Body, the Church, in true solidarity with all other members of Christ's Kingdom."[30] The sacraments are social realities, and participation in the worshipping community is the complete expression of the I-Thou-We pattern. Essentially this dynamic forms the basis for relationships that extend beyond worship. Assimilation to Christ through the sacraments forms the inner dispositions, which in turn enable persons to imitate Christ's actions in the world.

The following quotation from *The Law of Christ* especially summarizes Häring's sacramental-moral theology:

> The end and purpose of the sacraments is the sanctification of our lives. The sacraments usher us into the light of the divine majesty and most effectively bring home to us the obligation to seek our salvation in the glory of God; they link our lives with Christ and His salvific action in the history of salvation and caution us that our salvation can be wrought only through union with Him; they bind us to the community of cult, the Church, and give to our lives *ecclesial* foundation and assignment. Thus do they sanctify. Precisely insofar as the means of salvation do not leave us entirely to our own resources, they prevent us from clinging to a narrow and one-sided concept of our own salvation. The sacraments manifest the work of our salvation as true sanctification for the glory of God in Christ and the community of salvation, which is the Church.[31]

Häring retains the systematic structure of scholastic sacramental theology but replaces its philosophical base with biblical imagery and an alternative dogmatic theology. He makes a more dramatic shift away from neoscholasticism by incorporating theological insights of the liturgical movement into his sacramental theology. Thus the content of his sacramental-moral theology departs radi-

---

[29] Häring states that the sacraments are "God's plan for the salvation of the world" and through assimilation to Christ the person is set upon a path toward the fullness of God's kingdom. The sacraments, then, have an eschatological dimension. "Joyful and resolute anticipation of the end of time is constantly reawakened by the sacraments which order our lives to eternal glory and the Second Coming. The sacraments give form and meaning to the salvific events of the span of time which is the bridge between the resurrection and the Second Coming of Christ" (*LC* 2:50).

[30] Ibid., 2:143–44.

[31] Ibid., 2:183.

cally from the neo-Thomists. He draws three concepts from the liturgical movement to shape the sacramental theology in his system: the sacraments as visible and perceptible signs of faith, Christ as the supreme sacrament, and the Church as the Mystical Body of Christ that continues to make manifest through the sacraments God's saving grace in the history of salvation. These concepts expand Häring's sacramental theology beyond the scholastic categories and give his moral theology a new theological foundation.

Häring's Sacramental Theology and the Liturgical Movement

The dialog with God, in faith, hope, and love, is in no wise banished into the purely interior confines of contemplation without word or gesture. There is a reflection of God's invisible nature in the visible creation, which He created in His own Word, Who is the Image of His substance. In the splendor of His visible creation God reveals Himself, if only we harken to its inner voice and respond to the divine message. But mightier by far is the supernatural message: The Word of the Father willed to become visible and audible to us in a Person. . . . Christ is truly the basic, primordial sacrament. He is the sign in which and through which we experience the promise and the love of the Father. And in turn through and in Him we are able to speak effectively and worthily to God in response to His love.[32]

—————————————— Bernard Häring, *The Law of Christ*, vol. 2

Häring is the first Catholic moral theologian to incorporate the central tenets of the liturgical movement into moral theology. Even though the development of the liturgical movement parallels the rise of neo-Thomism in moral theology in the nineteenth and early twentieth centuries, there is little contact between the two movements. The neo-Thomist manualists ignore the ideas and issues raised by the liturgical movement. Over the course of the liturgical movement, reformers focus their academic and pastoral efforts on five main concepts: (1) a Christology emphasizing Christ as the sacrament of God, (2) an ecclesiology based on the Church as the Mystical Body of Christ, (3) a strong pastoral emphasis on lay understanding and participation, (4) the Eucharist as the center of the Church's life, and (5) a social understanding of the liturgy that responds to the prevailing individualism of modernity and Catholic

———————————

[32] *LC* 2:8.

piety. Each of these claims counters the neoscholastic theology that formed the Church's official sacramental theology and liturgical practice. When *The Law of Christ* was published in the early 1950s, liturgical reforms were well under way in Europe and North America, and the movement was granted official acceptance through the encyclicals of Pius XII. For example, scholarly research was growing in centers for liturgical study situated in Paris, Louvain, and Maria Laach; social action movements were directly related to liturgical reform in Belgium and Germany; new architectural expressions and experimentation with liturgical music were beginning; and revisions and experiments with the Easter Vigil were initiated.

The liturgical movement influenced both Häring's scholarly and pastoral work. Many of the leaders of the liturgical movement were centered in Germany in the first half of the twentieth century, and the German Catholic community was experimenting with liturgical reform through dialogue Masses, use of the vernacular in certain prayers and hymns (officially approved in Germany in 1953), retreats and conferences, and numerous publications.[33] As a student at Tübingen, Häring was taught by its two major figures of the 1940s, Karl Adam and Romano Guardini. In his pastoral work during and after World War II Häring implemented liturgical reforms in German parishes, encouraging greater lay understanding and participation, and as a scholar, he began incorporating the basic theological insights from the liturgical movement into moral theology.

Sacraments as Signs of Faith

Liturgical reformers observed that the liturgy had become a formal, static set of ritual actions that had lost its inner meaning and failed to cultivate the Catholic Christian's relationship with God. Romano Guardini in his path-breaking book *The Spirit of the Liturgy* and later in *Sacred Signs* argues that the inner meaning and essence of ritual actions, symbols, and material objects is the very presence of Christ.[34]

---

[33] Beginning in the Middle Ages, the priest began saying all parts of the Mass, even the responses assigned to the laity. Dialogue Masses restored the role of laity in responding to and praying with the priest.

[34] Guardini writes, "We must help ourselves to read in the outward from the inner state: to read from the body what is in the soul; to read from the earthly process what is spiritual and hidden. The liturgy is a world of sacred and hidden events which have taken visible shape—it is sacramental. The most important things to learn, then, are those living acts by which the believer grasps, receives and performs, the sacred 'visible signs of

Guardini draws this idea from Möhler, who defines the Church as an organic whole whose essence or inner spirit is expressed in outer forms; all external forms are valid and meaningful only to the extent that they animate this inner life.

Häring builds on Guardini's notion and connects the idea of sacraments as visible signs of God's redemptive, salvific love to other visible divine signs, such as creation, the incarnation, and the resurrection.[35] He draws on personalism to explain the relationship between material signs and divine realities, and he defines sacraments as "signs of faith" that relate to the whole person (i.e., the corporeal, spiritual, historical, social, and cultal dimensions of human personhood) because they are experienced through the five senses and utilize material objects. "In these visible and perceptible signs, which deal with things we can see and hear, there is the assurance of our faith that we encounter Christ in a manner suited to our human nature, composed as it is of body and soul."[36] According to Häring, sacraments relate to persons at their most natural and existential level because they engage the whole person, calling for response through bodily and spiritual action.

Häring's understanding of sacraments also links his theological anthropology and his Christology both of which emphasize the personal dynamic nature of the divine-human encounter. Häring's theological anthropology centers on his interpretation of the biblical notion of *imago dei*.[37] He strove to overcome the dualistic understanding of the relationship between the body and soul by emphasizing the goodness of the body and the complementarity of the

---

invisible grace.'" *Sacred Signs* (London: Sheed and Ward, 1937) x. This idea was also presented by Jungmann, *Liturgical Worship*, 24–25, and promoted by Pius XII in *Mediator Dei*, 23, 24. Jungmann argued that external forms and expressions are essential to liturgy precisely because liturgy is public, corporate worship and not individual prayer.

[35] *SEL*, 1–2.

[36] *LC* 1:406.

[37] Möhler argues that the Catholic understanding of human nature and life is that each person finds his or her source in the goodness of grace that is at the heart of creation. After the Fall, the image of God remains, but the "likeness" to God is lost. The image of God in each person is the necessary precondition for the incarnation and subsequent regeneration through Christ. Johann Adam Möhler, *Symbolism or Exposition of the Doctrinal Differences between Catholics and Protestants as Evidenced by Their Symbolic Writings*, trans., J. B. Robertson (London, 1843) 110. Karl Adam adopted this idea from Möhler and emphasized that God's image, though it remains, cannot be renewed and restored by human effort but only through communion with the God-man, Jesus Christ. (Guardini, *The Spirit of the Liturgy*, 163–70).

material and spiritual.[38] Häring follows the traditional understanding of *imago dei* but rejects the idea that the likeness of persons to God is based solely in their "spiritual nature." If that were so, he argues, moral action and responsibility would be narrow and limited to a "cultivation of spirit alone." Rather, the whole person—body and soul—reflects the divine image.

According to Häring the creation, Incarnation, and resurrection demonstrate the goodness of the body and the unity of body and soul. The sacraments also demonstrate how material elements "manifest and signify spiritual meaning" and make reference to both bodily and spiritual aspects of persons. According to Häring, "The sacraments with all the freshness of created nature in their use of material elements to manifest and signify spiritual meaning, and by reference to the visible body of man as well as to the spiritual soul, express most concretely and graphically the great truth: we in our whole present existence of body and soul stand before God and must respond to Him with the responsibility of our whole being."[39]

The sacraments are linked with other visible and perceptible signs through which God speaks and invites humanity to share divine life. Just as creation and the incarnation are Word of God, so the Church's sacraments continue the manifestation of God's life and will to humanity through concrete material existence. The sacraments continue the "concrete order of salvation," so that through creation, the incarnation, and the Church, "God's invisible nature is made visible."[40] The sacraments also contain an important eschatological dimension for Häring. Salvation history expresses God's ongoing revelation of the Word from the past (creation and Incarnation) to the present (the Church and sacraments) and into

---

[38] Adam argues for this same idea and emphasizes that Christ (and thereby the Church) affirms and reaches out to the whole man "body as well as soul, of the senses as well as the intellect" (*The Spirit of Catholicism*, 160–67).

[39] *LC* 1:63.

[40] *LC* 2:9. *SEL*, 12–20. In these passages quoted from *The Law of Christ*, Häring is sharply critical of the neo-Thomist philosopher Jacques Maritain, who argues that silent contemplation, with no words, signs, or gestures, is the highest and most perfect communion with God and source of the theological virtues. Häring regards contemplation as a special form of Christian prayer but sees it as neither the highest nor the most perfect way for persons to communicate with God. Rather Häring places the sacraments at the center of the Christian life precisely because they are "visible and perceptible signs of faith" and shared publicly in community. Sacraments express most completely, but not exhaustively, God's continual invitation to share divine life and the community and individual's response, manifested in both the theological and moral virtues.

the future (the Kingdom of God). Häring refers to the time between Pentecost and the Second Coming as the "age of sacraments" because sacraments are visible signs of the invisible future of the Kingdom of God.[41]

Christ as Supreme Sacrament

According to Häring what makes Christian morality distinct from other ethical systems is "the fact that it has its origin, form, norm, and goal in the priesthood of Christ and in the sacraments of the new law."[42] Jesus Christ as Word of God and High Priest is the "supreme sacrament," the central sign of faith in Christianity.[43] The Incarnation is part of the "continuing creation" of the "ongoing disclosure of God's presence in the world." Because Christ is God-made-visible he gives "all material, visible creation a sacramental quality."[44] Häring goes on to say that "In view of creation, in the Word of the Father, in view also of the Word Incarnate, we are entitled to ascribe to visible reality a sacramental quality, a capacity to make the presence of God perceptible to the eyes, ears, touch, reason, will, indeed to the whole man, and to predispose him to respond."[45]

As sacrament, Christ makes visible and perceptible the full dialogical character of divine redemption: Jesus makes the perfect response to God and through his life, death, and resurrection is the most complete and absolute sign of God's saving power. The sacraments, according to Häring, are the locus through which Christ remains present as Word and High Priest in the community of faith.

---

[41] *SS*, 7–8; *SEL*, 85–92. "In the last analysis our hope in the final splendor and glory of the loving majesty of God is sustained by the visible manifestation of the Kingdom of God. We look forward to the final unfolding of that which begins here on earth. It is already manifested in the incarnation of the Son of God, in the paschal mystery of the Lord, in the Church and her sacraments. . . . Made as we are, essentially of body and soul, we do not await an exclusively interior beatitude. Beatitude in the Christian sense of the word consists of the complete unfolding of the loving glory of God before us in a perfect dialog of love. In this the reflection of the divine majesty in our bodies and in the visible bodily fellowship is not something accidental. The life of grace here below is the germ of eternal glory. It is bestowed upon us in the sacraments, and unfolds in the dialog of faith, hope, and love" (*LC* 2:10). In his later works, Häring (*SEL*, 102) emphasizes that the sacraments and the Kingdom of God urge Christians to make visible God's love through service to others.

[42] Ibid., 11.

[43] *LC* 2:152.

[44] *SEL*, 21.

[45] Ibid., 22.

Sacraments, as both word and response, are the signs that Jesus gives the Church that continue to manifest the healing and saving power of God, and they incorporate Christians into the life of Christ and invite them to share with Christ in full praise of the Father.

Häring uses biblical imagery to explain the scholastic notion of symbol (matter) and form. He explains that Jesus used material objects as signs of God's power throughout his ministry (e.g., spittle to heal) and continues to be present through the union of the symbol and form of the sacrament.[46] This is not a cold and static presence, or one that is automatic, according to Häring. Christ is present personally through the sacrament, summoning each person to follow: "The sacramental sign in the unity of the symbol and word (matter and form) is in the dimension of the personal. It is the Word of Address, the summons of Christ directed to us personally."[47]

Not only does Christ transform all material reality, but through participation in the sacraments, the Christian is assimilated to Christ. Drawing upon Pauline and Johannine themes Häring emphasizes the indwelling of Christ to show how sacramental reality transforms the moral life.[48] First, the call and response to one's neighbor is grounded in this inner reality, which is experienced as gift and grace and not as an external mandate. Second, even if the Christian fulfills all the external laws, they do not, according to Häring, "live authentically according to his vocation in Christ. . . . His life bears witness only to laws and discrete values but not to Christ; he cannot be effectively and truthfully a sign of life in Christ."[49]

The Church as the Ongoing Sacrament in History

A dramatic shift took place in Roman Catholic ecclesiology in the mid-twentieth century. Since the Counter-Reformation, the Church

---

[46] *LC* 2:156. Also, see Adam, *The Spirit of Catholicism*, 25.

[47] *LC* 2:156. In the context of discussing the sacrament as the personal encounter with Christ, Häring raises the issue of validity and fruitfulness. He argues that it is incumbent on the minister to perform the ritual so that this encounter is brought forth fully and completely. Therefore, validity for Häring is far more than fulfilling the correct administration of the sacraments according to the rubrics; rather, it is the responsibility of the Church and minister to bring forth the true message and full reality of the symbols, as signs of faith and the invitation of Christ. See *LC* 2:159, for pastoral guidance on following rubrics under extreme situations. For discussion of valid and fruitful reception, see *LC* 2:159–66.

[48] Häring (*SEL*, 34) states that this concept is mentioned 160 times in the Gospel of John and Paul's epistles.

[49] Ibid., 35.

defined itself as the *societas perfecta;* in the 1940s and 1950s this model gave way to the Pauline image of the Church as the Mystical Body of Christ by the influence of Möhler and his followers.[50] The liturgical reformers adopted the ecclesial image of the Mystical Body of Christ, which was later supported by Pius XII in two encyclicals, *Mystici Corporis Christi* (1943) and *Mediator Dei et Hominum* (1947).[51] Häring's ecclesiology draws on central ideas in *Mediator Dei* as well as the work of Guardini, Jungmann, and Adam.[52] For example, many of the central ideas in *Mediator Dei* are found in Häring's work: Jesus Christ as High Priest, the obedience and sacrifice of Christ, the Church's role in continuing Christ's obedience and sacrifice, worship as both exterior and interior action, rejection of liturgical formalism, emphasis on interior devotion as the chief element of worship, the Church as a "living organism" that must adapt to "temporal needs and circumstances," and the imitation of Christ. He shifts from institutional and juridical language as the primary way of understanding the Church, to sacramental and biblical language.

Häring's ecclesiology is briefly developed in both *The Law of Christ* and *Free and Faithful in Christ*; in both works it is an extension of his Christology. Häring holds up the sacramental dimension of the Church that had been absent in moral theology. For example, in the one section on the Church in *The Law of Christ*, Häring places the legal aspects of the sacraments—valid and fruitful administration and reception—within the context of defining the Church as the Mystical Body of Christ, a community whose fundamental responsibility is to give praise and thanks to God. His purpose is to overcome the stark legalism of moral theology by placing the ecclesial norms in a larger theological and pastoral context. In a later work, *Sacraments in*

---

[50] For a discussion of the historical changes in ecclesiology, see Dulles, *Models of the Church,* 13–30. The Second Vatican Council drew on several biblical images to describe the Church, such as Body of Christ and sacrament, but the dominant view that emerged was the Church as the People of God. (*Lumen Gentium,* 2).

[51] *Mediator Dei*, the first encyclical to deal exclusively with the liturgy, expressed affirmation for liturgical reform but also objected to its abuses and errors. Pius XII encouraged lay participation in all Church rites, described the Church as the Mystical Body of Christ and placed the Eucharist at the center of the Church. He retained the scholastic emphasis on individual salvation and the special graces obtained through liturgical and private devotion.

[52] Häring's work also differs from the encyclical in several important respects. For example, *Mediator Dei* emphasizes Christ's role as Victim and the unbloody sacrifice of the Eucharist, rejects the "social character" of the liturgy, affirms the traditional understanding of *opus operatum* by stating that the faithful need not be present for the accomplishment of the Mass, and stresses the necessity of absolute obedience to church rules and rubrics.

a Secular Age, Häring offers a more substantial treatment of the Church, but the work is primarily descriptive and pastoral in tone and retains the same images and emphases as his other works. His ecclesiology emphasizes the social dimension of personhood, the relationship between Christ and the Church, and the Church as the sacrament of Christ.[53]

As noted, Häring's ecclesiology follows directly from his Christology.[54] As a sacrament, the Church makes visible Christ's ministry and "perfect synthesis" of the love of God and neighbor. Drawing from Aquinas, Häring states that the Church is born of Christ's sacrifice and is united with God and sanctified through the sacraments.[55] He writes of the Church, "Through her sacraments she is the temple of God (Eph 2:21; 2 Cor 6:16; 1 Cor 3:16), the true center of worship, the holy community. Through divine convocation (the *ekklesiá*) she is summoned in the unity of all the sanctified to chant with Christ the praise of the Father."[56]

His understanding of the Church—its purpose and activities—is based solely on sacramental realities.[57] According to Häring, the goal of the Church is the same as the goal of Christ: to give glory to God. Therefore the Church continues the activity of Christ's praise to God. According to Häring, Christ does not pass on the seven sacraments as they are known, but rather a fundamental cultic disposition. The Church has as its fundamental purpose this religious task.

Häring's use of the imagery of the Church as the Mystical Body of Christ is consistent with his emphasis on biblical imagery and draws out the social and corporal dimensions of personhood.[58] In addition to overcoming a legalistic mentality, Häring sought to understand the

[53] See Krieg's summary of Guardini's ecclesiology, 45–69.

[54] Adam, drawing on Augustine, argued that the incarnation and the Church are intimately bound: "The Incarnation is for Christians the foundation and planting of that new communion which we call the Church" (*The Spirit of the Liturgy*, 35–36).

[55] Through the sacraments which flowed from the side of Christ hanging on the Cross the Church of Christ is built." *ST*, III.64.2-3. Häring refers to this image several times (*LC* 2:143, 167).

[56] *LC* 2:167.

[57] Dulles describes five models of the Church that have been operative in the Christian tradition: the Church as institution, mystical communion, sacrament, herald, and servant. Häring (*SEL*, 36) adopts the sacramental model and argues that this is the central model for the Church and the vision of Vatican II and John XXIII.

[58] *LC* 1:73–87; *SEL*, 36–48. See also Adam, *The Spirit of Catholicism*, 31–45 and Guardini, *On the Meaning of the Church*, 1922. Guardini in particular emphasized the way in which the Church brings persons into full personhood and where one can discover the proper hierarchy of values.

sacraments as a social reality, thereby countering the individualism that had so long been a part of the Catholic sacramental tradition. He argues for the "social importance of the sacraments," which must be "celebrated and lived as a power for good in social life."[59] The liturgical movement sought to recover the patristic idea that the "Christian community is the essential fruit of the sacraments" and that the sacraments are "the stamp of unity of the whole Church."[60] For Häring, the social aspect of the sacraments also means that they symbolize and unify the community in order that the people may be bound together in mission and love for one another. The sacraments, then, cannot be only an exterior sign with no interior transformative power nor can they be an interior experience with no visible, external signs.

The Church's activity and its sacraments are interpreted within Häring's word-and-response model. The Church receives and is united through God's grace, but this gift also places an imperative upon the community. The Church is a social and communal reality— a "body," to use Paul's image—and the sacraments are the means through which the Church unites in communal worship: "The sacraments constitute for our entire moral and religious life a social imperative because they are essentially a social reality. They form an objectively real bond of all the members of the Church uniting us all in the one Mystical Body."[61]

The Church's social and communal bond has real religious, social, and material effects, according to Häring. The individual is no longer concerned for his or her salvation; rather, the sacraments signify the "solidarity of salvation," the joining together of Christians who live for each other. In addition, those who participate in the sacraments view material objects differently. Häring points out that "one who has partaken of the supersubstantial bread in the community of divine love, who has slaked his thirst on the Mystical Blood . . . can no longer remain in tranquil possession of superfluous earthly goods while his neighbor and fellow member of the sacred community lives in misery. Rather he will relax his tense grip on material things to offer them open-handedly for pious and worthy causes."[62] Finally,

---

[59] Bernard Häring, "Social Importance of the Sacraments," *Lumen Vitae* 13 (July–September, 1958) 416. Guardini also explained the Church as existing on a polarity between the individual and the community, a polarity that exists in perfect balance, as opposed to the extremes of individualism in Kant and the totalitarianism of communism.

[60] Ibid., 420.

[61] *LC* 2:168.

[62] Ibid., 169.

the community formed around the sacraments reaches beyond itself into the public realm. Häring rejects a strict separation between the supernatural life of the Church and the natural life of the public order. Christians who are formed within the bonds of sacramental unity carry this union and communion into the broader public: "Thus the sacraments, particularly those which imprint a character, give us not only for the strictly religious or sacred domain but also for the formation of the public itself a social mission, a participation in the mission of the Church in the sanctification of all creation."[63]

The sacraments are a continuation of God's word spoken to persons. Häring shares with earlier liturgical reformers the idea that a revitalized and vibrant liturgy would overcome modern individualism and alienation. Häring also believes that "ossified cult" or dead religion leads to alienation from the Church and therefore from God. He argues that the liturgy is the only place where the "true man" can emerge and develop and where true community can be found.[64] As signs of faith, sacraments are the place of encounter with Jesus Christ, the ultimate sign of God's love. The Church is also a visible sign, a sacrament of God's love, which is called to make visible God's love through worship and through concrete acts of love in relation to the neighbor.[65] As Jesus is a visible sign, the Church's sacraments are also visible signs of faith and community. Because persons are composed of body and soul, both aspects of personhood must participate in divine praise and worship. The body, as well as spirit, must enter into acts of love, obedience, sacrifice, and praise. The Church, according to Häring, is the primary locus for such action.

Häring also links the social aspect of personhood with the Mystical Body of Christ ecclesiology—a link that, for Häring, provides the theological foundation for the connection between the moral life and worship. But Häring further argues that the social character of

---

[63] Ibid., 171. Häring does not elaborate on this point. Häring's discussion of reception and participation in the sacramental life of the Church is subsumed under his discussion of the Church as sacrament. Häring argues that valid and fruitful reception of the sacrament constitutes far more than merely following the rules spelled out in the rubrics. He is concerned primarily with the interior disposition of the recipient, rather than the external forms: "From the standpoint of the person receiving the sacrament we must be concerned with the relation toward God in Christ, with the work of Christ in the Holy Spirit, and with the form of words and the efficacy of the sacred encounter itself" (*LC* 2:159–60).

[64] *SEL*, 3.

[65] *SS*, 278.

human nature is premised upon a fundamental condition—the dialogical capacity that defines human relationships and the divine-human encounter. The social character of moral and liturgical interaction, for Häring, is responsive and interactive relationship to God and neighbor; whatever form participation takes in the liturgy, it is always in response to God's initiative. The dialogical character of the I-Thou-We relationship provides a basis for the self-in-relation and a concrete way of defining the fundamental relationships that bind the community together. These bonds are not merely external, but constitutive of what it is to be a person. The dialogue initiated by God through Word and Sacrament with the community extends beyond the liturgy into every facet of daily life, carrying profound implications for social witness and action. Though Häring does not define the relationship between the liturgy and the Church's social mission in great detail, nor does he connect the sacraments to the work of justice, his dialogical model may expand the anthropological implications of the Mystical Body of Christ ecclesiology for both liturgical and social ethics theology.[66]

Sacraments of Conversion

We must make a further distinction, a much more profound distinction which is of great importance in explaining the tasks of moral doctrine and moral instruction: there is a very marked difference between moral as a "school of life" whose purpose is the formation of all spiritual domains in the mind and heart of Christ, and a moral slanted almost exclusively toward the sacrament of penance, a species of "confessional moral," whose principal ideal is the guidance of the confessor in the correct exercise of his role as judge in the tribunal of penance, and the guidance of the penitent in the task of "integral" confession. These latter are important functions of moral theology, yet it must be remembered that while penance plays a capital role in the whole spiritual life, it is not the whole of Christian life. Such a statement, however, is in no way designed to discredit the manuals of moral theology which aim primarily at the formation of good confessors and limit their goals primarily to this function.[67]

——————————————— Bernard Häring, *The Law of Christ*, vol. 1

---

[66] Kenneth R. Himes, "Eucharist and Justice: Assessing the Legacy of Virgil Michel," *Worship* 62/2 (March, 1988) 201–24.

[67] *LC* 1:468.

One of the creative turns that Häring makes in *The Law of Christ* is the introduction of the theme of conversion in the moral life and its relationship to the sacraments. Conversion is an essential category in Häring's sacramental-moral theology for several reasons. First, it is biblical. As has been shown, Häring's sacramental-moral theology is grounded in biblical themes, and so it follows that his explanation of sin, conversion, and life in Christ are drawn primarily from the New Testament, especially the Gospel of John and Pauline letters. Second, conversion points to a dynamic element at the center of the Christian life, one marked by continual renewal and growth in the *imago Christi*. According to Häring, conversion is not a single event, though it can be a powerful initiating event in the lives of certain people, such as Sts. Paul and Augustine. For most people, however, conversion is the ongoing dynamic process of moving away from sin and darkness toward a fuller embrace of life in Christ, a life marked by reconciliation, joy and gratitude. Third, this dynamic process is at the heart of the sacraments, especially the "sacraments of conversion": baptism, Eucharist, and penance. Conversion links these sacraments together, highlighting each as personal encounters with Christ.

Conversion marks the beginning of a life in Christ, and is marked sacramentally through baptism. But conversion is not a one-time occurrence; it continues throughout the life of faith. It embodies the continual movement away from sin toward the full embrace of God's will, a life marked by deeper assimilation in the imitation of Christ. Baptism is distinct because it symbolizes the "primary conversion"; Eucharist and penance are the sacramental expression of what Häring terms "secondary conversion."[68]

By placing the sacraments within the context of conversion, Häring highlights the experiential and personal dimensions of the sacraments, as opposed to the merely juridical. The manualists give considerable attention to the sacraments, with particular attention to Eucharist, penance, and marriage. The manualist's task is to define, in juridical terms, the licit and valid administration and reception of the sacrament, though most of the weight is given to the

---

[68] Häring calls baptism, Eucharist, and penance the sacraments of conversion, however, the other sacraments also play an important role in the life of ongoing conversion. See *LC* 1:404, 408. In *SS* (13–14), Häring refers to baptism as the "first repentance" and the other sacraments as the "sacraments of the second repentance," the constant striving for "purification and progress in grace." Häring is drawing upon Justin Martyr's reference to baptism as the "bath of repentance" and penance as "a second plank to cling to in a shipwreck."

priest's role. What is strikingly absent is any other consideration of the sacrament from a biblical, pastoral, or historical perspective. For example, two of the four volumes of Henry Davis's *Moral and Pastoral Theology* are devoted to the sacraments, with two hundred pages given to penance. Each sacrament contains a discussion of the sacrament and its effects, the matter and form, the minister and subject, and a variety of topics pertaining to each sacrament (e.g., in the case of penance Davis discusses jurisdiction, duties of the confessor, and various classes of penitents).

Häring does not reject the juridical approach to the sacrament, but subsumes it within a broader biblical and spiritual understanding of sin and reconciliation. Moral theology, then, begins not with the law—either moral or canonical—but with the divine-human encounter in Jesus Christ. Häring's theology of the sacraments of conversion provides an illustration of the way in which he brings new elements into moral theology. He describes the sacraments of conversion within the categories of his sacramental-moral theology, their biblical, personal and Christocentric aspects, as well as their social, salutary, and cultal dimensions.

Biblical Foundations

Chapter 3 demonstrates how Häring draws upon a wide variety of sources to construct his moral theology. In addition to phenomenology, history of religion, value theory, sacramental theology, he also appropriates the work of other alternative manualists, particularly Fritz Tillmann. Tillmann, a Tübingen scholar in the tradition of John Michael Hirscher, wrote one of the first alternative manuals in 1937 built entirely on Scripture; but unlike Häring, he did not try to reconcile these ideas with neo-Thomism. Tillman's moral theology is christocentric and biblical; he draws from themes in John's gospel, particularly ideas of imitation, rebirth into new life, and the religious-moral character of response in terms of obedience. Tillmann argues that the person of Jesus Christ is what makes Christian morality distinctive and it is through the imitation of Christ that a Christian is born anew.[69] Häring includes each of these ideas in his moral theology and expands them through his sacramental theology.

---

[69] See Fritz Tillman, *Die Idee der Nachfolge Christi*, vol. 2 of *Handbuck der katcholisen Sittenlehre* (Düsseldorf: Druckund Verlag L. Schwann, 1934). See also J. Gallagher, 162–66, for a discussion of Tillman's moral theology, and 172 for his comparison of Häring and Tillman.

Häring, like Tillmann, sought to recover a biblical understanding of conversion in order to overcome the excessively juridical approach that developed in the theology and practice of confession. The very name of the sacrament—penance—points to part of the problem. Not only had the sacrament come to be associated with one of its three parts, but the identification of the sacrament with penance meant that the juridical model predominated. Davis, for example, describes the sacrament solely in these terms: "Penance is a Sacrament, whereby sins committed after Baptism are forgiven by the judicial absolution granted by a legitimate minister to a member of the Church duly disposed to receive it."[70] Even though Häring retains aids for confessors, he turns primarily to the experiential basis of the sacrament—the experience and knowledge of both sin and the grace of forgiveness by the recipient. Häring, as did many others, identifies part of the problem with the sacrament of penance with the Latin translation of several New Testament texts (e.g., Mark 1:15, Matt 4:17): the Greek term *metánoia* is rendered in Latin as *poenitemini* or "do penance," which has a different connotation than the original meaning "to turn around" or "return home."[71] Throughout its long history, as chapter 2 recounts, the sacramental practice and theology replaced the biblical idea of *metánoia* with the idea of performing acts of penance. As Häring notes, "The Lord's call to *metánoia* is totally misunderstood if we see in it first of all a demand for works of penance (the call: do penance)."[72]

Häring places the New Testament Greek meaning of *metánoia* at the center of his understanding of conversion. There are two main elements of conversion in the biblical narrative that forms the basis of the sacraments of conversion. The first is found in Jesus' initial call to the sinner to repent and accept the good news of God's Kingdom (found in the parables, stories of John the Baptist, and Paul's conversion). Baptism is the sacrament of this primary conversion, marked by repentance of the "old man" and return to God to live as the "new man." The fundamental dynamic of baptism is one of invitation and response: "In baptism Christ Himself awaits the sinner to welcome him home to the Father's house, to give him a share in the fruits of redemption. . . . By baptism the sinner returns to

---

[70] Henry Davis, *Moral and Pastoral Theology,* 3:235.

[71] *SS,* 11.

[72] *LC* 1:392. Häring points out that the Greek term *metánoia* is a translation of the Hebrew term *schub,* meaning "to return" or "return home."

Christ in his repentance, and Christ turns to the sinner to welcome and accept him."[73] Baptism demands that each person respond to this initial call and continually return to Christ through "a constant deepening and maturing of our first conversion, of our return to Christ, of *metánoia.*"[74] Baptism, then, initiates us into the life of on-going conversion.

Secondary conversion refers to the continual movement away from sin toward ongoing assimilation and imitation of Christ. Conversion, then, is not a once in a lifetime event, but is the foundational dynamic of all Christian life. Inner assimilation to Christ takes place through the process of secondary conversion, the "growth and progress, the deepening of the first conversion," which is not the "mere work of man, but the 'heart,' the interior conversion to Christ, to the Kingdom of God."[75] This movement toward full assimilation and imitation is marked by progress from knowledge of and obedience to the external law to a deeper understanding of the inner law and growth in the love of God. Häring states that "interior progress may be characterized as gradual passage from simple observance of the commandments with their burdens and difficulties to the keen alertness for the directives of the Spirit of God, communicated to us through inspiration from within and the situation without, in an ever clearer appreciation of what is essential, the love and glory of God and the effort to promote His kingdom."[76]

Assimilation to Christ, then, takes place through Eucharist and penance, the other sacraments of conversion, because they invite the believer to a continual movement away from sin and deeper assimilation to Christ. The sacrament of penance "places the sinner anew before the mercy of Christ, if he has again turned his back to His Savior and Father after having received the grace of pardon and assimilation to Christ." The Eucharist is the sign of "unity and love of Christ in the Church" and so conversion has as its goal "love of unity with the Church and all her members, a love which grows increasingly vigorous day by day."[77]

---

[73] *LC* 1:409
[74] Ibid.
[75] *LC* 1:400.
[76] Ibid.
[77] *LC* 1:409, 414.

Social, Salutary, and Cultal Dimensions

A biblical understanding of conversion is both personal and Christocentric. The call to renounce sin and return home is a divine invitation to the person, calling for a full response, not a mere "changing of one's mind" or actions. For Häring "conversion is in every way the most utterly personal movement, the restoration of the bonds of personal intimacy with God."[78] The invitation to return to the Kingdom and to divine friendship comes in and through Christ. Conversion, for Häring, is "essentially Christocentric." There is both an incarnational and eschatological dimension to conversion: through his preaching, cross, and resurrection Jesus makes known God's invitation to repent in the here and now, and the promise of fulfillment in the Kingdom points to the final and complete conversion in the future.

Häring's definition of sacraments as personal encounters with Christ links the biblical call of conversion with the sacramental life of the Church because sacraments are "divinely instituted revelation and development of the way of salvation itself."[79] The sacraments of conversion, then, have the "structure" and "essential features of conversion." They are personal encounters with Christ, they draw one into the community of faith and thereby the Kingdom, and through participation the Christian becomes part of the "sacred cult of the Church," carrying the full moral and religious obligation of divine worship. Neither conversion nor participation in the sacraments of conversion is solely interior and personal; but rather social, salutary, and cultal.[80]

Häring stresses the social character of the sacraments of conversion in order to overcome the individual character of Catholic sacramental life. Baptism, as well as being a sacrament of repentance and new life for the individual, also initiates one into membership in the Body of Christ. Penance, likewise, has an ecclesial dimension: the sinner repents before the community and returns to the community

---

[78] *LC* 1:392.

[79] *LC* 1:404.

[80] "There is an essential relation of conversion to that great reality which is the kingdom of God. To understand this relation, we must study in detail the holy sacraments not merely as instruments of salvation, used by the individual, but under their social-ecclesial aspects as well. The entire work of conversion and salvation is not a matter of mere individual relation between man and God; it possesses a dimension of community; it is a matter of the kingdom of God" (*LC* 1:412).

as a full member. And Eucharist is the ultimate sign of "unity and love of Christ in the Church." The sacraments of conversion are not meant, then, to focus solely on the individual. They are ecclesial acts of the community that demand a response by the individual that expresses one's participation in the Body of Christ. "Individual salvation, individual encounter with Christ, in every instance depends altogether on union with the community of the kingdom of God, on conversion to the community of the Body of Christ. Individual and community are not in antithesis. They form one indivisible totality."[81]

The salutary effects of the sacraments of conversion extend far beyond removal and forgiveness of sin. For Häring divine grace is "operative" from the "first impulse" of conversion, but the conversion is not yet complete without the "free consent and cooperation of the individual." The gift of grace through conversion aids the person in responding to the "two basic imperatives" that flow from the invitation: to be reconciled to God and "to live in accordance with the new creation God has wrought within you." This inner transformation is described in the writings of John and Paul as rebirth, birth in the Spirit, a new creature, and a new freedom to be a child of God. Through all these images, Häring argues, the Scriptures stress that new life in Christ is lived according to a New Law, an inner law written by the Holy Spirit onto the heart. The external law still exists as a guide, but it is through the inner workings of grace that the child of God can live fully in imitation of Christ:

> The negative precepts of the decalog, the two tables of the law, are not a perfect and adequate expression of the inner law written in the heart through our assimilation to Christ. This is manifested rather by the Sermon on the Mount, the new law of the kingdom of God promulgated by Christ, the law of disinterested and unbounded love, humility, and love of the cross. The prohibitive precepts (contained essentially in the decalog) lay down the minimum requirements. They fix the boundaries which all must respect (prescriptive precepts). The Sermon on the Mount determines the ideals and goals toward which we must strive (purposive precepts). Unlike the prescriptive precepts of the external law, these purposive precepts emerge and clearly reveal their obligatory boundaries only as one progresses interiorly in the new life. The movement toward the goal, toward the full realization of the law of Christ, is a strict duty arising from the new existence, the life in Christ. The approach, the progress

---

[81] *LC* 1:416–17.

toward fulfillment, must be an expression of the interior growth and the inner guidance of the Holy Spirit.[82]

Finally, the sacraments of conversion orient and reorient the Christian to cultal participation and obligation. "Conversion must result in a new orientation of the sinner's entire life toward the glory of God." Participation within the community leads to a "cultal orientation and obligation" on behalf of the individual. As in the Old Testament, the law shapes and forms the community's obligations of worship. Under the New Law, however, the believer is not only a member of an external cult, but the sacrament of conversion "produces inner dispositions for the perfect worship of God in Jesus Christ."[83] Through the baptismal character the believer is consecrated in a "profound interior assimilation to the priesthood of Christ." The cultal orientation and obligation is the primary effect of conversion—the sinner's life is turned toward God's glory within the cultal life of the community. The character conferred in baptism, confirmation, and holy orders, is directly related to cult because it is the mark of Christ the High Priest. Häring writes: "To return to Christ and His Church through baptism, sacrament of the divine home-coming, implies, therefore, the honor, the right, the duty to orientate our whole life toward the glory of God in holy priestly cult and constantly renew it through the liturgical realities." The conversion, effected through baptism, Häring argues, points to the Eucharist as the "heart and summit of all divine worship: the consecration received in baptism as fruit of the sacrifice of Christ confers on the recipient of the sacrament the fullness of power and the mission to participate in the sacrifice of Christ and the Church. The principle of conversion as well as its end and purpose resides in sacrifice, which gives glory to God. Conversion as the gift of sacrifice of Christ essentially engages one in cult."[84] Likewise, penance restores the sinner to the dignity and worth of the sacramental character, restoring one to the "holy altars." The goal, then, of conversion is cult, the participation in the community of faith giving praise and honor to God.

---

[82] *LC* 1:403–4. Penance also has salutary effects, primarily as an "antidote" against evil that is foundation in sin. Penances can work to counter self-will that tends toward sinful behavior.

[83] *LC* 1:417.

[84] *LC* 1:418.

Confession as the Sacrament of Ongoing Conversion

Unlike the manualists Häring does not discuss each sacrament according to the canonical norms in *The Law of Christ*.[85] He offers an analysis of penance and marriage.[86] He takes up penance in the section on conversion and places the juridical aspects within a biblical and theological framework. He gives far less attention to the priest's role as confessor and a great deal more weight to the penitent's role in conversion and the ways in which the sacrament facilitates this movement.[87] For example, after a biblical and sacramental view of conversion as the basis of the three sacraments of conversion, Häring turns to the "convert's share in conversion" where he takes up the traditional aspects of the sacrament of penance: contrition, confession, and satisfaction.

The priest's role is primarily as spiritual guide who assists the penitent along the path of conversion rather than judge who determines the proper procedure for the sacrament.[88] Like the liturgical reformers, Häring is placing the primary emphasis on the free and active participation of the Christian in the sacramental encounter, rather than the juridical role of the priest and Church. He places the three traditional aspects of the sacrament within his sacramental theology,

---

[85] Davis (3:353) defines the sacrament of penance as: "In this Sacrament, the acts of the penitent which, with the absolution given by the priest, constitute it, are contrition, confession, and satisfaction. Reconciliation of the sinner with God requires the will to be reconciled, which means the act of contrition and purpose of amendment; subjection to the judgment of the priest, who acts in God's place, means confession; compensation in accordance with the judgment passed by the priest, who judges in God's place, means satisfaction. These acts of the penitent are required by divine institution for the integrity of the Sacrament and the complete and perfect remission of sins. That these three acts of the penitent are required is matter of defined Catholic Faith."

[86] See *LC* 1:421–81 for a discussion of penance, and *LC* 2:267–378 on marriage. Häring wrote one book on penance, *Shalom: Peace, The Sacrament of Reconciliation* (New York: Farrar, Straus, and Giroux, 1967). He developed a longstanding interest in marriage and family arising out of easy early work, *The Sociology of the Family* (Cork, Ireland: Mercier Press, 1959). Other books on marriage include: *Marriage in the Modern World* (Westminster, Md.: The Newman Press, 1965); The Nobility of Marriage (Chawton, Alton: Redemptorist Publications, 1966); *Married Love: A Modern Christian View of Marriage and Family Life* (Chicago: Argus Communications, 1970).

[87] Davis (3:235–39), for example, commits 125 pages to the jurisdiction and duties of the confessor, emphasizing under what conditions the priest may hear confessions, assign proper penances, and grant absolution. At the end of the section on penance, he turns to the "acts of the penitent" and discusses contrition, confession, and satisfaction.

[88] Interspersed throughout the discussion of the sacrament of penance are pastoral guidelines for priests who should act as "spiritual judge" and "physician of souls." See *LC* 1:449, 453–63.

emphasizing their role in the dynamic process of conversion. He highlights the sacramental encounter within the experience of each movement, drawing in elements from his Christology, ecclesiology, and anthropology.

In his discussion of contrition, confession and satisfaction Häring first states the Church's teachings from the Council of Trent and interprets each within his sacramental-moral theology. Several other sources outside of neo-Thomism are included: Scripture, Max Scheler, Alphonsus Liguori, John Michael Hirscher, the Eastern spiritual tradition, and psychoanalysis. Even though these strikingly different sources are intermingled throughout the discussion, his purpose is not to bring these sources into conversation with each other, or reconcile their methodological differences, as much as it is to describe the human experience, especially the spiritual psychology, that constitutes the sinner's progress from sin toward healing and forgiveness: "The 'law of progress' is a fundamental norm of life. Even the life of grace is a law of progressive conversion. Therefore it must also be a basic norm of all our efforts in the pastoral care of our fellow man."[89] Häring's argument for retaining the categories of contrition, confession and satisfaction is that they constitute the "dispositions and acts which properly are elements of every genuine religious conversion."

Contrition, rooted primarily in the virtue of humility, is the initial recognition of sinfulness and desire for forgiveness and change.[90] It "assumes the form of a 'sacramental encounter' with Christ" by the mutual recognition of sins in the face of "divine judgment which Christ took upon Himself on the cross" and "repentance and sorrow for sin in the light of the infinite redemptive love of Christ."[91] Contrition is a twofold movement: the movement away from sin and the embrace of a new freedom born of God's forgiving grace. That is why, as Häring states, the Council of Trent places such strong emphasis on the purpose of amendment, which he interprets through Pauline themes: contrition leads not just to sorrow for past sin, but

---

[89] *LC* 1:437.

[90] Humility is one of the central virtues of the Christian life, according to Häring. He opens the discussion of contrition with an analysis of humility: "It is the acknowledgment, perfected in freedom, of one's own sinfulness and consequent misery. And the more profoundly the sinner is moved by contrition, the deeper will be the descent of humility into the abyss of his own sinfulness through a purified vision and appreciation of all that is holy and good." *LC* 1:422.

[91] *LC* 1:427.

to the free choice to live "a new life in the spirit of the liberty of God's children."[92]

Confession, the second element of the sacrament, is essential to conversion because of the need to acknowledge fault and guilt to God and the community. Häring is concerned with distinguishing, for both priest and penitent, the "positive divine and ecclesiastical law" that focuses on the minimal observance of the law, from the "lofty ideals," which point beyond mere obedience to law to the highest level of divine-human encounter. The highest ideal of any sacramental encounter is to enter into divine worship. In the case of confession, Häring emphasizes the penitent's direct relationship with God through Christ in the act of confessing, especially the intent of the penitent's action: "Our self-accusation is an element of the efficacious sacramental sign and thereby partakes of the effective act of Christ the priest. For this reason our confession must be more than mere recital of our sins, even though it be contrite. It must be raised to the dignity of the divine worship by which God is praised, his justice acknowledged by our contrite self-accusation, and His mercy glorified."[93] Obviously Häring is encouraging the fullest participation in the sacrament on the level of spiritual and moral growth; this is the "spirit of obedience to the inner guidance of grace," which had been lost to the almost singular attention to "the measure of the rigid demand of the law."[94]

However confession is never a solely interior, silent process; it demands social and auricular expression. It is an expression and manifestation of the "unreserved manifestation of our heart" as well as the body, which also shares in fault and sin. Just as sin is visible and public in its manifestation, so must be confession and the grace of forgiveness: it is appropriate therefore that "man . . . externally acknowledge his sinfulness in order to proclaim salutary union and solidarity with the Church . . . confession before the visible Church imparts to contrition a deeper dimension in its most basic components, humility and sincerity."[95] The bodily, material, and social character of the sacrament, in other words, heightens the spiritual effect of conversion.[96]

---

[92] *LC* 1:435.

[93] *LC* 1:450.

[94] *LC* 1:467–68.

[95] *LC* 1:452.

[96] Häring (*LC* 1:453) places confession to "a good father confessor" within this broader context and encourages priests to "contribute much toward deepening of the penitent's

The third stage of the sacrament is satisfaction, or what traditionally is called penitential works, which is intimately related to the first two movements of conversion, contrition and confession. Häring observes, "The penitential effort initiated in sorrow and self-accusation is completed and perfected by the actual satisfaction in bearing up under penitential suffering *(satispassio)* and the performing of the penitential work itself *(satisfactio)*. Since the humiliation of self-accusation and the pain of satisfaction are the development of what is implicit in all sorrow, it must follow that through them contrition grows and matures, for it is the actual conversion of the heart."[97] He opposes identifying the sacrament with acts of penance; for him the spirit of satisfaction is part of the overall movement of conversion. "If Christ speaks of repentance in 'sackcloth and ashes' (Matt 11:21), this does not imply that penitential works are the very essence of the *metánoia* proclaimed as the glad tidings of salvation, but rather its spontaneous expression flowing from it with increasing spontaneity as the repentance itself grows deeper and richer."[98]

Penance, according to Häring, is first an inner disposition of the heart that recognizes God's justice and mercy. Penance arises out of love rather than a "rightful claim to pardon," it seeks rather the "transcendent mystery of the consuming and saving 'justice of God' rather than the "petty or narrow commutative justice of law."[99] Hence, Häring grounds his understanding of penance in a "theocentric orientation which places God in the center of religion and morals." Penance is first of all a *religious* experience that implies the virtue of religion—it is first of all directed to God, and secondly to moral improvement.

In an interesting way, Häring places penance within his historical understanding of human action. The past and future are drawn together in the present penitential act:

> The hour of grace, the hour of moral decision, sustains the entire weight and burden of the past and, through the right grasp of the past, an infinite fruitfulness for all the future. The more completely the moral-religious decision captures and "elaborates" the past, the more it opens up new domains of freedom previously closed. Every

self-knowledge and sorrow, abstracting altogether from the supernatural effectiveness of the words of absolution freeing him from his sins."

[97] *LC* 1:468.
[98] *LC* 1:469.
[99] *LC* 1:470.

decision imparts new meaning, not merely to the particular act, but also to the whole past. . . . Just as the disposition of sorrow kills the life nerve of the evil sentiments and attitudes of the past, so the spirit of penance gives to the particular acts the sense of atonement, freeing and redeeming the past, the sense of prayer for pardon, the sense of the virtue of religion which looks to the past in the form of gratitude for pardon attained.[100]

The historical character of sin and conversion are parallel to Christ's acts in salvation history and are another way in which the Christian becomes assimilated to Christ. "His action is the law of history and the norm for our penance. Really and effectively He entered into the very heart of the history of mankind, opening up the new era of salvation (the new aeon) through the work of redemption. Precisely in so far as and only in so far as it is work of satisfaction, redemption of the old aeon . . . does it open the new era of salvation to mankind."[101] Finally, penance moves the sinner to "interior objective assimilation to Christ through the sacrament." Drawing upon Sts. Albert and Thomas Aquinas, Häring envisions penance as directly related to Christ's suffering and redemptive love.

> And this assimilation to Christ is actively and spontaneously expressed in acts of penance. Our sacramental assimilation to Christ, constantly deepened and enriched by works of penance, perfects and ennobles our entire life in the imitation of Christ. . . . Among the most sublime forms of the imitation of Christ is expiation through love, manifesting itself in self-renunciation and willingness to suffer in union with Christ.[102]

* * * *

Many other aspects of Häring's theology of conversion and the sacrament of penance could be highlighted and discussed.[103] This brief summary points out some of the ways in which Häring's ideas anticipate the theology within the revised sacrament of penance in 1973: The biblical foundation of the sacrament in *metánoia;* the shift

---

[100] *LC* 1:471.
[101] *LC* 1:472.
[102] *LC* 1:472–73.
[103] See Mark James O'Keefe, "An Analysis and Critique of the Social Aspects of Sin and Conversion in the Moral Theology of Bernard Häring" (S.T.D. diss., Catholic University of America, 1987).

from penance to reconciliation, and the juridical aspects of the sacrament placed within a broader theology. He draws out the theme of conversion in his sacramental-moral theology, a concept virtually absent from the neo-Thomists' manuals, and connects it to the invitation-and-response model. He replaces the legal and juridical language for a pastoral approach, and gives attention to the religious and moral approach of the Christian to the sacrament. He is interested in demonstrating the theological foundation that connects the sacraments to each other, especially the way in which baptism, Eucharist, and penance share a similar dynamic intent.

For all the ways in which Häring departs from the manualist tradition, there are many ways in which he remains squarely within it. In this regard, *The Law of Christ* is an uneven manual. The scholastic structure is present as a framework for his system. He also retains moral theology as a pastoral discipline that serves priests to be good confessors; of course, he adds to this the idea that moral theology should help guide the Christian in faithful living, but he does not abandon the discipline's pastoral focus. His later book *Shalom: Peace* is also intended to help priests understand the changing character of the sacrament of penance during the turbulent changes of the 1960s.

Within his system Häring continually departs from the manualists insofar as he drops juridical language in favor of a biblical and pastoral approach. New concepts are developed, but they often sit side-by-side with other ideas; conversion, for instance, is not mentioned in the treatment of sacramental character, grace, and causality. Likewise, another major idea at the center of Häring's system—the virtue of religion—is explained and interpreted through the categories of word-and-response, but is not explicitly connected to sacramental character, grace, and causality, nor to the idea of conversion.

Part III

The Christian Moral Life
and the Virtue of Religion

Chapter 5

The Theological and Moral Virtues and the Virtue of Religion

In other words we face the world with a moral task which flows from the virtue of religion. This assumption can have only one meaning in the light of the following principle: our entire activity in the world must have a religious formation, for all our acts must be ordered to the loving majesty of God. This means that all our moral tasks are at the same time religious tasks.[1]

———————————————— Bernard Häring, *The Law of Christ*, vol. 2

Responsibility, understood as word-and-response, is the dominant theme of Häring's writings on the Christian moral life for his fifty-year career. Responsibility influences not only his theology but also each part of his moral theory, including law, conscience, and virtue. Häring retains much of the structure and the central categories of the neo-Thomists' moral system, but interprets and defines the content according to his word-and-response ethic. A central feature of his accomplishment as a moral theologian is the way that this theme unifies the theological, moral, and sacramental dimensions of his thought.

At the heart of his interpretation of traditional moral categories is the concept of the virtue of religion. He takes an obscure, minor category and places it at the center of the Christian religious-moral life. The virtue of religion is interpreted by Häring as those actions that are sustained by and bring to expression the theological virtues within the world of both cult and morality. Most importantly, the virtue of religion becomes a way of describing the relationship between the religious (theological virtue) and the moral (moral virtue)

[1] *LC* 2:124.

in a quite different manner than that of the manualists, who maintained a sharp distinction between the two categories. At the heart of Häring's interpretation of the virtue of religion is his understanding of religion as dialogical, cultal, and social; the liturgy and sacraments, then, become the primary place of encounter with Christ and formation in the life of virtue.

Within the history of Catholic moral theology, the virtue of religion is a minor category. Aquinas introduces the concept as a quasi-potential part of justice defined under the moral virtue of justice as rendering to another their just due. In the case of religion, this means rendering to God what is due God, a task Aquinas deems to be not entirely possible according to the requirements of justice and the imbalance between God and humanity. The neo-Thomist manualists follow Aquinas and place religion under justice but after the dissolution of the manuals in the mid-twentieth century, the virtue of religion rarely appears again in Catholic moral theology.[2]

In *The Law of Christ* Häring uses the virtue of religion to explicate the relationship between religion and morality, and the theological and the moral virtues. His presentation of the virtue of religion draws together the central concepts of revelation as word-and-response, the imitation of Christ, and the sacramental formation of the religious-moral life. Häring understood the task of the moral theologian to be one of discerning an answer to the question: How can the Christian respond to the love of God expressed through Jesus Christ?[3] The answer to this question, as presented in *The Law of Christ*, is the cultivation and practice of the virtue of religion.

In order to understand Häring's contribution to moral theology, it is necessary to compare his virtue theory—what is virtue and what is the distinctive between theological and moral virtues—to that of Aquinas and the manualists. In moving beyond the manualists, he

---

[2] A survey of contemporary moralists demonstrates that the virtue of religion is a forgotten concept. J. Gallagher, for example, discusses the manualists' treatment of the virtue of justice (106–12) but makes no mention of the virtue of religion. A few contemporary studies of Aquinas summarize his teaching on the virtue of religion; see Etienne Gilson, *The Christian Philosophy of St. Thomas Aquinas* (Notre Dame, Ind.: University of Notre Dame Press, 1956) 333–37; Josef Pieper, *The Four Cardinal Virtues* (New York: Harcourt, Brace & World, Inc., 1965) 104–10; Alasdair MacIntyre, *Whose Justice? Which Rationality?* (Notre Dame, Ind.: University of Notre Dame Press, 1988) 188, 201. Mahoney (250–52) gives a devastating critique of the impact of Aquinas' placement of religion under justice for contributing to the legalism of moral theology.

[3] *LC* 2:xvii.

often presents his ideas as a return to the original meaning found in Aquinas, yet rarely makes an explicit rejection or critique of the manualists' position. In the end, however, Häring's analysis of the virtue of religion goes beyond Aquinas by combining his phenomenological understanding of religion, his personalist understanding of the divine/human encounter, and the Christology, theological anthropology, and sacramental theology he draws from the liturgical movement.

Aquinas and the Manualists on Virtue

Human virtue is a habit perfecting man in view of his doing good deeds. Now, in man there are but two principles of human actions, viz., the intellect or reason and the appetite. . . . Consequently every human virtue must be a perfection of one of these principles. Accordingly if it perfects man's speculative or practical intellect in order that his deed may be good, it will be an intellectual virtue: whereas if it perfects his appetite, it will be a moral virtue. It follows therefore that every human virtue is either intellectual or moral.[4]

——————————————————— Thomas Aquinas, *Summa Theologica,* I-II

Aquinas' Virtue Ethic

Thomas Aquinas synthesized ideas from several ancient sources to construct his virtue ethic, drawing especially from Aristotle, the New Testament, Augustine, and Cicero, each of whom understood virtue in somewhat distinct terms and defined a particular set of virtues as central to the moral person.[5] Häring illustrates how Aquinas adopts Aristotle's teleological method and his emphasis on the role of natural reason, as known through creation, for the moral life; he adopts the "content and ultimate intention" of morality from the

[4] *ST* I-II.58.3.

[5] Alasdair MacIntyre argues that even though Aristotle and Paul differ considerably in their understanding of the content of virtue, they share the "same logical and conceptual structure," which consists in the notion that virtue is a human quality, the practice of which leads to a goal or telos. This "parallelism" is what allows Aquinas to bring together Aristotle and the New Testament. "A key feature of this parallelism is the way in which the concept of *the good life for man* is prior to the concept of a virtue. . . ." Alasdair MacIntyre, *After Virtue,* 2nd. ed. (Notre Dame, Ind.: University of Notre Dame Press, 1984) 184. MacIntyre provides an overview of Greek, Stoic, and the New Testament understandings of virtue (121–80); his analysis of Aquinas is much briefer (178–80).

New Testament and Augustine. In Aquinas' system, Aristotle's understanding of virtue is no longer a form of self-perfection, but rather the sharing in divine life; "happiness" is reinterpreted as the Beatific Vision.[6] Aquinas' understanding of the moral virtues, informed by Aristotle, and the theological virtues, informed by Augustine, rests upon his distinction between the natural and supernatural levels of human existence, which each have their own distinct telos.

Aquinas understands persons as possessing the natural capacity to obtain a natural end or goal, but as receiving from God a supernatural principle to obtain the supernatural end of the Beatific Vision. He defines the virtues as good operative habits that strive toward a particular end and through the course of repetitive action move to a level of perfection. The virtues enable persons to lead a good moral life on earth and these habits or practices are therefore acquired since the virtues develop from human choice and action.[7] But the end which they achieve—earthly happiness—is imperfect because it does not consist of the full and complete vision of the Divine Essence.[8] Only through the infused or supernatural virtues does a person have the grace-filled capacity to move beyond the proximate ends of earthly life to the ultimate end of heavenly existence.

Aquinas defines two types of virtue: human or natural (which were further distinguished as intellectual and moral virtues) and the theological virtues. The four cardinal virtues—prudence, justice, fortitude, and temperance—are natural virtues and are determined to be "cardinal" because all other natural virtues fall under one of these categories. The three theological virtues of charity, faith, and hope are supernatural virtues because they are gifts of divine grace. According to Aquinas, there are three primary differences between natural and theological virtues.

First, their formal object is different: the object of the moral and intellectual virtues is the perfection of human action, which is moved by both the intellect and will, whereas the object of the theological virtues is God. Second, moral virtues are a direct result of human intention, will, and action, whereas theological virtues are given by God, infused with grace and cannot be obtained through

---

[6] *LC* 1:13.

[7] "Human virtue which is an operative habit, is a good habit, productive of good works" and "Man's virtue perfects him in relation to the good." *ST*, I-II.55.3, 4. See *ST*, I-II.49-67 for Aquinas' treatment of habits and virtues.

[8] On imperfect and perfect happiness, see *ST*, I-II.5.1-8.

human effort. In other words, no act of the will can elevate natural capacities to a supernatural level. Third, persons come to knowledge about the moral virtues because they are rational, but knowledge of the theological virtues exists only through divine revelation.[9]

Aquinas' distinction between nature and grace is the foundation for the moral and theological virtues. For Aquinas, human nature is such that the human person can grow in virtue by his own will and reason, because the mind is oriented toward truth and the will toward the good, an orientation created by God.[10] Grace, according to Aquinas, is a "quality" that both acts upon the soul to move the intellect and will and is a habitual gift that is infused by God so that persons may acquire "supernatural good." Grace does not obliterate or replace nature, but perfects it, transforming the human person's last end into the true and final end. For Aquinas grace makes persons "born again sons of God" who by the "light of grace" participate in the "Divine Nature." He states that "for as man in his intellective power participates in the Divine knowledge through the virtue of faith, and in his power of will participates in the Divine love through the virtue of charity, so also in the nature of the soul does he participate in the Divine Nature, after the manner of a likeness, through a certain regeneration or re-creation."[11]

Virtue in the Neo-Thomists' Manuals of Moral Theology

The manualists' summarize Aquinas' virtue ethic; they do not attempt to expand the definition by drawing upon other sources nor do they attempt a critique of Aquinas' system.[12] Their deductive

---

[9] Ibid., I-II.62.1-2. "Now man's happiness is twofold . . . . One is proportionate to human nature, a happiness, to wit, which man can obtain by means of his natural principles. The other is a happiness surpassing man's nature, and which man can obtain by the power of God alone, by a kind of participation of the Godhead, about which it is written (2 Pet 1:4) that by Christ we are *made partakers of the Divine nature*. And because such happiness surpasses the capacity of human nature, man's natural principles which enable him to act well according to his capacity, do not suffice to direct man to this same happiness. Hence it is necessary for man to receive from God some additional principles, whereby he may be directed to supernatural happiness, even as he is directed to his connatural end, by means of his natural principles, albeit not without the Divine assistance. Such like principles are called *theological virtues*: first, because their object is God, inasmuch as they direct us aright to God: secondly, because they are infused in us by God alone: thirdly, because these virtues are not made known to us, save by Divine revelation, contained in Holy Writ."

[10] Ibid., I-II.110.2.

[11] Ibid., I-II.110.3, 4.

[12] J. Gallagher's (32) close analysis of the moral theology manuals are the basis for the analysis provided here. He restricts his inquiry to those manuals written or translated into

approach takes Aquinas' definitions as a starting point, from which conclusions are derived, conclusions usually in conformity with Aquinas' position. As discussed in chapter 2, the neo-Thomist manuals share a common structure, method of argumentation, and basic content. The structure of the manuals, a result of combining sections from Aquinas' *Summa Theologica* and topics discussed in the *Summae Confessorum* consists of three parts: general and special moral theology and the sacraments.[13] General moral theology treats basic categories of moral anthropology: the human act, conscience, law, and sin. Special moral theology explores the problem of sin, either in relation to the Ten Commandments or the theological and cardinal virtues. Whether or not a manualist chose the Ten Commandments or the virtues as the overarching structure to discuss moral actions, the content is relatively the same.[14] The main emphasis rests upon discrete analyses of moral acts and the rules that determine acts as good or sinful. Because the main context of the manuals is the proper administration of the sacrament of penance, the problem of sin and its absolution is viewed largely in juridical terms. Consequently, this emphasis on sin as rule-breaking weakened the manualists' virtue ethic.

English and Latin and relies on a representative sample from the Jesuit, Redemptorist, and Dominican traditions. His selection is a "reliable sample" because they represent those "manuals which directly influenced the moral theology of priests and thus indirectly the Catholic laity of the pre-Vatican II Church. Although more exhaustive investigations may modify and refine the conclusions drawn here, I am confident that the limited number of manuals examined in the research for this essay provide sufficient clues to the content of the theological genre to justify the findings offered below." The manuals most often cited by J. Gallagher include: Henry Davis, *Moral and Pastoral Theology*, 4 vols. (London: Sheed and Ward, 1935); H. Noldin, s.j. and A. Schmitt, s.j., *Summa Theologiae Moralis*, 2 vols., 27th ed. (Oeniponte: Sumptibus et Typic Feliciani Rauch, 1940); Thomas Slater, s.j., *A Manual of Moral Theology*, 2 vols., 3rd ed. (New York: Benziger Bros., 1908); and, John A. McHugh, o.p., and Charles J. Callan, o.p., *Moral Theology: A Complete Course Based on St. Thomas Aquinas and the Best Modern Authorities,* 2 vols. (New York: Joseph F. Wagner, Inc., 1929). In this study I rely primarily on McHugh and Callan, but also Davis and Dominicus M. Prümmer, *Handbook of Moral Theology* (Cork, Ireland: Mercier Press, 1956). McHugh and Callan enjoyed widespread popularity in English-speaking countries and was used for over thirty years in moral theology courses.

[13] See McHugh and Callan, 1:8. "The arrangement of his matter made by St. Thomas Aquinas in the *Summa Theologiae* is admittedly unsurpassed and unsurpassable in the qualities that good distribution should have viz., clearness, connection between parts, completeness. Hence, we cannot do better than follow the order he has used in his treatment of moral subjects."

[14] J. Gallagher, 56–57.

The third section on the sacraments outlines the valid and licit administration of the sacraments and obligation on the Christian for valid and licit reception. This section is also legalistic because it draws primarily from canon law and lacks a dogmatic foundation.[15] J. Gallagher concludes that "the second and third parts of the manuals of moral theology provided generations of priests with the preparation needed for their roles in a sacramental ministry."[16]

The neo-Thomists retain important aspects of Aquinas' moral thought, but they also depart from his system and these departures affect their presentation and understanding of moral theology in significant ways. For example, the manualists retain Aquinas' teleology and define human existence as having both an ultimate end, defined as the beatific vision or union with God, and "proximate ends," the material or earthly ends achieved within this world through loving God and one's neighbor. The neo-Thomists also retain Aquinas' distinction between the natural and supernatural levels of existence, which informs their understanding of human action, virtue, and merit. Because natural moral acts, determined by the will and reason, can achieve only proximate ends and not the final end of human existence, grace is necessary in order to raise human actions to a supernatural level in order that a person merits eternal happiness.

One of the most significant differences between the neo-Thomists and Aquinas is that the neo-Thomists treat moral theology as a discrete and separate discipline from dogmatic theology and make few references to dogmatic themes.[17] Even though the manualists retain Aquinas' framework as a unifying theme, they sever the theological foundation that provides a systematic unity to Aquinas' explanation of how all things come from and return to their divine source.[18] For example, the manuals contain few theological arguments or explanations about God, Christ or the Holy Spirit; further, as J. Gallagher points out, an explanation of the final end is absent.

[15] Ibid., 29–30.

[16] Ibid., 44.

[17] This does not mean that neo-Thomist manualists do not acknowledge a relationship between dogmatic and moral theology. See, for example, McHugh and Callan, 1:1. Many, however, make no mention of the relationship; see Prümmer, 3 and Davis, 1:xxviii.

[18] J. Gallagher, 69–70. "This unity within the plan of the two *Summae*, the essential interdependence between systematic theology (for Chenu, dogma) and Christian notions of morality was *de facto* destroyed by the manualists. The idea of dividing the contents of the *Summa Theologiae* into a number of philosophical and theological treatises may have been well-intentioned, it may have met a pedagogical need, but it undermined the unifying schema of the theological vision of Aquinas."

Dogmatic theology does inform the manuals, but it is implied and the manualists assume that the reader is cognizant of the neo-Thomist and neo-scholastic theological worldview. The language and method is largely deductive: statements of fact about human nature, the world, and salvation are concluded from reason and revelation. One consequence of separating dogma and morals is that greater emphasis is placed on law and merit, reducing the moral life to a set of duties and obligations required to merit sanctifying grace that eventually leads to the rewards of eternal life.[19]

The first section of the manuals—general moral theology—is organized around four basic concepts: human acts, law, conscience, and sin. The person, defined as a rational being, acts both consciously and freely toward the attainment of a goal or end. An action is morally good if it is done freely and with a good intention. A *good* act is defined by the manualists as having a good object (the essence or nature of the act), a good end (the reason or intention), and good circumstances (whom, where, when).[20] The manualists rely on Aquinas' idea that God assists persons to be good in two ways: through law and grace. Laws are required to determine whether an act is good or evil, giving guidance to the actor to make the right choice.

Manualists define two categories of law: human law, which is derived from reason and guides the community toward the common good and divine law, which is composed of eternal, natural, and positive law and is made known through revelation and the natural order. Conscience is the internal subjective guide for moral action and is based primarily on the dictates of the natural law. Sin is defined as a "thought, word, deed, or omission, against the law of God" and therefore, like all human actions, must be both consciously known and intended.[21]

The second and largest section of the manuals shifts to what is necessary for moral actions to be good and salutary in order to achieve the final end of heavenly existence. What is necessary for actions to be good are virtues and knowledge of the moral law and what makes virtues and good actions salutary is grace. Virtue, ac-

---

[19] As discussed in ch. 1, J. Gallagher argues law and grace are separated from the doctrine of providence and "[verge] toward positivism" in the manuals. In addition, the manualists do little to explain the positive moral duties of the Christian life. For Gallagher's analysis of Aquinas' understanding of providence, see, 68–69.

[20] McHugh and Callan, 1:9–36.

[21] Davis, 1:19. McHugh and Callan treat sin under the category of bad habits and vices, 1:56–89.

cording to the manualists, is a "good habit of the free powers of the soul that is a principle of good conduct, and never of conduct that is evil."[22] The manualists make several distinctions regarding virtue: there are natural and supernatural virtues, moral and theological virtues, and acquired and infused virtues. The manualists retain Aquinas' basic distinctions between these various categories, but expand and elaborate them considerably.

Natural virtues are those which persons exercise by their own reason and will; they are further distinguished as either intellectual or moral virtues. Intellectual virtues strive toward truth and the moral virtues guide the will and desires toward the good.[23] Supernatural virtues are natural virtues that exist on a different plane or level because they are infused with divine grace so that persons may attain their final end in God.[24] Davis states,

> The moral virtues would have remained natural in the state of pure nature, but man has been raised to the supernatural state, and has a supernatural destiny which he is bound to achieve. That he may do so, God enlightens his mind by faith, and gives him graces to enable him to raise above mere nature, and to travel along the highway that ultimately reaches heaven. This destiny is beyond all the exigencies and achievement of mere nature. But man retains his human nature, though he has received new potencies, which are brought into operation by grace, so that if man cooperates with that grace, he will merit the destiny which God has appointed for him. Man's natural virtues have been, as it were, sublimated; their objects are no longer natural, they are supernatural, his motives are no longer natural, they are supernatural.[25]

Moral virtues, as stated above, are "those habits that perfect the will and the sensitive appetite with reference to their immediate and respective objects; that is, they are habits concerned with acts as means to the Last End."[26] The manualists treat four central or cardinal

---

[22] McHugh and Callan, 1:49.

[23] The intellectual virtues are further distinguished as speculative (wisdom, knowledge, understanding) and practical (art and prudence).

[24] McHugh and Callan, 1:51.

[25] Davis, 27.

[26] Ibid., 54. "The four moral virtues were defined as follows: (a) in the intellect there is prudence, which guides all the actions and passions by directing the other moral virtues to what is good according to reason; (b) in the will there is justice, which inclines a person to make his actions accord with what he owes to others; (c) in the irascible appetite is fortitude, which subjects to reason the passions that might withdraw from good, such as fear of dangers and labors; (d) in the concupiscible appetite is temperance, which represses the motions of passions that would impel one to some sensible good opposed to reason."

virtues: prudence, justice, fortitude, and temperance. Theological virtues are infused by divine grace to raise the natural abilities to a supernatural level in order that reason and the will might be directed toward God. The theological virtues of faith, hope, and charity, are distinct from the moral virtues because God is their immediate object, whereas the moral virtues have a proximate end as their object. As Davis states:

> The theological virtues are those that perfect the intellect and will with reference to God, their ultimate supernatural object. They are three: (a) *faith*, which is a virtue infused into the intellect, giving man supernatural truths that are perceived by a divine light; (b) *hope*, which is a virtue infused into the will, enabling man to tend towards the supernatural destiny disclosed by faith as towards an end possible of attainment; (c) *charity*, which is a virtue infused into the will, uniting man's affections to the object of his hope and transforming him into its likeness.[27]

Their orientation is essentially interior, which means that the gift of the virtue imposes a duty on the person to elicit interior acts of faith, hope, and charity within the will. Some authors argue that the theological virtues are to be expressed through external actions, but most believe that they serve to orient the interior life and that the moral virtues guide external acts in the world.[28]

The third distinction made by the manualists is whether or not a virtue is acquired or infused. Acquired virtues are attained through habits and are asserted by the will; infused virtues are those which have been given by grace. Therefore, the theological virtues are infused and according to most neo-Thomist moralists there is a category of supernatural or infused moral virtues.[29] Infused refers to the

[27] Ibid., 55. McHugh and Callan, 1:52–53. See J. Gallagher, 56–58, for a discussion of the manualists' understanding of the theological virtues.

[28] See Davis, 1:25, and Prümmer, 80, for a discussion of natural and supernatural virtues. For a similar discussion see Francis J. Connell, C.Ss.R., *Outlines of Moral Theology* (Milwaukee: Bruce Publishing, 1953) 57–61.

[29] Davis, 25; McHugh and Callan, 2:51. There is a long and substantial debate about the category of infused moral virtues. Most neo-Thomists accepted the category because they understood the soul to be animated with grace and therefore able to affect all thought and action. Infused sanctifying grace assists faith in accepting the truth of the supernatural end and assists hope and charity in grasping and loving God as the final end. Because God's grace affects persons on a supernatural level, this grace must also move the reason and will toward to the good on the natural level. See *New Catholic Encyclopedia*, "virtue," 706–7, for the history of debate about infused moral virtues. See also *ST,* I-II.63.3.

gift of the Holy Spirit (also understood as the New Law) that aids reason and the will, but does not replace it.[30] Moral virtues are good but imperfect because they do not "make man perfectly good."[31] Perfection is attained, according to the manualists, when infused virtues are practiced and sanctifying grace increases. In other words, the practice of infused virtues, either moral or theological, is a meritorious act and is rewarded by an increase in sanctifying grace and finally eternal life.[32] Because the ultimate end extends beyond human existence, the manualists spoke of proximate ends as obligatory because they allow a person to live a life of service, gain merit, and obtain a final state of perfection. A Christian moved along this path by receiving habitual grace and the infused virtues through the sacraments.

Another consequence of the manualists' separation of theology and morals is the heightened importance given to the concept of merit.[33] Actions receive God's merit, according to Aquinas, because man chooses the moral good of his own free will. For choosing what God has ordained and because God is just, God rewards man's actions.[34] J. Gallagher argues that the manualists did not believe that man was able to make such a free choice apart from God's grace. For an act to be meritorious it must be supernatural. J. Gallagher explains that

> for a human action to be proportionate to its ultimate goal and fitting to the 'love and service of God' it must be a supernatural act. The consistent position of the manualists was that three things were required

[30] Several manualists discuss the gifts of the Holy Spirit—wisdom, understanding, knowledge, counsel, piety, fortitude, and fear—as part of infused virtue. These gifts aid and support the four cardinal virtues and the theological virtues. See Prümmer, 78–79.

[31] Prümmer, 79–80.

[32] Ibid., 80.

[33] The concept of merit does not receive a great deal of space from the manualists in proportion to its overall importance in their system. They claim that morally good acts are supernatural and therefore meritorious. As Davis states, "These three conditions on the part of the act itself, namely, moral goodness, freedom, and the influence of actual grace, appear to be quite sufficient to constitute an act meritorious." The manualists argued that the Christian is obligated to obtain a supernatural goal, which cannot be achieved without the help of divine grace. Free acts merit grace so that a person can move toward and achieve the supernatural goal of eternal life. Several aspects of Aquinas' treatment of merit are not explicit in the manuals, particularly the notion of divine justice and mercy and the fulfillment of divine promises. The manualists place the individual's actions at the forefront, largely because the dogmatic foundations of moral theology are absent from their work.

[34] *ST*, I-II.114.1-2.

for an act to be supernatural: 1) it must be a morally good act; 2) it must be supernatural, i.e. elicited by the help of a supernatural principle; and 3) it must have a supernatural motive. These three characteristics of the supernatural/meritorious act are essential to an adequate comprehension of this system of morality.[35]

The act is supernatural because of habitual grace, which is God's constant aid and help which "excited" the will to choose the good. Again, J. Gallagher states,

> Grace cooperated with the human will in that it elicited the supernatural act, i.e., it moved the will itself to conform to a good befitting the ultimate end of human nature. The will then commanded what was required for the external performance of the act, thereby maintaining human freedom and establishing the grounds for a notion of human merit.[36]

The primary way that habitual grace "works" is through the theological virtues. The presence of grace, moving the will to act, raises faith, hope, and charity to a supernatural level. As "infused virtues" these are gifts given by God, and cannot be attained by good habits or actions. In the case of supernatural virtues, the will is moved to perform both elicited acts (an interior act of the will) and external actions. Charity is considered to be the central theological virtue that operates within the will and is "turned to God as infinite goodness."[37] Charity commands the other two virtues—it commands the intellect to accept in faith the beliefs of the Church and it commands hope to attach itself to God as the final end. J. Gallagher concludes:

> The theological virtues in general and the virtue of charity in particular, provided moral theology with its religious and supernatural foundation. When the manualists turned their attention to the requirements of the ten commandments or the cardinal virtues their focus would be on sin, aversion from the plan of God, and only secondarily on moral evil. Positively, a life lived in accord with the commandments or virtues was not esteemed principally because of the moral good which was produced, but rather for the supernatural and meritorious character of such a life. The *a priori* condition for such a

---

[35] J. Gallagher, 55. See McHugh and Callan, 1:37–39. McHugh treats merit as part of the section on human acts and makes no reference to a theology of grace. He refers the reader to dogmatic books that deal with the topic of grace.

[36] J. Gallagher, 56; McHugh and Callan, 1:52–53.

[37] J. Gallagher, 58; McHugh and Callan, 1:53.

life, this tradition strongly maintained, were that one's heart be turned to God as the ultimate good and the final end, and that one's mind and will be turned to revelation as the source of one's knowledge of the means to that end. The Christian operated not on natural, but on supernatural principles.[38]

The manualists' understand the moral and theological virtues as representative of the natural and supernatural realms. The model of the two realms eventually becomes constrained in several ways. First, by holding to a sharp division between the natural/moral and supernatural/theological, the unity between the moral and theological virtues is lost. The debate over whether there is a category of infused moral virtues indicates this very problem. Second, by defining virtue as a means to the Last End, virtue loses its dynamic quality as a means for transforming human action in the present time. Nearly exclusive emphasis is placed on the final goal, so that all action becomes defined according to those acts that move toward that goal (and merit the grace to keep moving forward) or those actions that move one away from that goal. Third, the manualists explain that grace is necessary for the practice of virtue, and is rewarded for its practice, but grace is understood largely as a metaphysical reality, not in personal or experiential terms. The sacraments are reduced to a means of grace, as was the case in the medieval sacramental system, but the gift did not need to be experienced in order to be effective. Further, the manualist's concept of virtue is both private and individualistic and is not connected with the sacramental or ecclesial life of the Christian community. Each of these constraints can be found in the manualists' treatment of the virtue of religion.

The Virtue of Religion According to Aquinas and the Manualists

In the second part of the second part of the *Summa Theologica,* Aquinas treats, at considerable length, the moral virtues of prudence, justice, temperance, and fortitude. Of the 123 questions devoted to the cardinal virtues, sixty-five (the largest number) pertain to justice, and thirteen of these address religion. Drawing upon Aristotle's concept of justice, Aquinas defines this cardinal virtue as a habit "whereby a man renders to each one his due by a constant and

---

[38] J. Gallagher, 58; See McHugh and Callan on merit, 1:37–39.

perpetual will."[39] In the questions devoted to justice, Aquinas considers injustice, judgment, the parts of justice (subjective parts such as distributive and commutative justice), the quasi-integral parts (to do good and to decline from evil) and the quasi-potential parts (those virtues which are connected with justice but do not reach its perfect state).

Religion is simply defined as a moral virtue that renders to God the honor that is due him.[40] According to Aquinas' overall understanding of virtue, religion is a special virtue and is distinct among the moral virtues, but it is not a theological virtue. Religion is unique because the good to which it is directed is God; it is a moral virtue because religion is "about things referred to the end" and not to God as an end in itself. It is distinct from and preferred over other moral virtues because "its actions are directly and immediately ordered to the honor of God. Hence religion excels among the moral virtues."[41]

The nine virtues that make up the potential parts of justice according to Aquinas are religion, piety (familial obligations), observance, gratitude, vengeance, truth, friendship, liberality, and equity. They are considered potential because they cannot obtain the full perfection of justice and "fall short" in two respects: by the "aspect of equality" and by the "aspect of due."[42] In terms of equality, there are certain relationships in which one cannot render the other the full or equal measure of what is owed to them because of the nature of the relationship, for instance, in relation to God or one's parents. Thus, religion, piety, and observance are only quasi-potential parts of justice. In regards to falling short of just due, Aquinas distinguishes between legal and moral due and discusses the other quasi-potential parts of justice in relationship to these two categories.[43]

Aquinas divides the virtue of religion into interior and exterior acts. The interior acts consist of devotion and prayer; the exterior acts are adoration, sacrifice, oblations and first fruits, vows, oaths, and the taking of God's name in adjuration and praise. Aquinas' distinction between the two types of acts of religion is simple: interior

---

[39] *ST*, II-II.58.2. The virtue of religion is treated in II-II.80.1-8. Aquinas draws primarily from Augustine's understanding of religion in Book X, chs. 1–5, of *The City of God* (New York: Penguin Books, 1984) 371–79.

[40] The essence of religion is defined in *ST*, II-II.81.1-2.

[41] Ibid., II-II.81.6.

[42] Ibid., II-II.80.1.

[43] Ibid.

acts belong to the "heart" and are the primary expression of religion and exterior acts belong to the "flesh" and are secondary.[44] The distinction between interior and exterior acts is based upon Aquinas' understanding of the body and soul and their relationship to each other. First, persons give honor and reverence to God for "their own sake" and not for God's sake, since persons cannot add to the glory of God. This honor and reverence is based upon the recognition that "our mind is subjected to Him; wherein its perfection consists, since a thing is perfected by being subjected to its superior." The mind (soul) alone cannot be perfected, but rather it requires the sense world, the material and visible, to guide and stimulate it:

> Now the human mind, in order to be united to God, needs to be guided by the sensible world, since *invisible things . . . are clearly seen, being understood by the things that are made,* as the Apostle says (Rom 1:20). Wherefore in the Divine worship it is necessary to make use of corporeal things, that man's mind may be aroused thereby, as by signs, to the spiritual acts by means of which he is united to God. Therefore the internal acts of religion take precedence over the others and belong to religion essentially, while its external acts are secondary, and subordinate to the internal acts.[45]

Aquinas indicates in the discussion of religion that he will treat the sacraments in a later section of the work. In the third part of the *Summa,* Aquinas makes a brief reference to the relationship between the virtue of religion and the sacraments: "The sacraments are ordered to perfecting man in what belongs to the worship of God according to the religion of the Christian life."[46] As is the case with each discussion of a virtue, Aquinas considers religion in itself, the actions pertaining to religion, and the vices or opposites of religion.

The manualists rarely depart from Aquinas' understanding of the virtue of religion.[47] Three characteristics are common to the manualists' treatment of religion: (1) the virtue of religion is considered to be a potential part of justice; (2) it is a moral and not a theological virtue; and, (3) it consists of internal and external acts along with

---

[44] Ibid., II-II.81.7.

[45] Ibid. After discussing internal and external acts, Aquinas (Ibid., II-II.92-101) enumerates the vices opposed to religion: superstition (those things which agree with religion in giving worship to God) and irreligion (those things that show contempt for God).

[46] *ST*, III.65.1.

[47] See Connell, 142–54; McHugh and Callan, 2:291–420; Davis (37) does not discuss the virtue of religion, but treats religion under the first commandment.

vices against religion including both excesses and defaults. Most manualists make mention of religion, but some give fuller treatment to the subject than others. For example, McHugh and Callan devote over one hundred pages to religion and Prümmer close to fifty pages, and most of their attention is given to an analysis of vows and oaths.[48]

An example from a neo-Thomist manual will illustrate the common treatment of religion. According to McHugh and Callan, the virtue of religion must consider and "pay" what is owed to God. It is considered to be a "potential part of justice" because the habits that make up the activity are "subsidiary to justice, partaking in some degree, but not entirely of its nature or activity."[49] The reason is that some activities pertaining to justice cannot fulfill two of the essential aspects of justice, "a return is given which is equal to a debt, and that the debt is owed on account of a strict or legal right."[50] Religion fits this category since the debt owed to God can never be fulfilled. "Thus, to God man owes whatever honor and veneration he manifests, but with all his efforts man can never pay to God a worship that is equal to the debt."[51] McHugh and Callan state:

> Religion takes its rank among the moral, not among the theological, virtues. A theological virtue has the Last End for its immediate object or subject-matter (e.g., faith is concerned directly with God, since it believes Him and in Him), and has no mean of virtue (e.g., faith cannot go to extremes by believing God too much); whereas a moral virtue has the means to God for its immediate object (e.g., justice is concerned directly with actions we owe to others) and it must observe the golden mean (e.g., justice must pay the just price, neither more nor less, and at the proper time, place, and to the proper person, etc.). Now, it is clear that religion has for its immediate object the due performance of worship, although God is the person for whose sake it is offered and His excellence the foundation of its necessity; and also that one must observe moderation in worship as to circumstances of place, time, etc., although it is impossible to be extreme in the quantity or fervor one gives to worship, since even the best efforts will fall short of the honor God deserves (Ecclus., xliii. 33).[52]

---

[48] See McHugh and Callan, 2:291–420 for a discussion of religion and 2:309–54 on vows and oaths; Prümmer, 165–210, on religion and, 175–92, on vows and oaths.

[49] McHugh and Callan, 2:287. See *ST* II-II.80.1 on potential parts of justice.

[50] McHugh and Callan, 2:287.

[51] Ibid., 2:288.

[52] Ibid., 2:291.

McHugh and Callan claim religion as the greatest of the moral virtues for two reasons: "the person in whose favor it is exercised is God Himself, and its obligation is correspondingly stricter than that of the other virtues."[53] According to the authors, this does not contradict the placement of religion under justice because "it is more correct to speak of the integral and potential parts of virtues as quasi-parts" and it is not inferior to justice since "in matters of virtue good will takes precedence over the ability to pay."[54] In terms of moral virtues, however, the authors claim that religion is superior to legal justice, humility, mercy, repentance, and external offerings to God.

In nearly every detail the manualists' treatment of religion mirrors that of Aquinas, except for two points: a shift in language and a more extensive treatment of acts such as oaths and vows. The language shifts from Aquinas' idea of rendering (or giving back, restoring, returning) to God to the idea that a debt or payment is owed to God. The manualists' language reflects a juridical and commercial understanding of the divine-human relationship; Aquinas' language reflects his *exitus-reditus* model.

The extensive treatment given to actions such as making vows and oaths demonstrates the extent to which casuistry shapes the manuals. For example, McHugh and Callan devote fifty-two sections to vows; they discuss various kinds of vows, the necessities for a valid vow, circumstances that make vows invalid, the obligation of certain vows and the time to fulfill them, doubtful vows, and the annulment and dispensation of vows. This careful scrutiny of all the potential ways that certain acts fulfill a vow demonstrates the precise manner in which moral action was legally defined by the manualists.

The manualists' treatment of vows and oaths is a good illustration of how Häring shifts from the neo-Thomist tradition. For example, the consideration given to the multiple aspects of each type of act allows the manualists to examine every possible circumstance or action that might or might not constitute virtue or vice. The weight given to a casuistical examination of topics and the relative absence of dogmatic themes creates an image of the Christian moral life as composed primarily of rational discernment of the natural and divine law; the image of God is one of law-maker, dispenser of grace to those who merit it, and one who exacts a price for the gift.

---

[53] Ibid. See *ST*, II-II.80.6.
[54] McHugh and Callan, 2:291.

In contrast, Häring drops the Greek and scholastic definition of virtue in favor of a biblical and dialogical view. Rather than considering numerous circumstances and acts that contribute to or detract from virtue, Häring defines the virtues within his word-and-response system, placing particular emphasis on the revelation of God, the imitation of Christ, and the sacramental formation of the life of virtue. The theological explanation replaces the casuistic analysis and the image of God as divine life-giver replaces the law-maker image.[55] He shifts to explaining the divine initiative and human encounter rather than carefully delineating human acts.

The Theological and Moral Virtues in Häring's Moral Theology

The Christian ideal of virtue is not man himself and human prudence or the mere balance and harmony of human life. The fount of virtue, the center and measure of virtue, the goal of virtue is the love of God. For the Christian, virtue in its most comprehensive sense is love. To be virtuous means to abandon oneself to the love of God which gives itself to us. It is the imitation of the love of Christ, the heroic renouncement of self, the outburst of love for God and neighbor.[56]

—————————————————— Bernard Häring, *The Law of Christ*, vol. 1

Defining Virtue

Häring, unlike the manualists, draws upon several sources in addition to Aquinas to define virtue, especially Augustine and Max Scheler, and thereby draws the virtues into his larger theological and moral framework. In defining virtue, Häring emphasizes three main points: Christian virtue is distinct from Greek and Stoic virtue be-

---

[55] J. Mahoney's (252) critique of Aquinas' placement of religion under justice has largely to do with the central interpretation of God as law-maker: "But to consider that this non-Christian, indeed, atheistic, category of justice can be an adequate and completely enlightening means of conceptualizing and expressing the reality of man's relationship to the God of Israel and to Jesus Christ is both a travesty of the Gospel and an ignoring of the fact that all our discourse about God (and here the voluntarists have a point) is severely limited. Moral theology has in this respect considered itself exempt from the limiting axiom of all theology, that of analogical predication about God and all his activities—that is, the inherent limitations of applying directly to God terms and ideas which are in the first instance derived from more mundane human experience. . . . This is the ultimate literalism and legalism of moral theology and it is, in that respect at least, profoundly untheological."

[56] *LC* 1:487.

cause it is ordered and unified by divine love; Christian virtue is christocentric; and, Christian virtue requires not mere repetition of good habits, but free, conscious response to the divine word. Drawing from the common tradition that defines virtue as a power within the soul that orientates the human person to the good, Häring defines virtue as "steadfastness and facility in doing good springing from the very heart of man . . . . inner equipment of the forces of the soul that is turned exclusively to the good life that cannot be misused. It transcends noble endowment and capacity. It is a permanent capacity *(habitus, héxis)* of the soul's powers assuring that constancy in good action that makes a man true to himself in the multiple hazards of decision and in the most diverse situations of life."[57]

Theologically speaking, the orientation to the good is an orientation that is given by God and directed to God. Häring shares the Greek understanding of virtue as the power to do good, but rejects the end and purpose of virtuous action as self-fulfillment, harmony, and happiness. The Greeks also held prudence to be the central or highest virtue, but Häring, following Augustine and Aquinas, places love at the center of the virtues. All virtue springs from love and is oriented by love to God:

> Virtue in its fullest sense is that which places the life of the soul in order, for the right order in living is consequent on the right order in loving. To love rightly is to possess perfect virtue, for the order of love is the order of charity *("ordo amoris, ordo caritatis")*. Only the love of God with the noble retinue of virtues animated by it can establish this order in the soul, so that it can rightly perceive the true hierarchy of all the values of love and respond to them.[58]

Häring integrates value theory into the virtues in order to show that virtue involves the realization of the order of value and the free choice to actualize value: "The unity of virtue rests in the unity of good in God. Plurality of virtue corresponds strictly to plurality of moral values."[59] Häring also draws upon value theory to show that there are different virtues, but that all are ordered and unified in the highest virtue, "obedience to God and love for Him," in much the same way that diverse values are ordered and unified in ultimate

---

[57] *LC* 1:285.
[58] Ibid.
[59] Ibid., 1:488–89. J. Gallagher (174) discusses Häring's use of value theory to explicate the virtues.

value. Häring points out Aquinas' argument that virtue is diverse but reaches perfection only when it "takes its place in the integral hierarchy of all the virtues and is rooted in the primary and basic virtue in which all are centered." This is similar to Scheler's notion of the hierarchy of values.[60] The Christian recognizes many virtues to be practiced and realized in relationship to particular situations and ends, but the foundation, center, and orientation of virtue is love.

If virtue rests on love and strives toward perfect love, then Christ is perfect virtue and Christian virtue is the imitation of Christ's virtue. Similar to his argument that Jesus is the perfect embodiment of religion as word-and-response and the perfect manifestation of the worship of God, Häring presents Jesus as the perfect embodiment of virtue because he is perfect selfless and obedient love: "Christ taught us what virtue is, above all in His own all-embracing love. What virtue is appears in the very excess of his loving sacrifice by which He offered Himself for the glory of God and the salvation of mankind."[61]

Häring also relates Christian virtue to his theology of the Trinity: God the Father creates persons in his image and likeness so they have the capacity to do the good; Christ is the example of perfect virtue; and, the Holy Spirit is given as a gift, infused within the believer, to enable imitation of Christ and cooperation with the Father's grace. Therefore, the ideal of Christian virtue is the full participation, in love and obedience, in the divine life and not the Greek ideal of harmony, balance, or perfection of the mean.[62]

The source of Christian virtue is God's divine love infused in the soul. Häring reinterprets the doctrine on infused virtues to mean that God is the source and dynamic power that shapes the inner person. "God does not merely confer supernatural character and value on the various acts of virtue through the cooperation of actual grace, but He sanctifies the very root and source of these acts through the infusion of the supernatural virtues."[63] Häring challenges the scholastic emphasis on "habitual repetition of acts" because the aspect of free

---

[60] *LC* 1:489–91. Häring admits that this is good theory, but very difficult to see in reality when many people are a mixture of both virtue and vice.

[61] Ibid., 1:485.

[62] See Ibid., 1:486–87.

[63] Ibid., 1:491. In a later work (*SS*, 77) Häring adopts the biblical idea of "sanctification by the Holy Spirit" in order to describe both the "work of God in us making us holy" and the "command to live a holy life; grace brings with it the order, 'Be holy.'"

choice is lost. He draws on his word-and-response theory to show how virtue is always conscious striving for love: "Habit and exercise can never take the place of the decision, always fresh and free, for the good, based on the inner spirit with its intimate sentiment for good."[64] Virtue is another category for explicating both free choice of value and the word-response pattern of the religious-moral life: "For the Christian it is the abandonment to God's loving self-giving which demands the free response of our gratitude in return."[65]

Moral Virtues

Despite Häring's integration of virtue theory into his overall theological and moral scheme, the category of moral virtue is not central in his work after *The Law of Christ*. In fact, moral virtue is briefly considered at the end of the first volume and the introduction of the third volume. It is replaced with what Häring terms the biblical or eschatological virtues in later writings;[66] humility is considered along with the moral virtues in *The Law of Christ* and gradually moves

---

[64] Ibid., 1:493.

[65] Ibid., 1:488.

[66] In *Free and Faithful in Christ* (1:201–2) Häring includes a brief examination of the moral virtues but introduces the category of the "eschatological virtues." These include gratitude/humility, hope, vigilance, and serenity/joy. According to Häring, these virtues are the true biblical foundation of the Christian moral life, rather than the four cardinal virtues borrowed from the Greeks. "The four cardinal virtues are by no means characteristic of biblical ethics. They are taken from the Greek culture in a creative effort by the evangelizing Church to be faithful to the promptings of the Lord of history in that culture. The purpose was to bring home the valuable ethos of those who turned to Christ. However, the emphasis of the Bible is on the eschatological virtues. . . . My intention here, is to show that a return to the biblical vision can generate and release energies of creative liberty and fidelity in today's world." See also *HR*, 142–51 and *Called to Holiness* (Slough, United Kingdom: St. Paul Publications, 1982) 26–58. In *Timely and Untimely Virtues* (Slough, United Kingdom: St. Paul Publications, 1986) Häring writes that different virtues are required at different times and analyzes the Hebrew Bible, New Testament, and early Christian literature for examples of the kinds of virtues that were needed in order to respond to the various conditions social challenges. The main virtues he identifies are grateful memory (from Augustine and Alphonsus), readiness, vigilance, discernment, serenity, and courage. Häring's category of the eschatological virtues is very similar to Romano Guardini's list of virtues in *The Virtues: On Forms of Moral Life* (Chicago: Henry Regnery Company, 1963). Among the virtues Guardini identifies are truthfulness, acceptance, patience, reverence, asceticism, kindness, and gratitude, but unlike Häring he does not reject the Greek understanding of virtue and does argue for this list of virtues to be found solely in Scripture. Rather he (8) offers them as a "series of such structures of man's relation to the good" that is based on "image upon image as these present themselves in the manifold varieties of human experience."

to the center of Häring's moral thought.[67] The theological virtues, on the other hand, are prominent throughout his works.

Häring's ambivalence about the category of moral or cardinal virtue is related to several issues. He recognizes that the cardinal virtues arise from Greek philosophy and culture, and even though he can locate some biblical support for them, they are not the primary virtues of the New Testament.[68] Second, he rejects the sharp distinction between the theological and moral virtues in neo-Thomist moral theology and strives to show how the moral virtues are related to theological virtues. Based on his reading of Aquinas's *Secunda Secundae,* Häring argues that the theological virtues are the true "hinges" of the Christian moral life and that he only considers the moral virtues as "fundamental attitudes" that he will treat as "intrinsic tasks according to the theological virtues."[69] He is critical of what he perceives as a "too anthropocentric concept of virtue" and argues that "human virtues need redemption by being integrated into true adoration of God."[70] Third, the scholastic and neo-Thomist debate over infused moral virtue makes little sense in light of his doctrine of grace.

Häring's presentation of the moral virtues in *The Law of Christ* retains some elements from the Catholic moral tradition, but overall they take on a new character when incorporated into the themes of his moral theology. First, he considers each in light of biblical texts. For example with reference to prudence, he surveys the Hebrew Scriptures and New Testament and concludes that: (1) prudence is a gift from God, who is Eternal Wisdom, (2) prudence must also be acquired through prayer, observance of the commandments, the exercise of prudence, and observance of the wise, (3) prudence is part of the teaching of Jesus to his disciples, and (4) Jesus is the supreme example of prudence.[71]

Häring also explains how each moral virtue is related to the theological virtues, especially charity. Following Augustine's teaching

---

[67] Häring (*LC* 1:492) treats humility similar to the way he treats religion as a basic and fundamental virtue which is related to all other virtue. "Only through humility, which attributes nothing to oneself but, on the contrary, with a perfection of loyalty far transcending the demands of mere law, refers all to God, does virtue attain the noblest splendor of beauty." The final section of volume 1 is devoted to humility; see *LC* 1:546–57 and *CRCW,* 278–85.

[68] *CE,* 20.

[69] *LC* 1:497.

[70] *SEL,* 158.

[71] Ibid., 1:499–500.

that the moral virtues are the path to the love of God, Häring shows how justice and love are related, with love preceding and supporting justice. He writes that

> justice in the first place really and directly regulates the relation to objects, the use of material goods and the relation to one's fellows in regard to the material order and material possessions, not in regard to man's interior value in love. But it is love which unfolds the actual I to the Thou and discovers the living fountain of value in the Thou. Then only comes what is second—and no one doubts that it is also very important—justice between the I and Thou, between the I and the We of society, justice which establishes the right order regarding the goods of the individual and the community.[72]

In a similar manner, the Christian understanding of fortitude is defined by the love of God. "Only love for a higher good justifies the sacrifice of lesser goods. One who is prepared to suffer and die must be aware of what he is sacrificing and of the reason for his sacrifice. . . . Fortitude must serve the love of God, if it is to be perfect virtue."[73]

Häring's doctrine of grace attempts to return to biblical descriptions and understandings of God's active presence, replacing the two-tier language of the neo-Thomists. He states: "Our doctrine on the infused moral virtues clearly reveals the source and basis and also the end and goal of Christian virtue: the foundation and source is the Holy Spirit with His transforming and renovating grace; end and goal are Christ and the Father, the imitation of the spirit of Christ through the force of His Spirit."[74]

Häring's moral virtue is distinct from the neo-Thomist because it is trinitarian and the emphasis is on the dynamic, personal relationship with God in the present moment. The Holy Spirit acts upon the Christian in three ways: transforming the natural abilities into supernatural abilities, directing the energies and actions of the person toward imitation of Christ, and changing the motive for action from self-perfection to love of God.[75] For example, in regards to prudence, the Holy Spirit guides the believer in discerning the will of God in concrete particular moral situations in which general principles, according to Häring, cannot always aid in making decisions: "Prudence

[72] Ibid., 1:514.
[73] Ibid., 1:527. See also 1:530 for a discussion of love and temperance.
[74] Ibid., 1:491.
[75] Ibid., 1:493.

is accompanied by a sense of the will of God (subjectively this is the "*Gnóme*") in the concrete circumstances of particular instances, which is not learned *a priori* or from a simple scheme or outline of the virtues. Docile and completely responsive to the gift of counsel conferred by the Holy Spirit, this virtue of prudence does not apply a mere universal norm, but rather directly senses that the loving will of God is immediately embracing and moving it in the hour of grace."[76] Because the Christian is "grasped by Christ," all action, both interior and exterior, "has its source of power in Christ and tends with exalted end and aim toward Christ" and this means that both the moral and theological are "divinely given powers."[77] The moral virtues, according to Häring, are never separated from their divine source or from the theological virtues and find their full and complete expression when they arise from this source. For example, prudence is a divine gift, but requires free choice and response to the divine gift in order to be complete. Häring writes:

> As such, the theological virtues are not directly influenced by prudence, for their activity is orientated directly and immediately toward God without concern for the measure and balance provided by prudence. But in so far as these same virtues must manifest themselves in acts of the virtue of religion and the other moral virtues, they also have need for the guidance of prudence. On the other hand, prudence is the noble handmaiden of the noblest mistress, wisdom. It is the role of prudence, in the light of wisdom and in the service of wisdom, to discern the true reality of the moment, perceiving in each situation the hour of grace (*kairós*) granted by God, seeing in it the divine message and mission, with practical concern for the ways and means of becoming active for love of God.[78]

Häring emphasizes through his teaching on the moral virtues that moral action is never separate or distinct from its religious source in Christian morality. There is no separation from an interior, religious sense and an exterior, moral sense. Rather they are integrated and bound together by the word-and-response dynamic of divine-human life.

---

[76] Ibid., 1:503.
[77] Ibid., 1:492.
[78] Ibid., 1:502.

Theological Virtues

In *The Law of Christ*, Häring retains the traditional Roman Catholic doctrine on the theological virtues of faith, hope, and charity as supernatural infused virtues that elevate and transform the human person's natural capacities to a supernatural level: faith elevates reason, and hope and charity elevate the will. But Häring also expands this definition to emphasize that the theological virtues are related to the moral virtues as "basic endowment, equipment, orientation, capacity. They are qualifications for action."[79] Häring presents the theological virtues as the religious core and foundation of the Christian moral life and links faith, hope, and charity to three essential concepts in his moral system: The theological virtues are the foundation for dialogue between God and humanity, they are the basis for the imitation of Christ, and, the sacraments provide the sustenance and nurture of these gifts within the community.

The theological virtues have traditionally been defined as interior acts oriented toward God as the final end and not directed to external expression in the world. Häring slightly shifts away from Aquinas and the manualists' exclusive emphasis on the Supernatural End of the theological virtues and indicates that they are a present reality that points to a future reality: "The primary purpose of the theological virtues is not to equip man for a mission or vocation in the world . . . but to open the sacred dialog between God and man which is to be completed and perfected in eternal bliss."[80] The three theological virtues are a person's basic orientation toward God. According to Häring, "These fundamental activities are not world betterment, not striving for self-perfection, but orientation to God, participation in the fullness of divine life." God's sanctifying grace initiates a dialogue and creates the possibility for human response. "The dialog always begins with God, who reaches out to man with His transforming grace endowing him with the capacity to respond."[81]

Häring carefully retains the tradition's teaching on the theological virtues as focused toward God and not to external acts, but he

---

[79] "Thus in the virtue of divine faith, reason is elevated as a faculty made capable of participation in the divine fulness of truth. In hope the will, reaching out toward happiness, is directed toward the divine inheritance of the child of God, the heavenly bliss. In love man's power to love, the power that says *yes* to value, is made capable of a joyous response to the absolute love-value which is God Himself" (Ibid., 2:3).

[80] Ibid., 2:5-6.

[81] Ibid., 2:6.

does not want to create a strong division between the theological and moral virtues as though the former were solely interior and other-worldly and the latter exterior and this-worldly with no relation between them. He defines their relationship through his concept of response and responsibility:

> But since these virtues are infused in this earthly life and lay hold of man on his pilgrim's sojourn in this world, they must bear a relation to his activity here below. They place man, the pilgrim, with all his external activity, with all his tasks in the world (that is, in his total moral bearing and orientation) before God His final end, in his response and responsibility. This implies that all the vital manifestations of the moral virtues of man in the state of grace are laid hold of by the divine virtues and transformed and placed into dialog with God. . . . But such is the vital dynamic of these three virtues that they render the entire earth their sphere of activity, transparent with the countenance of the Christian always shining through earthly realities and turned to God. *In consequence, once man lives from the dynamism of the theological virtues, there no longer exists a mere moral life for him, but hence-forth only a religious-moral life. This is the yes of world-responsibility spoken to God, arising from the gift of divine love within us (italics mine)*.[82]

There is a dynamic relationship between the theological and moral virtues that mirrors the word-and-response model: the theological virtues are divine gift summoning and empowering the person's response to enter into the divine life and live according to Christ's example in the world. The person's response to the divine is manifested in all aspects of thought and action.

For Christians, the theological virtues form what Häring calls the "inner dynamism of the imitation of Christ." God's grace transforms the inner life to conform to Christ and by "being in Christ" external actions also take on the character of Christ. The inner source of the Spirit's power does not obliterate or replace free choice, but guides and assists the person to respond in obedient love.

Christ, as Word and High Priest, is the perfect manifestation of divine gift and response and so through Christ, faith, hope, and love are made manifest: faith is "attuned" to Christ, the Teacher, hope looks to Christ as source of redemption and glory, and love is manifested through the outpouring of God's love through Christ and the

[82] Ibid., 2:7.

Holy Spirit. The love which unites the Trinity, binds one to Christ through the power of the Spirit to God, the Father.[83] Häring states that the "theological virtues give to us an interior relationship to Christ, our Teacher, Redeemer, and Friend. They are the inner capacity, the divine invitation and obligation to imitate Christ, because Christ is for us the sole cause of this God-like life. Life flowing from these virtues is nothing other than actual imitation of Christ, harkening to Christ, hoping in Christ, obediently loving Christ."[84] Drawing on Johannine and Pauline themes (Christ as word-and-response and the Christian life as incorporation into the life of Christ), Häring's Christocentric virtue stands in stark contrast to the manualists, who make no mention of Christ in relationship to the virtues.

The theological virtues are the inner capacity for dialogue, response, and imitation of Christ, but for Häring they are not exclusively private and individual. Drawing on personalism, Häring argues that the theological virtues, which are formed in and through the sacraments, are personal encounter with Christ that are also public and communal. The theological virtues are shaped and sustained by the Christian community through worship and sacraments, the visible, communal acts of the church.

The sacraments are an extension of the divine signs beginning in creation and culminating in the Incarnation and extending to the Church.[85] The basic, primordial sacrament is Christ who fully reveals God's redemptive love: "He is the sign in which and through which we experience the promise and the love of the Father. And in turn through and in Him we are able to speak effectively and worthily to God in response to His love."[86] The Church continues to make manifest and visible the divine love of Christ for the world:

> The Church is a visible sign of the continuing love of Christ in the world. Precisely as visible and perceptible does the Church, linked with Christ in the covenant of love, live from His redemptive words. She is His full response to the Father, the basic, primal sacrament of

---

[83] Ibid., 2:7–8. Häring' relies on the gospel of John for his theology of inner divine life and transformation in Christ. The gospel and the First Letter of John are quoted extensively in *LC* 2, ch. 1, on the theological virtues. There is no reference, however, to the Synoptic Gospels in this section.

[84] Ibid., 2:8.

[85] See Ibid., 2:8–9 for a discussion of the creation, incarnation, the church and sacraments.

[86] Ibid., 2:8.

Christ, the redemptive sign of Christ's love which saves all and embraces all in loving response. She is the sacrament of Christ as He, the Incarnate Son of the Father in His visible Sacrifice and in the visible sign of His resurrected humanity, is the basic, primordial sacrament, the redemptive sign of the love of the Father.[87]

As Christ was visible to his followers, so the Church uses visible and tangible signs to express God's love and unite the community in love. The visible sign is essential, according to Häring, because God expresses love of man through the visible created order and through Jesus, and so persons hear and respond to divine love through signs and symbol.[88]

Häring sharply criticizes the argument put forth by the neo-Thomist philosopher Jacques Maritain on the formation of the theological virtues. Maritain maintains that the theological virtues are nurtured through contemplation and prayer without word, sign, or gesture. Contemplation must transcend material signs and objects, according to Maritain, because it is a higher and more pure encounter with God than the liturgy.[89] Häring criticizes Maritain's understanding of the liturgy as secondary to contemplation and argues that the theological virtues must be formed and sustained by the public and communal expression of the liturgy and cannot be solely nurtured through the individual's contemplative experience of God. He states that "only because Maritain places the divine virtues primarily in contemplation—wordless, motionless contemplation—and looks upon the external common form of the liturgy as an obstacle to purely spiritual contemplation, is he able to hold and defend the 'primacy of contemplation' over the liturgy. Participation in the liturgical life appears to Maritain as neither the only nor the necessary way to contemplation. For him the community celebration of the sacred mysteries is of

---

[87] Ibid., 2:9.

[88] Ibid.

[89] Jacques and Raissa Maritain, "Liturgy and Contemplation," *Spiritual Life* 5 (June 1959) 120. Maritain makes this same point in two small books. Contemplation is achieved, according to Maritain, when the soul "leaves the reign of sensory images for the sphere of the Pure Intelligible . . . while the operation of the intelligence grows more perfect in proportion to its emancipation from sensory images." Jacques Maritain, *Prayer and Intelligence* (New York: Sheed and Ward, 1943) 5. In *Liturgy and Contemplation* (New York: P. J. Kenedy & Sons, 1960) 22, he argues that the Christian experiences full membership in the Church when "along with Him Whom he loves, he is united to God in an ineffable union of person to person, and enters into the depths of God."

less significance than solitary contemplation."[90] Häring further argues that "union with Christ and the Mystical Body of Christ is not actuated less in the liturgical celebration than in quiet meditation but rather that it there finds clearer expression."[91]

The sacraments, as visible signs of faith, hope, and love, are an extension of salvation history and continue as God's external expression in the world. They are essential for persons who both need visible signs to receive God's word but also must express their response to God through visible realities. In addition, the very nature of the liturgy and sacraments as communal and public rites is essential: they bind the community together in faith, hope, and love and call upon the Christian to respond to the summons of divine love through love of neighbor. Häring writes in the introduction to the second volume of *The Law of Christ*:

> It would be utterly false to assume that community with God (in the three divine virtues, faith, hope, love, and in the worship of God through the virtue of religion) removes man from human fellowship and places him exclusively in solitary personal encounter with God. Quite the contrary! Life in the community of the brethren is rooted in the fellowship of faith, in the good tidings of salvation, in the solidarity of the one hope, in the love of the one Father and the one Lord Jesus Christ, in the unity of the Holy Spirit, in the community of praise offered to the Triune God. The very first objective above all others in our scientific moral theology is to present this fundamental structure of the Christian life. In other words: the Great Commandment of love is the foundation for Christian personalism and as well the deep source of the Christian spirit of fellowship and family. The divine summons to us, which is something utterly personal, and its acceptance on our part, which must likewise be altogether personal, is the foundation of fellowship with God and at the same time of

[90] "We cannot refrain from expressing our surprise and shock over the attitude of such a noble spiritual thinker as Maritain. Undoubtedly misled by certain critics of the liturgical renewal and a few incidental excesses which everyone should deplore, he goes so far as to protest against too intense a cultivation of the liturgy. His concern is for the purity and vitality of the theological virtues. Not only does he go so far afield as to make of religion a second-rate virtue constrained to accept its subordinate position in the Aristotelian scheme of virtues, he is also completely oblivious of the fact that the celebration of the divine mysteries is exercise of the theological virtues as well as of the virtue of religion" (*LC* 2:523). Häring also critiques Maritain in *SSA*, 157–58 and in an article that appeared in a special issue of the journal *Worship* devoted to the topic of liturgy and the spiritual life, sparked by Maritain's article a year before. See Bernard Häring, "Liturgical Piety and Christian Perfection," *Worship* 34 (October 1960) 523–35.

[91] Ibid., 529.

brotherly community with men. All authentic responsibility of man for his fellows and all responsibility for the social order in the world flows from our response to the redemptive Word of God. From this response it draws its life and inspiration; to this response it constantly returns.[92]

The sacraments are essential to the formation and expression of the theological virtues. Faith is both heard and expressed in the sacraments.[93] In hearing and responding in faith, the Christian person accepts the promise of salvation and receives it in hope.[94] And finally, love is expressed through the sacraments both by the power of divine love to unite the follower to God and to the neighbor: "It demands of us a loving response to Him, peace and harmony with our fellows, for we are all given a share in the love of the Lord which makes all things one."[95]

The theological virtues become, in Häring's system, the center of the divine-human dialogue because they are biblical, they are a divine gift, and as gift they demand a response. The theological virtues become the foundation of the religious-moral life, and even though the moral virtues are still part of his system in *The Law of Christ*, it is obvious how the category of the theological virtues draws together the religious and moral through the Trinity, Christ, and the sacraments. Häring's reinterpretation of the virtues overcomes several of the constraints found in the manuals of moral theology: the word-and-response motif gives theological unity to the Christian life; a balance is achieved by focus on the present, earthly life, and future anticipation of the eschatological reality of the Kingdom of God; strong emphasis on the personal and experiential through the sacraments redefines the liturgy as the center of the encounter with Christ, the sacrament of God; and, recalling the liturgy as the formative sphere of the virtues emphasizes the social bond between God and neighbor.

---

[92] Ibid., 2:xviii–xix.

[93] Ibid., 2:12.

[94] ". . . [I]t follows that we must be eschatologically formed, altered, and renewed with all the vigor of Christian hope through the sacramental celebration, through the sacred and solemn signs which stimulate and strengthen hope" (Ibid., 2:12–13).

[95] Ibid., 2:13.

The Virtue of Religion in Häring's Moral Theology

The doctrine—we cannot speak of it as absolutely convincing—that religion is a moral virtue implies that acts of religion must enter into the temporal sequence of our lives. They must form the warp and woof of the whole texture of our earthly existence including the communal life among men (thus is the community sanctified). Consequently it belongs essentially to our activity in the world to fulfill the moral tasks imposed by the virtue of religion. In other words we face the world with a moral task which flows from the virtue of religion. This assumption can have only one meaning in the light of the following principle: our entire activity in the world must have a religious formation, for all our acts must be ordered to the loving majesty of God. This means that all our moral tasks are at the same time religious tasks.[96]

—————————————————— Bernard Häring, *The Law of Christ*, vol. 2

The virtue of religion plays a special role in Häring's moral theology. In a similar way to other concepts he inherits from the Catholic moral tradition, he retains some aspects of the category but integrates and expands the concept with his word-and-response theology. Häring's understanding of religion has two ideas in common with the manualist tradition—he defines the virtue of religion as a moral virtue and retains the distinction between internal and external acts and the vices against religion. He departs from the tradition by treating religion as separate from the moral virtue of justice. For example, in discussing the moral virtues in the first volume of *The Law of Christ*, Häring briefly alludes to religion under justice, but his full treatment of religion takes place in the second volume after his consideration of the theological virtues. He devotes a separate section to the virtue of religion with chapters on the virtue of religion in the Bible, an analysis of religion in relation to the theological and moral virtues, the sacraments and religion, sins against religion, and an analysis of four acts of religion.[97]

Häring also departs from the manualists' legalistic definition of religion, which emphasizes one's duty and obligation to worship because one "owes" payment to God, and defines religion as communion and dialogue with God that finds expression in external acts of worship. Häring presents his theory of religion as a return to

[96] Ibid., 2:124.
[97] Ibid., 2:111–346; nearly half of this volume is devoted to the virtue of religion.

Aquinas' relational understanding of religion but also expands it to include a biblical and christological focus. The virtue of religion is central for Häring because it serves as the foundation for the religious-moral life of the Christian.[98]

Defining the Virtue of Religion

Like the other moral virtues, Häring's analysis of the virtue of religion begins with a survey of Scripture. In the Hebrew Scriptures and New Testament, he identifies three concepts that form the "presupposition, the object, the content" of religion. These are the sanctity, the name, and the glory of God.[99] Drawing upon the word-and-response theme as his main interpretative framework, Häring finds in the Scriptures stories about God's revelation that point to God revealing God's holiness, name, and glory: the Exodus and revelation on Mount Sinai, the calling of the prophet Isaiah, stories about the ark and temple, and manifestations of God's judgment and wrath. The revelation of God's glory elicits an initial response of awe, fear, and adoration; a full response of love and obedience grows from Israel's experience of divine love and mercy.[100]

In the New Testament, Häring turns to John's Gospel, in which glory is a central theme, to emphasize Christ's glory of the Father through his life and work and the full glory of Christ in the resurrection and *parousia*.[101] He also highlights the Pauline theme of the full glory of Christ in the second coming, which Christians participate in to some degree in the present, through the power of the Holy Spirit. Häring writes, "The light and warmth of God's love for His elect will be fully revealed in the Second Coming of Christ in His glory (Rom 8:18; 21). But through the Holy Spirit, the Spirit of Holiness and Majesty, infused into our souls by divine grace, the glory

---

[98] Bernard Häring, letter to the author, July 2, 1997: "My particular attention to the virtue of religion has very much to do with the liturgical renewal but always in the context of the whole life. St. Thomas was for me an inspiration for the virtue of religion. More than theory and speculation it was simply the life of "prayer in everyday life" that inspired my thinking."

[99] Ibid., 2:111; *SSA*, 159.

[100] Häring relies on Otto's analysis (12–24) of the *mysterium tremendum*; the name of God will be discussed in the next chapter.

[101] *LC* 2:113–16. Häring also returns to a theme advanced by Jungmann and Adam: Christians give glory to the Father with Christ; they also give glory to Christ for his obedience and love. For an analysis of the theme of glory in John's gospel, see Raymond E. Brown, *The Gospel According to John, I–XII* (Garden City, N.Y.: Doubleday, 1966) 503–4.

(dóxa) of God is already active in us (1 Pet 4:14), establishing the 'inner man' (Eph 3:16). The Holy Spirit is the pledge and earnest of our participation in the glory *(dóxa)* (2 Cor 3:18)."[102]

Häring concludes from the analysis of Scripture that there are three parts to the definition of religion: religion as union or communion with God, cult and worship, and community. The first and most essential understanding of religion relates to the divine-human dialogue. Religion ultimately is union with God, which is first initiated by God's gift of divine grace; it is received and manifested in the theological virtues, which form the intimate bond of religion. He states that "the dialog which binds man to God is basically perfected in the theological virtues and their acts. Therefore the essence of religion is found above all in these virtues. Religion is the bond *(ligare, relegere)* uniting us with God through the God-formed life of grace and the personal encounter with God in the acts of the theological virtues."[103] The virtue of religion, in this sense, is similar to the theological virtues because of its basic orientation to and relationship with God. It serves as a unifying dimension of the interior life of faith, hope, and charity. For Häring, all external forms of religion must arise from this interior foundation or they fall prey to formalism.

The second and more common understanding of "religion" is what Häring calls the "restricted" or "technical" definition—religion as cult or worship, the external expression of adoration for God. Worship and divine cult are not the essence of religion but a manifestation of the essence, the acts that flow from it. Religion is essentially life in communion with God that demands cult or worship as its direct manifestation, the "first mandate of religion." Third, Häring regards religion as community, the joining together of people who share faith and cult and who seek to express relationship with God and each other through visible, public, communal worship. He summarizes the three aspects of religion: "Religion is the bond with God mutually joining together in community of faith and worship all those who are thus united with God and acknowledge their union with Him and with one another. Nothing manifests and sustains this common bond more perfectly than community of cult. The Mystical Body of Christ forming one community in the life with God, which is the very essence of religion, offers to God the perfect cult of sacrifice

---

[102] Ibid., 2:116.
[103] Ibid., 2:119.

and sacraments."[104] These three aspects of religion are essential to Häring's understanding of the internal and external acts of religion, which are the topic of the next chapter.

The Virtue of Religion: A Moral or Theological Virtue?

Häring is ambivalent about categorizing religion as a moral rather than theological virtue. On the one hand, he wants to claim that religion is a theological virtue because it shares an immediate and direct relationship with God. On the other hand, because he retains the traditional idea that theological virtues are interior acts and moral virtues are exterior acts, he retains the definition of religion as a moral virtue, but not without some hesitation, since religion, like the theological virtues, draws the believer into communion with God. For example, Häring states that the theological virtues form the interior life of the Christian and serve as the foundation for the virtue of religion, which "flows from the divine virtues as a property or essential demand from the essence or nature."[105] He notes the tension within the tradition regarding the placement of religion under justice and raises the question of the virtue of religion as only a moral virtue under justice and argues that religion, more so than any other moral virtue, is the "primary manifestation" of faith, hope, and charity:

> Reference to the three virtues as three and only three does not settle the question regarding the position of the virtue of religion: must it be reckoned among the theological or moral virtues? This much is certain: the theologians of the school of Salamanca and many other writers very strongly opposed the opinion that the virtue of religion should be subordinated to the moral virtue of justice. It can very cor-

---

[104] Ibid., 2:120. Häring also recognizes the use of "religion" in canon law to refer to the special vows made by people in religious communities.

[105] Ibid. Häring (Ibid., 2:121) turns to Aquinas to make the point that love is the most important theological virtue in relation to the virtue of religion because it forms the interior response and longing of the human person for spiritual union with God. The inner spirit of devotion and love for God calls for an external expression through cult and worship, but cult becomes formal and legalistic if separated from religion. "Without charity and the interior spirit and disposition flowing essentially from it there can indeed be external and legal performance of the acts of worship, but not the virtue of religion with the fully worthy and fruitful acts of cult." Häring (Ibid., 2:123) agrees with Aquinas that religion is the superior moral virtue and "plays a role of leadership which is analogous to charity. While dependent on the theological virtues, particularly on love, it is the religious form of all the virtues."

rectly be considered a component part of the divine virtues and as their primary manifestation.[106]

And again Häring notes the problem of defining religion within the narrow category of the quasi-potential parts of justice: "Thus one may look upon the essence of religion as simply and exclusively the divine worship or cult, only to be perplexed by the fact that St. Thomas and with him most modern moral theologians place this same virtue of religion in the realm of the moral virtues. If in consequence we should form a false impression and reduce religion entirely to morality, how could we continue to look upon religion as the virtue of the divine worship or cult?"[107]

Häring retains the traditional definition of religion as a moral virtue because its basic orientation is toward external expression of the glory of God, but he does not place religion directly under justice because it expresses the intimate and primary dialogue with God found in the theological virtues. Häring states that "it is sound and reasonable to reckon religion among these moral virtues: this virtue does not directly and immediately give the value-response to the hidden holiness of God as do the theological virtues. *Its object is rather the holiness of God as manifested externally. In its content there must be a task for man in space and time, in the body and in the community, a task which belongs to it necessarily and immediately* [*italics mine*]. Such is the nature of the virtue of religion by contrast with the strictly theological virtues. It follows that we may correctly place it among the moral virtues."[108]

Even though he accepts the traditional teaching of religion as a moral virtue, Häring does not hold to an absolute, rigid division between the theological and moral virtues. In fact, he argues that his position is closer to Aquinas' and defends his placement of religion

---

[106] Ibid., 2:5. In *SEL* (158), Häring argues that the virtue of religion is "an essential and integral part and perspective of the theological virtues themselves."

[107] Ibid., 2:119. Aquinas, Häring argues (*SEL*, 160–61), was concerned to bring religion and life together and by placing religion under justice was attempting to draw an analogy between human justice and religion in order to emphasize the impossibility of giving back to God in equal measure what God has given to humanity. "While St. Thomas takes the human experience of justice as point of departure, he transcends it in his concept of the virtue of religion. . . . The statement of St. Thomas that *the virtue of religion 'is not perfect regarding justice'* is not a very happy one. However, we ought to note immediately the truly theological explanation which the saint gives: it is not possible to give to God what is his due."

[108] Ibid., 2:122.

under justice.[109] Rather, the theological and moral virtues are joined together by the virtue of religion and through religion the theological virtues strive to find external expression. Häring states:

> This line of reasoning for placing religion and the divine worship under the moral virtues and obligations is not by far as convincing as it might first seem. For that matter even the theological virtues themselves do not exist entirely apart from the visible experiences in this world of time and space. . . . *From this it is evident that the theological virtues reach out to meet the virtue of religion establishing the foundation for its extension into time and space [italics mine].* This very expansion, of course, is broadened and accentuated progressively by the virtue of religion. But it cannot be denied that the virtue of religion and the divine worship which belongs to it are as closely allied to theological virtue as to the moral.[110]

Recalling that Häring's moral theology is designed to counter moral systems in which ethics is autonomous from religion and Catholic moral systems that divide the theological from the moral, Häring finds a way of expressing the relationship between religion and morality through the virtue of religion.[111] For Häring, the Christian moral life is grounded upon the religious, so that all moral action arises from the religious response to God's initiative. He states that

> true morality may be said to accept all earthly tasks only in their relation to God. If the *religious* in the narrow sense of the term is *response*

---

[109] "In the external systematization of the virtue of religion, St. Thomas follows Aristotle, nevertheless, with regard to its interior dynamism, he emphasizes the initiative of God. Therefore, we can assert that St. Thomas has a truly sacramental vision of it in the perspective of the biblical concept of justice (*dikaiosyne*) . . . . the angelic doctor succeeds in expressing well the dynamism of the sacraments for a life which, in its totality, is worship of God. In his thought, the whole of liturgy and of prayer are explicit and direct expressions of the virtue of religion ('*actus eliciti virtutis religionis*') dynamically tending to make of the whole Christian life an expression guided and shaped by adoration ('*actus imperatus virtutis religioinis*')." *SEL*, 161. Mahoney (251–52) would vehemently deny Häring's generous reading of Aquinas: "As a matter of justice God has dominion over us and we are his servants—owing reverence and honour to his supreme transcendence and subjecting ourselves to him who is our superior. It is only a logical consequence of this mental straightjacket that Aquinas should then develop as so many expressions of justice towards God the activity of prayer and other 'duties' or religion, and should complete his treatise on justice with an examination of the Ten Commandments, 'precepts of justice' which are naturally also 'first precepts of law.'"

[110] Ibid; see also, *SEL*, 158.

[111] See Ibid., 2:124 for Häring's discussion of Otto's understanding of sacral and sanction ethics as a possible alternative to his approach. His aim is to find a way of communicating with people who have rejected religion because of its legalistic morality.

directed immediately to God, then the *moral* is *response-ability* as to the spatial-temporal before God and toward God. For the religious man morality is a summons issuing from the immediate encounter with God. It is a call for action in the world. It is not merely a task commanded by God but a task which must be ordered entirely to the glory of God.[112]

Therefore, the virtue of religion is the bridge between the theological and moral virtues and it gives expression to the theological virtues and is the foundation for all moral virtues. By holding to the traditional distinction between theological and moral virtues, Häring is forced to define the virtue of religion as a moral virtue because of its external expression. He attempts to soften that distinction and emphasize the inter-relatedness of the theological and moral virtues by placing the virtue of religion outside justice and alongside the theological virtues. Eventually, when he drops the category of moral virtue in favor of biblical and eschatological virtues, the problem is eliminated and the virtue of religion stands as its own virtue.

The Virtue of Religion and the Sacraments

Häring, in contrast to the manualists, and to some extent Aquinas, makes explicit the relationship between the virtue of religion and the sacraments. The sacraments must express all three aspects of religion in order to be a complete and perfect expression of the virtue of religion: they are dialogical (salutary), cultal, and social. The sacraments are first of all intimate dialogue between God and persons in community through the sacraments, particularly those sacraments that impart a character insofar as the believer receives the gift of divine grace. The sacraments are secondly the expression—in time and space—of communion with God. The virtue of religion demands external expression, or cult, because they are extensions of God's revelation through the creation and Incarnation and because persons need visible signs in order to respond to God's invitation.[113]

The sacraments, according to Häring, are the extension in the present, of Christ, who is the basic sacrament of God, and they point to the full eschatological reality of the Kingdom of God. The sacraments are also communal—they join together the Christian community

[112] Ibid., 2:123.
[113] *SEL*, 158.

and express the unity between the love of God and the love of neighbor. In this sense, religion is primary among the moral virtues because it shapes and directs all motives, desires, and choices to express God's glory: "for the Christian must esteem the acts of religion properly so-called above all the acts of the other moral virtues, in order that the firmness and vigor of his inner spirit of worship may effectively direct all else to the glory of God."[114]

Religion, as dialogue and imitation of Christ, also consists of the free response to the divine gift of grace and the obligation to respond in obedience and love. The sacraments consecrate the human person "manifesting both his significance as creature and his dignity as child of God" and through baptism the believer enters into the "priesthood of Christ."[115] Through the empowerment and indwelling of the Holy Spirit, the Christian lives with a new awareness of his relationship to God strives in all action to give honor and praise to God. The honor and praise of God is expressed both through cultal and moral action. Regarding cult, the Christian is obligated, as a holy subject, to consecrate all things to God. Häring states:

> In consequence the Christian has the mission first of all to sanctify himself in the service of cult and for the service of cult. In other words, through a personal acceptance of his objective sacral holiness he must consecrate (through devotion or submission to God) himself and all his activity to the service of God. Moreover, he receives the mission of exercising in the created world a priestly service. This means that he is to impart to the things of earth a cultal or religious formation through places and seasons set apart for cult, through the oblation of the fruits of his labor, specifically the fruits of the earth itself.[116]

Regarding morality, the Christian is obligated to extend the sanctification of all earthly reality into moral relationships. For Häring, "the total morality of man must bear the stamp of consecration, must 'be made holy.'"[117] Religion, then, as expressed through the sacraments of the Church, infuses all action—moral acts and acts of worship— with holiness, so that all action arises from the divine gift and in response to the divine gift.

Therefore, the goal of the moral life is not reduced to fulfilling a set of obligations and laws demanded by God. The goal, as stated by

---

[114] Ibid., 2:126–27; *SS*, 38.
[115] Ibid., 2:127.
[116] Ibid.
[117] Ibid.

Häring, is "moral perfection," the striving to obtain through all one's actions the perfect loving response to God: "Thus moral perfection becomes religious morality or holiness, that is, a moral rectitude sustained by the love of God and consecrated to the divine glory. The cultal sanctification of man, caught up as he is by the loving majesty of the Most High, to which the virtue of religion corresponds as response, demands by its very nature moral holiness in man."[118] In a later book Häring stresses that because the sacraments "insert us into the community of worship" and the "Christian participates in the consecrating power" of the paschal mystery, the Christian is sanctified, made holy, and therefore is consecrated for a life of "social worship" that is carried out through justice and charity.[119]

* * * *

The category of virtue has always been central in Catholic moral theology. Within Aquinas' system, and later for the neo-Thomist moral theologians, the virtues are a way of describing how human action is oriented teleologically toward God, the ultimate good. The manualists used the category of virtue in a particular and somewhat narrow way in order to emphasize how good acts (either theological or moral) cooperate with grace to merit the rewards of eternal life. In Häring's moral theology, virtue continues to be important, although he clearly departs from the neo-Thomist tradition. Virtue becomes the full response of the whole person to God's invitation to participate in the divine life through Christ by the power of the Holy Spirit. Because Häring's primary concern in *The Law of Christ* is how religion and morality are related to one another, he reinterprets a minor category—the virtue of religion—as the bridge or link between the theological and moral virtues.

The virtue of religion, within Aquinas' system and the manualists', consists of both internal and external acts. The distinction, according to Aquinas, is between the interior person, the "heart," and the exterior person, the "body." For the human person, the interior acts are primary because they reflect the higher part of human nature; external acts are necessary to incite the interior acts and therefore are secondary. Häring's analysis of the acts of religion attempts

[118] Ibid., 2:128.
[119] *SEL*, 163.

to overcome the separation between the two types of acts, to show their mutuality and inter-relationship, and to demonstrate that external acts go beyond merely exciting the interior acts because they are in fact response to God's external manifestation in the world.

Chapter 6

The Interior and Exterior Acts of the Virtue of Religion

If we regard prayer as a listening and a response to God, we will under-stand morality in terms of responsibility in the fullest sense of that word, namely, listening to God speaking to us in those circumstances of life in which we encounter our neighbor, his love, and his needs. Responsibility takes the stuff of life, our own self with its talents and weaknesses, and above all the Thou of neighbor and community, and includes it all in its response to God. Thus life becomes a prayer. Prayer is watchfulness, docil-ity, openness, and a valiant effort to bring all things back to their source in God. This is the full meaning of the Christian ethic of responsibility.[1]

——————— Bernard Häring, "A Modern Approach to the Ascetical Life"

Devotion, prayer, and adoration are aspects of the Christian life that are most often associated with the spiritual and not the moral tradition. Few, for instance, would turn to Catholic moral theolo-gians for insight on how to pray or progress through the various stages of spiritual and mystical practice. This is partly the case be-cause consideration of spiritual practices, such as prayer and con-templation, became the purview of another discipline—spiritual theology—at the same time that moral theology was developing its own distinct approach. After the Council of Trent, the two realms of theology separated—moral theology turned to a consideration of the minimum requirements for the Catholic Christian to fulfill in order to receive the graces necessary for the supernatural life and salva-tion, and spiritual theology moved beyond the minimum duties out-lined for the lay believer to consider the practices, disciplines, and

---

[1] Bernard Häring, "A Modern Approach to the Ascetical Life," *Worship* 39 (December 1965) 644.

stages of growth toward perfection in the love of God, a process intended for vowed religious men and women or monastics.[2]

Despite the extensive treatment of spiritual practices by spiritual theology manualists, the neo-Thomist moral theology manualists did not ignore the subject of devotion, prayer, and other religious practices. Following Aquinas' outline closely, the manualists considered aspects of the spiritual life under the virtue of religion. Their analysis is characterized by precise definitions, legal parameters for fulfillment of required duties, casuistical examinations of actions that fall between fulfillment of the law and vice, and extensive discussion of the sins contrary to religion. For example, the manualists give considerable attention to whether or not attention is required for prayer to be efficacious and meritorious.[3] Also, examination of sins against religion can be twice as lengthy as discussions on how to fulfill the virtue.[4]

An important distinction made by Aquinas, and followed by the manualists, is that the virtue of religion is comprised of different types of actions—interior acts that pertain to the individual, the "heart," and are not expressed in word, sign, or action, and exterior acts that pertain to the body and are expressed through word, sign, and action.

---

[2] There are several neo-Thomist spiritual theology manuals written in the early part of the twentieth century that are quite similar in theology and format to the moral theology manuals. Several of the more popular manuals include Adolphe Tanquerey, *The Spiritual Life: A Treatise on Ascetical and Mystical Theology,* 2nd. rev. ed. (Tournai, Belgium: Desclée & Co., 1930); R. Garrigou-Lagrange, o.p., *The Three Ages of the Interior Life: Prelude of Eternal Life,* 2 vols. (St. Louis: B. Herder Book Co., 1947); Joseph de Guibert, s.j., *The Theology of the Spiritual Life* (New York: Sheed and Ward, 1953).

[3] The neo-Thomist manualists elaborate upon this distinction between intention and attention at great length, but their treatment of the issue turns away from Aquinas' discussion of the problem of human frailty to how to fulfill one's obligation to pray in a right and proper manner and assure that merit is gained from the act. McHugh and Callan (2:289), for example, argue that prayer is a duty for all adults and quote Scripture to show that prayer is a divine precept and that prayer is necessary as a means for salvation. There is a duty to pray at the outset of the moral life, frequently during life, and at the time of death. Prayer is also commanded when one "needs to have recourse to God to fulfill some command or avoid something prohibited." McHugh and Callan (2:293) devote nine of the twenty sections on prayer to issues of intention and attention and give consideration to such topics as external and internal attention and what is considered to be sufficient for both; the problem of distractions, which can be either acts or omissions, voluntary or involuntary, and venial or mortal sins. Intention refers to the purpose of an act and is itself an act of the will that is elicited by devotion. Thus, "A man who, while reading aloud from a novel, recites the words of a prayer contained in the novel, does not pray, for his intention is pleasure or instruction, not worship."

[4] See Davis, for example, 2:2–41; nine pages are given to religion and prayer and over thirty pages to the vices against religion.

Interestingly, Aquinas does not make the distinction between interior and exterior acts in regards to the other moral virtues. The interior and exterior acts of religion are not virtues under religion, but actions that comprise the full expression of the virtue of religion.

Aquinas defines interior acts as principal and exterior acts as secondary. The distinction rests on the difference between the heart and the flesh; the interior acts pertain to the heart, or soul, and are more primary because they relate to and express a higher aspect of human nature. But, according to Aquinas' Aristotelian anthropology, the soul is dependent upon the body to orient the mind to higher realities, and so external acts are necessary for the intellect and contemplation. The primary purpose, then, of exterior acts is to give rise to interior ideas. The manualists follow this same line of thought.

Aquinas lists nine acts of religion, two interior and seven exterior. The interior acts are devotion and prayer, and the exterior acts are adoration, sacrifice, oblations and first fruits, tithes, vows, oaths, and the use of God's name. Aquinas further divides the exterior acts into three categories: the use of one's body to reverence God (adoration), acts that involve external things offered to God (sacrifice, oblations, first-fruits, tithes, and vows), and acts by which something is used to honor God (oaths, God's name, and sacraments).

Häring retains some features of the virtue of religion from the tradition. For example, he describes both interior and exterior acts and agrees that exterior acts aid in exciting interior acts, particularly devotion. By placing the acts of religion within his word-and-response theology, however, Häring goes beyond Aquinas and the manualists in several important ways. First, interior and exterior acts are mutually related to each other, though one is not higher or more primary than the other. Häring describes the categories of interior and exterior acts in much the same way as he does the theological and moral virtues—the orientation of action is primarily internal to the person or external to the world, but each realm is never entirely distinct or separate from the other and, in fact, they are mutually dependent upon one another.

Second, Häring presents exterior actions as fundamental to religion precisely because God's expressions of divine love and will are exterior: God expresses the divine self through the creation, Incarnation, and the sacraments. Because God's expression of the Word is exterior, human persons respond through exterior action. As detailed in the previous chapter, Häring defines the "presupposition, the object, the content" of the virtue is religion as the sanctity, name, and glory of God—God reveals divine holiness, glory and the divine name and so human persons respond with acts of praise and honor and appropriate use of God's name. The various acts of religion are brought together in his moral theology by the dogmatic themes of divine word and human response, his Christology that focuses on Christ as the perfect adorer, and his anthropology that defines the "very nature of man as an adorer."[5]

Third, exterior expression of the virtue of religion is essential for community. Häring goes beyond the individualistic conception of the virtue and highlights the social aspects of human personhood and the sacramental expression through the Mystical Body of Christ. In this way, Häring links the virtue of religion with the sacraments.

Häring does not discuss all nine acts of religion in *The Law of Christ*, but selects three—prayer, vows, and the use of God's name; he also adds a fourth category, observance of the Sabbath, which for Aquinas and the manualists falls under the precepts of justice.[6] Häring also discusses devotion and adoration, although he defines them not as separate acts but as foundational dispositions of religion from which all other acts flow. In later works, adoration replaces religion as the category by which he explicates the relationship between worship and morality. Häring does not explain his choice of these three acts of religion from the list of nine, but their definitions indicate that they are closest to his understanding of religion as dialogue and responsibility. Because devotion and prayer, and adoration and the use of God's name, are central to Häring's presentation of religion in *The Law of Christ*, and continue as part of his moral theology in later writings, they are analyzed here. His interpretation of these categories will be compared with both Aquinas and the manualists in order to show where his thought is continuous with the tradition and how he transforms these concepts within his own system.

---

[5] *CRCW*, 267.

[6] The precepts of justice are outlined in the Decalogue, according to Aquinas (*ST*, II-II.122.2). The first three precepts pertain to religion, the fourth pertains to piety, and the remaining six laws pertain to justice among equals.

Interior Acts of Religion

Prayer is not a unilateral act but bilateral: it is God's word and man's word. It is an encounter of God and man in word and response, in word of love with response of love, in incitement of grace and cooperation with grace. Prayer is colloquy, dialog.[7]

—————————————————— Bernard Häring, *The Law of Christ*, vol. 2

Devotion to God

Aquinas identifies devotion and prayer as the two interior acts of religion and distinguishes them by the faculty of the soul to which they relate: devotion is a "special act" of the will that consists of surrendering oneself to the service of God and prayer belongs to the "intellective power of the soul" and derives from practical reason because it consists of "spoken reason" that seeks to ask or beseech.[8] Thus, devotion belongs to the appetitive part of the soul and prayer belongs to the intellect which is moved by "the will of charity."

Aquinas states: "The will moves the other powers of the soul to its end, as stated above (q. 82, a. 1, ad. 1), and therefore religion, which is in the will, directs the acts of the other powers to the reverence of God. Now among the other powers of the soul the intellect is the highest, and the nearest to the will; and consequently after devotion which belongs to the will, prayer which belongs to the intellective part is the chief of the acts of religion, since by it religion directs man's intellect to God."

Devotion has two causes: God is the extrinsic cause of devotion because God determines who is called to be religious and holy. The intrinsic cause is contemplation, since by thinking about God one considers giving their life in service to God. In this sense, devotion, as an act of the will, is led by reason but it also serves to direct reason to its final object or end. Aquinas states that "every act of the will proceeds from some consideration, since the object of the will is a good understood. Wherefore Augustine says that the will arises from the intelligence. Consequently meditation must be the cause of devotion, in so far as through meditation man conceives the thought of surrendering

———

[7] *LC* 2:247.

[8] "But to the practical reason it belongs in addition to cause something by way of command or of petition" (*ST,* II-II.83.2). The purpose of prayer is not to alter divine providence, but to accept that which God has ordained and by "praying confesses that he needs Him as the Author of his goods" (Ibid., II-II.83.3).

himself to God's service."[9] Two thoughts give rise to devotion: the "goodness and loving kindness" of God, which "awakens" charity and the realization of humanity's weakness and absolute dependence on God. Further, devotion has two effects on the person: the experience of spiritual joy in considering the love of God and a deep sense of sorrow through considering one's failings and separation from God.[10]

The neo-Thomist manualists' definition of devotion is drawn directly from Aquinas. For example, according to McHugh and Callan, devotion consists of "an act of the will, that is, an offering of oneself to the service of God." It contains "a ready willingness, that is, the devout person is quick to choose the divine honor as a purpose, quick also to select and employ suitable means for this purpose." In addition, they note that devotion has both an external and internal cause. Externally, devotion is caused by God's grace that moves the will and internally devotion is caused by mental prayer or a "consideration of divine things, for will follows on the intellect."[11]

The authors add to Aquinas' treatment a discussion of what is not authentic devotion and give pastoral guidance for how to sustain a spirit of devotion. For example, McHugh and Callan state that devotion should not be confused with emotion or pleasure of a non-religious kind, spiritual consolation, or external devotional practices that are performed without the true spirit of devotion, e.g., the rosary. The authors encourage the reader to nourish devotion through daily or frequent mental prayer, which consists of a consideration of the love of God and human weakness.

Häring retains the traditional understanding of devotion as involving human choice but places devotion within his personalist framework and emphasizes the free choice to surrender oneself to divine service, rather than distinguishing between devotion as related to the will and prayer as related to the intellect. Devotion, Häring emphasizes, includes the whole person in the act of responding "yes," which includes the body, emotions, the will, and the intellect.[12] For Häring, devotion is the "heart of religion" and animates all interior and exterior acts.

---

[9] Ibid.

[10] According to Aquinas (Ibid., II-II.82.1-2), charity and devotion are mutually related: charity is the source of devotion but it also needs devotion in order to unify the theological virtues. "Charity causes devotion" (love causes one to will their total surrender to God) and "feeds on devotion" (charity requires a will that is devoted).

[11] McHugh and Callan, 2:284–85. Davis, 2:2, calls devotion the foundation of all religious acts.

[12] *LC* 2:260.

Häring expands the idea of devotion through the biblical understanding of "piety," which is understood as a gift of the Holy Spirit. Aquinas discusses piety twice under the moral virtue of justice, first as a quasi-potential part of justice concerned with giving to one's parents and country their due worship and respect and second, as a gift of the Holy Spirit that "we pay worship and duty to God as our Father."[13] Häring makes an explicit connection between devotion and Aquinas' second definition of piety in order to emphasize the inner sentiment and emotion of religion, not as a distinct act necessarily, but as a precondition to religion as dialogue and exterior act. He emphasizes Aquinas' notion of piety as a gift of the Holy Spirit because it is a biblical concept and it captures the affective qualities of relationship with God. Häring writes: "Related to devotion is piety. According to St. Thomas piety as a gift of the Holy Spirit is an interior disposition, a sentiment of filial affection toward God. It manifests itself immediately in the interior life of prayer, in filial protestations of faith, hope, and love addressed to God our Father."[14]

It should be noted that Häring does not connect his discussion of spirit, disposition, and emotion in the first volume of *The Law of Christ* with his treatment of devotion in the second volume. Häring discusses emotions in relation to value theory and describes emotion as "something of the heart, a thinking of the heart *(cogitationes cordis)*." Emotion is "a re-echoing response to value or non-value centering in the subject which is the very depths of the human soul. . . . Our dispositions can place us in a much more intimate relation with an object, with a person, than the most intensive thinking or willing. For in the disposition one strikes the most intimate chord in the heart of man. As in the case of the intimate experience of conscience, the whole soul participates. The response of man's heart to value re-echoes within the object itself, and all the forces of man's soul are in some measure affected."[15]

---

[13] *ST,* II-II, 121. Aquinas (*ST,* I-II.68.1) refers to the gifts of the Holy Spirit as the divine cause of virtue, the divine aid that helps man perfect virtue in relationship to God. "Human virtues perfect man according as it is natural for him to be moved by his reason in his interior and exterior actions. Consequently man needs yet higher perfections, whereby to be disposed to be moved by God. These perfections are called gifts, not only because they are infused by God, but also because by them man is disposed to become amenable to the Divine inspiration."

[14] *LC* 2:129.

[15] *LC* 1:198. See *LC* 1:195–213 for a discussion of disposition, emotion, and an analysis of the concept of the "heart" in Scripture.

If connected more explicitly with his value theory and understanding of emotion, devotion would be defined as the ongoing transformation of the disposition, intention, and emotions toward God, the ultimate value. Devotion then would more clearly be an experience of the whole person. As it is, Häring emphasizes that the will to devote one's self to God's service and the filial affection for God as Father form the inner sentiment that forms a constitutive part of religion by "nourishing" religion and the theological virtues.

Prayer as Dialogue and Imitation

Prayer is for Häring the *"par excellence"* act of the virtue of religion and involves each essential aspect of Häring's moral theology: dialogue with God, imitation of Christ, and sacramental formation and expression. Prayer is interpreted by Häring as dialogue, the most intimate and personal expression of the divine-human dialogue that is centered in the Word of God: "Prayer is a dialogue with God, a communion in word and charity. It is the expression of our union with Christ and our adoption as children of God."[16] Häring redefines the category within his own framework so that it is a clear departure from the manualist tradition. For example, Aquinas and the manualists define prayer as an act of practical reason, rather than speculative reason, because it does not involve apprehension, judgment or reasoning, but "the arrangement and presentation of requests, plans, etc. before God with a view to their acceptance by Him."[17]

Practical reason discerns what one needs and presents this to God and in this sense prayer is speaking directly to God. As McHugh and Callan emphasize, "Prayer in its origin is an act of the will, for the practical reason presents before God only such things as are desired by him who prays. Prayer is the interpreter of desire."[18] Häring drops the language pertaining to the appetite and intellect in favor of his personalist understanding of the human person as dialogical and social. He also emphasizes the mutually-related dialogue of God and the human person in prayer—God and humanity speaking and listening to each other.

Another major difference between the neo-Thomist tradition and Häring on the issue of prayer is a point of emphasis. For example,

---

[16] *CRCW*, 288.
[17] McHugh and Callan, 296.
[18] Ibid.

Aquinas' discussion of prayer (II-II.83) consists of seventeen articles, which may be grouped into six general categories: prayer as an intellective power (a. 1); God in relationship to prayer (a. 2-4); the content of prayer (a. 5-9); what kind of beings pray (a. 10-11, 16); how to pray (a. 12-15); and, the different kinds of prayer (a. 17).[19] The manualists consider all of these issues with particular attention to the issue of prayer as practical reason and how to pray, especially the acts that constitute the observance or duty to pray.[20]

Häring, on the other hand, turns attention to the dogmatic dimensions of prayer and the place of prayer within the entire religious-moral life. Prayer is not a minor part of the virtue of justice, in other words, but involves the three inter-related parts of religion: prayer is dialogical, cultal, and social. Häring draws out several themes not found in the manuals, such as Christ as teacher of prayer and perfect model, the relationship between both the theological and moral virtues and prayer, and finally, the dynamic relationship between interior and exterior forms of prayer.

According to Häring, the possibility of prayer—hearing God's word and speaking with and to God—is based upon the *imago dei*: "that a man can speak with God is the noblest evidence of his resemblance to God."[21] Similar to Aquinas and the neo-Thomists, Häring states that prayer requires both a double experience of humility and dignity: the Christian stands before God with a sense of "his own pettiness" combined with a sense that one is elevated to be "face to face" with God.[22] Häring also emphasizes the personal dynamic of God's word spoken to the whole person and the power of God's grace that enables the person to respond. Häring also argues that the person is never an isolated individual but a member of a community: being called by name means that the believer is drawn into the Mystical Body of Christ as well as becoming a participant in

---

[19] An overview of Aquinas' teaching on prayer that places his ideas within the larger context of his work and those he drew from can be found in *Albert and Thomas: Selected Writings*, trans. and ed., Simon Tugwell, O.P. (New York: Paulist Press, 1988) 271–79. The editors' footnotes to the excerpt on prayer from the *ST* are also helpful; see 476–519.

[20] The manualists vary greatly in amount of attention they give to prayer. Davis, for example, summarizes Aquinas' conclusions in six pages (2:6–11), whereas he devotes almost four times more space to sins against religion (2:11–41). McHugh and Callan (2:286–300) devote considerable attention to prayer, with special attention to practical issues such as the times and frequency of prayer and pastoral help with issues such as what things may be prayed for and the problem of inattention and distractions in prayer.

[21] *LC* 2:246, *CRCW*, 288.

[22] *LC* 2:247.

the divine life of the Trinity. He states: "Grace has made us vital members of the Mystical Body of Christ and participants in the divine nature. We have been accepted into the blessed dialogue between the Father, the Son, and the Holy Spirit. . . . The fact that we ourselves are enveloped in God's own eternal dialogue of love finds its most fitting expression in prayer, in the mutual loving discourse with God."[23]

Speaking to God, Häring emphasizes, is not merely thinking about God or "detaching one's self from all created things in mind and heart" but "real converse with God." "Not merely our thoughts are with God, but we ourselves are really with Him in prayer because God really bends down over us, addresses us, responds to our response."[24] Prayer is turning the whole person—body, mind, affections—toward God in order to completely communicate with God.

In their definition of prayer as speaking to God Aquinas and the manualist's state that God does not need prayer since God already knows human desires. Rather, prayer is for human persons because it requires the person to express their needs to God. It is primarily a human effort expressed toward God and is a necessary means to maintain a deep love for God and feeling of dependence.[25] For the manualists, prayer becomes a duty that must be fulfilled in order that a person may move along the spiritual path toward the final supernatural end. Thus, religious acts become closely associated with both law and merit. Häring shifts attention away from the obligatory and meritorious aspects of the act to the relational. Religious acts such as prayer express and foster the full dialogue between God and human persons which is based on love. "Prayer is meant to be a heart-to-heart colloquy in humble and joyful love, the expression of a union sealed by charity and expressed in the spoken word."[26]

Häring goes beyond the notion that the human person speaks to God and emphasizes the dialogue between God and the human person as the essence of prayer. Of course, the dialogue of prayer is initiated by God's word, which must be accepted, listened for, and discerned: "Prayer is rooted in the word of God, draws its life from

---

[23] *CRCW*, 289.

[24] *LC* 2:247; *CRCW*, 288–89.

[25] McHugh and Callan (2:296) go further and argue that since God already knows what persons want or desire, God still prefers a request: "Although God could and sometimes does grant favors unasked, He wishes that ordinarily we should have the double benefit of the prayer and of the favor given in answer to the prayer."

[26] *CRCW*, 290.

the word of God, and in its growth and development constantly turns again to the divine word."[27] The Word of God is experienced in many ways, according to Häring, but the primary time and place is the celebration of the liturgy and sacraments of the Church, because God's word and grace is experienced and received directly through the sacraments and through them the Christian participates in Christ's response of "love, thanksgiving, adoration, expiation—the response which He as the new Head of mankind offered the Heavenly Father on the cross." It is through the sacraments, according to Häring, that Christian prayer becomes part of the "eternal dialog of love in the Trinity itself" and is expressed in the community, the I-Thou-We relationship.[28] Sacraments involve two aspects of human personhood: God's word spoken to the individual person and God's word spoken to the community. The sacraments are the most significant expression of prayer, according to Häring, because they unite the love of God and love of neighbor.

> All the sacraments are direct and personal encounters with Christ, and through Christ with the Father in heaven; but at the same time they are effective signs of the unity of the Church, the unity of all the redeemed in Christ. So they call us to a fully self-conscious and individual existence, to an entirely personal prayer, and to personal responsibility in the sight of God. But this fully personal and individual life to which the Bible and the sacraments call us, is based on the heavenly Father's love for his family—on the *pietas* of God—in Christ. Our fully personal prayer and our consciousness of being responsible to God are only truly Christian when they are based on the part we play as members of that family, on our praise of God in common and on our responsibility for each other.[29]

Häring's understanding of prayer is shaped by his Christology and the *imitatio Christi* model: Christ is the perfect teacher and exemplar of prayer, the imitation of Christ consists of praying as Jesus prayed, and imitation is not merely an external act but is incorporation into the life of Christ so that, by the influence of the Holy Spirit, the believer prays with Christ to the Father.

Häring analyzes New Testament texts in order to demonstrate the importance of prayer in the life of Jesus—prayer marked his "entry

---

[27] *LC* 2:248.
[28] Ibid.
[29] *SS*, 38.

into the world," the forty days in the desert at the beginning of his ministry and other significant moments, especially the passion and crucifixion. Prayer is a central part of Jesus' teaching to his disciples and the person who follows Christ must become "a great man of prayer." The primary criterion for a saint, according to Häring, is their imitation of Christ in prayer.

Christians learn from Christ and the saints how to pray (primarily from the Lord's Prayer) and what prayer is.[30] But the imitation of Christ's prayer is not external copying in Häring's judgment. It is primarily incorporation into the life of Christ so that with the gift of the Holy Spirit the Christian is able to conform entirely to Christ. Prayer arises from the power of the Spirit to transform the "inner man" so that one's entire being participates in divine life: "It is in truth a participation in the eternal dialog between the Word of God with God the Father in the Holy Spirit."[31] For Häring, it is essential that the Christian pray with and in the name of Christ.

It is interesting to note that the neo-Thomist manualists make no mention of Christ in their discussion of prayer, except for stressing the importance of the Lord's Prayer. For example, in his discussion about who it is right to pray to, Davis mentions "God, to the Blessed Mother of God, to all the Saints and Angels" and goes on to include "children who, after Baptism, died before reaching the use of reason" and "the Holy Souls in Purgatory."[32] He makes no mention of praying to or with Christ.

Prayer is, according to Häring, the *par excellence* virtue of religion, and in fact, Häring equates prayer and religion in several places. For example, he states that "without prayer religion cannot survive . . . all prayer is cult or divine worship."[33] He defines both prayer and religion as listening to and receiving the Word of God and responding to the divine word. He states that "to pray is nothing less than to harken reverently to the Word of God and to attempt, however falteringly, to respond to it. Religion thrives on prayer because *religio* (bond with God) cannot exist without the Word of God and our

---

[30] *LC* 2:245–46. The Lord's Prayer is "perfect" according to Aquinas (*ST*, II-II.83.9) because it expresses "rightly desire" and in the right order for which human needs should be asked. Häring also places the Lord's Prayer at the center of his theology of prayer with particular emphasis on Jesus' invitation to address God as "Abba." See *LC* 2:249; *CRCW*, 289–90; and *SS*, 37–39.

[31] *LC* 2:246.

[32] Davis 2:10; see also McHugh and Callan, 2:290.

[33] *LC* 2:249.

power to respond."[34] Prayer cannot be restricted to the four traditional expressions of prayer—praise, thanksgiving, propitiation, and
petition—because even these distinctions do not grasp the heart or
essence of prayer, according to Häring. Prayer "is a vital manifestation of religion in its totality, in its fullest and richest sense" because
it involves the full expression and exercise of all the theological
virtues in relationship to God. Prayer expresses the three theological
virtues so that they become united with the virtue of religion:
"Prayer gives expression to all three theological virtues, and they in
turn through prayer become cult or the exercise of the virtue of religion: they adore God in His infinite truthfulness, fidelity to His
promises, and His loving-kindness."[35]

Prayer also expresses the moral virtues in the sense that through
prayer a person is attentive to sin (the "moral values he has violated
by sin") and attends to the love of God and obedience to God through
all one's actions. The most important aspect of prayer in relation to
the moral life is the turning of all desire and intention to conform to
God's will and to imitate Christ's actions of radical obedience and
love. Further, the sacraments are the expression of prayer within the
community of faith and bind the members of the Body of Christ together by praying in Christ's name for the needs of one another.

The manualists do not link prayer to either the theological or
moral virtues, except in the case of the content of prayer they follow
Aquinas' question. If prayer derives from practical reason then for
what does a Christian pray? He states that it is acceptable to pray for
temporal things if we need these to support the body or activity of
virtue, but never as an end in itself. Likewise, we are to pray for both
our friends and enemies, which are required by charity. He concludes
that the Lord's Prayer is the most adequate prayer to express all that
is necessary: praise and adoration of God and what is needed to fulfill human life.[36] According to McHugh and Callan, it is right to pray
for one's self, other persons, enemies, the excommunicated, sinners
("unless they are already lost"), and souls in purgatory. A Christian
should not pray for the "success of the evil projects of an enemy" or
a moral or physical evil; however praying for a physical evil such as
death, illness or poverty is acceptable if one requests them as a
"means of correction, improvement, merit, penance, or escape from

---

[34] Ibid., 1:37.
[35] Ibid., 2:250. Häring relies on Hircher's theology of prayer in this section.
[36] *ST*, II-II.83.

sin."[37] A person should not pray for either indifferent things (e.g., to win a game) or temporal goods, if they are an end in themselves. Prayer for temporal goods is acceptable if they are a means "that assist us to attain spiritual goods." The most perfect request consists of prayers for salvation and the means to attain that end.

Häring demonstrates that prayer is not only an internal act for the individual, but involves both internal and external acts, which are mutually related to one another. Häring emphasizes that interior prayer is superior to exterior prayer not because it is higher or better but because it proceeds from and animates exterior prayer. Häring states that "for man taken in the totality of his nature it is not the interiority itself which is the more perfect. It is rather the prayer of the heart which expresses itself spontaneously in forms of external prayer more or less frequently, more or less warmly, and which is constantly renewed and re-enkindled in such manifestation."[38]

Häring discusses the various "species" of prayer but rather than juxtaposing the interior against the exterior, he points to how the interior and exterior are mutually related in each category. He distinguishes between cultal, apostolic, and mystical prayer; active and passive prayer; interior and vocal prayer; common and private prayer; and, informal and formal prayer. In discussing the first three groups Häring considers the place of contemplation and mystical prayer in relationship to other forms of prayer; in discussing the last two groups he considers the individual's prayer in relationship to the community's prayer.

As was noted in the previous chapter, Häring disputes the traditional idea, as presented by Maritain, that contemplation or mystical prayer is the highest and most perfect form of communion with God. For Häring, mystical prayer is "really passive prayer or the prayer of contemplation, the exercise of the virtue of religion in the most sublime and exalted sense of the word. It is truly the triumph of the soul in its submission to God, the most profound experience of the glory of God. In a manner hitherto undreamed of man experiences the love of God drawing nigh to him, enkindling the zeal of the divine honor and the spread of His Kingdom."[39]

Mystical prayer, then, has an important place in the life of Christian prayer, but it is not separate from or radically distinct from

---

[37] McHugh and Callan, 2:291.
[38] *LC* 2:253.
[39] *LC* 2:252.

other forms of prayer. For example, Häring notes that cultal and apostolic prayer are focused on different aspects of the reality of God, yet each embrace the fullness of the life of faith. Cultal prayer is focused on divine glory and holiness, particularly through the expression of the divine name, and apostolic prayer "flows from" the desire and expression of the adoration of God to the "spread of His Kingdom among men." Mystical prayer is a kind of "self-absorption" in divine love, an overpowering by the "intimate closeness" of God so that it is passive and interior, whereas cultal and apostolic prayer are expressed in both interior and exterior forms. The difficulty, according to Häring, is discerning whether or not mystical prayer is authentic; one indication is whether or not mystical prayer relates to and returns to cultal and apostolic prayer. In other words, mystical experiences are not separated from the full life of faith but are integrated with other forms of prayer and discipleship. Häring states that mystical prayer "is genuine precisely by shunning the narrow circle of its own needs, even spiritual needs, and touched by the divine love, opens itself with ever increasing love to all the needs and interests of the honor of God and His Kingdom."[40]

Similarly, interior and vocal prayer are mutually related: interior prayer requires "mental words and images" and vocal prayer, which is also exterior prayer, must be "sustained by interior prayer or at least by a desire to awaken interior prayer." Again, Häring dismisses the notion that exterior prayer is insignificant or unnecessary; he backs up this point with evidence from both Augustine and Aquinas, who argue that vocal prayer expresses devotion and in turn encourages and incites devotion. An individual prays aloud, according to Aquinas for three reasons: (1) the voice, as an external sign, excites interior devotion, (2) the mind and body, together, are serving God, "as though to pay a debt," and (3) it is a necessary outcome when the soul "overflows" with an excess of feeling. Aquinas also concludes that prayer is vocal for both common prayer (when ministers pray on behalf of the Church) and individual prayer.[41]

Häring also discusses the relationship between individual and communal prayer which "must mutually complement and enrich each other." The individual is called as a person through the sacraments and must respond to the divine initiative as a unique individual.

---

[40] Häring, "Liturgical Piety," 528.
[41] *ST*, II-II.83.12

But this personal calling and dialogue takes place within the context of a "collective summons of love by which Christ draws the Church and each individual to Himself."[42] Both individual and collective prayer is taught by Jesus and recorded in the Scriptures (Matt 6:6, 18:20) and according to Häring, one cannot exist without the other because the human person is both a unique individual and a social being:

> Just as man himself may not be totally absorbed in the community to the loss of his individuality nor, on the other hand, hold himself aloof and isolated from the community, so must his prayer bear the mark of individuality and of community. It must take place in his own heart and in the privacy of his chamber. . . . It must likewise have the constant assurance of the community of those who pray and help to sustain and support their fellows in the community of prayer.[43]

Without individual prayer, communal prayer runs the risk of becoming "externalistic, mechanical, or at best entirely vapid and impersonal" and likewise without communal prayer, individual prayer becomes narcissistic and separate from the "right manner and correct forms" of the Church.

The difference between informal and formal prayer is not that of interior and exterior expression, but rather different modes of expression that are again mutually related and dependent upon one another. Informal prayer is the "free and spontaneous outpourings of the soul to God" as expressed by the individual. It is the essence of dialogue and conversation, the expression of what is deep and hidden in the heart. But informal prayer may also be used in the assembly and is important, according to Häring, in the "task of forming and educating the faithful in the spirit of prayer" because it is the "most direct and effective means of setting the heart on fire for God."[44]

Formal prayer is needed for both the individual and the community. It is modeled by Jesus throughout the New Testament stories in his use of standard Israelite prayers at the Last Supper and teaching the disciples a prayer formula such as the "Our Father." Häring opposes any rigid application of a formula prayer without the inner spirit and devotion of informal prayer or prayers that are unintelligible to the community.[45]

---

[42] *LC* 2:253.

[43] Ibid.

[44] *LC* 2:254; *CRCW*, 290–92.

[45] Häring (*LC* 2:255–56) argues for the use of the vernacular in the liturgy for the purpose of greater understanding and participation on the part of the people.

Devotion and prayer were traditionally understood as the two interior acts of religion related to the will and intellect, respectively. Häring drops this distinction in favor of a personalist understanding that emphasizes a unified response to God through the will, emotions, thoughts or reason, and the body. There is, then, according to Häring a fully human response to God that is not located in any one aspect of anthropology.

The Exterior Acts of Religion

The first and highest end and purpose of creation and redemption is the external glory of God. In His external works God Himself manifested His holiness, His majesty, His name to men. Christ is the all-holy God dwelling our midst. By this very fact He demands loving adoration of His holiness. In Christ creation has received its High Priest with whom it could share in the most tremendous adoration and glorification of the triune God. Christians, sanctified by the Holy Spirit, incorporated in the priesthood of Christ, may and must look upon the glory of God as their sovereign honor and their most consecrated vocation.[46]

———————————————— Bernard Häring, *The Law of Christ*, vol. 2

The external expression of the virtue of religion is fundamental to Häring's understanding of the divine-human relationship as dialogical, the manifestation of God as external expression in the world, and the response to God through sign, symbol, and sacrament within the believing community. The two external acts Häring considers are adoration and the use of God's name. Adoration, much like devotion, becomes the foundation for all other actions and for Häring is closely related to devotion as a disposition or fundamental attitude that shapes the inner life and is expressed in the outer life. Häring discusses the use of God's name in relationship to the revelation of God's name and essence to persons, and humanity's response to God by invoking the divine name, and thereby the presence of God.

Adoration

For Häring, adoration is to the exterior acts of religion what devotion is to the interior acts: it serves as the foundation and the

[46] *LC* 2:111.

spirit of the exterior acts. In *The Law of Christ*, adoration is considered as an exterior act of religion, which Häring defines within his word-and-response framework, but in later works adoration replaces religion as the organizing concept for the religious-moral life. For example, in *Christian Renewal in a Changing World* adoration and charity are the two foci that are mutually related to one another and link together the theological aspects of the religious-moral life such as Christology, theological anthropology, and the sacraments. In his later systematic work, *Free and Faithful in Christ*, adoration again replaces the virtue of religion and defines both the internal spiritual transformation that finds expression in free and faithful actions formed by Christ.

For Aquinas, adoration is the first exterior act of religion and consists of reverence shown to God "on account of His excellence" that is expressed through the body. Following Aristotle's understanding of cognition as moving from the senses to the intellect, Aquinas argues that adoration through the body leads to the interior acts of devotion,

> since we are composed of a twofold nature, intellectual and sensible, we offer God a twofold adoration; namely, a spiritual adoration, consisting in the internal devotion of the mind; and a bodily adoration, which consists in an exterior humbling of the body. And since in all acts of latria that which is without is referred to that which is within as being of greater import, it follows that exterior adoration is offered on account of interior adoration, in other words we exhibit signs of humility in our bodies in order to incite our affects to submit to God, since it is connatural to us to proceed from the sensible to the intelligible.[47]

According to Aquinas, adoration is secondary to devotion because it is located in external, bodily acts, which exist solely to excite interior acts such as devotion.

The manualists follow the same definition of adoration as Aquinas and stress the idea that adoration proceeds from devotion; also they add several varieties of adoration. For example, McHugh and Callan place great emphasis on the higher expression of adoration that is internal and "does not depend on bodily acts or places, and it is offered by Angels as well as by man" and the lower expression of adoration in bodily acts such as "genuflections, prostrations, prayer with face to the east, and the use of sacred places for worship,

---

[47] *ST*, II-II.84.2.

all of which externals are employed as aids to devotion and symbols of the divine glory."[48] The manualists also distinguish between the type of honor given to God because of his "supreme dominion" *(latria)* and that given to Mary, the Mother of God *(hyperdulia)* and the saints *(dulia);* further, adoration is absolute if given to God and saints as persons or relative if offered to images or relics.[49]

Adoration is the external expression of devotion and religion, for Häring, but its importance goes beyond bodily expression for the sake of exciting interior devotion—it also has anthropological, theological, and ecclesial dimensions. Adoration is connected to three inter-related actions: the expression of the whole being (body and soul); exterior expression that follows from God's external manifestation of glory and love; and the union of community as signified through external expression of gathering and worshiping.

Häring agrees with Aquinas that adoration and devotion are mutually related. In other words, devotion gives rise to adoration—it must express itself in external form because human persons are bodily creatures. In the same way, external expression must be fed by devotion and can nourish and excite devotion. Häring writes: "External cult flows necessarily from the very nature of man. By his very nature as composed of body and soul, man must render service to God with his whole being. Therefore he must serve Him with body and soul. It follows that the interior sentiment of adoration must also be expressed exteriorly. In fact it could not long survive without some form of external expression or manifestation."[50] Even though Häring stresses the unity of the body and soul, and the importance of the body in expressing adoration of God, he does not give attention nor specify how particular bodily acts are expressions of adoring love.[51]

Second, the reason that external expression is fundamental to religion is because God has manifested the divine to humankind and so external expression in response to God's glory is essential to the life of faith. Häring states, "Religion in the heart must essentially find an external expression in word and gesture with a presentation

---

[48] McHugh and Callan, 2:300–1.

[49] Davis, 2:3–5. Davis gives detailed guidelines to the right and proper adoration of saints and relics.

[50] *LC* 2:130.

[51] See Guardini, *Sacred Signs*, for a discussion of several bodily gestures such as the hand, the Sign of the Cross, kneeling, standing, walking, and striking the breast.

in time and place and community, because its proper object is the *kabod,* the *dóxa* or glory of God, the visible manifestation of the invisible majesty of God." God's glory is manifested in a particular way through the cross and continues in the Eucharistic celebrations of the Church. Thus, through Christ's suffering and resurrection, which involve his bodily self-renunciation and bodily exaltation, the Christian believer joins with Christ in giving herself bodily "through the sacred rites and ceremonies in which perceptible acts and movements manifest the glory of God filling the heart and soul of man" so that the "Christian offers in his very body an essential element of true religion."[52]

The connection between the sacrifice of Jesus and the celebration of the liturgy is material as well as spiritual. Häring states that "the sacramental consecration of the whole man, including also his body, implies an essential relation to the high-priestly passion of Christ and to His glory in the resurrection, ascension, and the parousia. This relation we find expressed in the sacred signs and symbols of the liturgical cult. Until the great day when the eternal liturgy begins, our liturgy is the manifestation and expression, perpetually renewed, of the glorification of God through Christ, of the visible glorification of Christ by the Father, and of our participation in both through divine grace."[53]

Third, the liturgy unites the believer with the Mystical Body of Christ, the whole Church. Again, the social bond of religion is essential and because religion is a communal act, external expression is fundamental. "As individuals and social beings they must pay honor to the source of their being, for not only the individual but also the community has been created by God for His own honor and glory."[54] Turning to the Old Testament, Häring argues that formalistic cult or external expression is one of the most serious dangers of religion and an expression that God abhors and rejects. The prophets warn that external religion must remain connected to both a love for God and love for neighbor. The warning is not against external worship, which God accepts and Jesus encourages, but it is the right form of external worship by the community that is essential.

These three ideas—adoration as an expression of the whole person, as response to God's external expression, and as communal re-

[52] *LC* 2:130.
[53] *LC* 2:130–31.
[54] *LC* 2:131.

sponse—form the essence of Häring's understanding of adoration in *The Law of Christ*. As noted, adoration becomes the central category for interpreting the religious-moral life and replaces the virtue of religion in later works. For example, in *Christian Renewal in a Changing World*, Häring uses adoration as a qualifier for the theological virtue of charity: "Our true relationship to God is fittingly expressed in the phrases: *adoring charity* and *loving adoration*." Through these two phrases, Häring joins together worship and the theological virtues in much the same way he does through the concept of religion in *The Law of Christ*. Häring's interpretation of "adoring charity" is identical to that of the virtue of religion.

First, Häring emphasizes how Jesus Christ as High Priest gives worthy praise and adoration to God and, secondly, that Christ reveals the name and holiness of God, and finally, how sacraments sanctify the Christian and unite him to Christ's priestly adoration of the Father. The central acts of adoring charity are prayer, vows, the oath, and the Sunday liturgy. What is different from Häring's discussion of these acts in *The Law of Christ* is that they are no longer defined according to interior and exterior acts of religion. He drops this terminology and expands the notion of adoration in two important ways. First, he emphasizes humility as the "appropriate attitude for an adoring love" of God and "unselfish service towards our fellowman." Second, he draws out more explicitly how charity forms the center of all virtue and worship.

Fifteen years later in the multi-volume work *Free and Faithful in Christ*, Häring shifts the definition of responsibility to emphasize "creative freedom and fidelity." Responsibility still is a religious-moral term for Häring, but in this work the idea of creative freedom and fidelity is closer to central biblical themes and the life of Christ.[55] Adoration (religion) is central and serves as "a matter of synthesis" of all the various concepts in the three volumes. He states at the end of volume 1:

> I do not intend to treat here the virtue of religion side by side with faith, hope and charity. Rather, my concern is to make clear to the reader that the theological virtues are the adoring response to God's self-revelation and self-bestowal. Adoration of God, our Father, in spirit and truth is faith, hope and love of God, insofar as they mark and transform our life. . . . I speak of worship, and especially of the Eucharist and the sacraments, in this dimension of adoration that

[55] *FFC* 1:5–6.

frees all our energies for the service of God, for love of our neighbor and for faithful commitment to justice and peace.[56]

Häring uses the category of adoration in the same way as he uses religion in *The Law of Christ*, but with greater emphasis on the freedom of God and humanity and the faithfulness that binds them together in love. The substance and meaning have changed very little, however. For example, Häring states that adoration is dialogical: God, in God's freedom, reveals divine glory, name, and holiness and human persons are totally free to respond to God's invitation to share in divine life. The Word of God, Jesus Christ, is the "sacrament of the Father's freedom to be for us and with us" and the "perfect adorer in spirit and truth."[57] Through the power of the Holy Spirit, each person shares in the life of Christ and becomes an adorer and worshipper. Adoration constitutes the free response of faith, hope, and love so that all of one's actions join with Christ's praise and glory of the Father. The Church expresses this through the sacraments: "Gathered by the sacrificial love of Christ, the Church is, in him and through him, the primordial sacrament of adoration."[58]

Häring ties adoration to each of the main themes of his word-and-response theology and in later works it becomes the central idea. As important as the concept of the whole person is to Häring, he does explicate under the category of adoration how particular bodily acts, e.g., gestures, movements, express the full dialogical relationship, in the way that Guardini highlights, for example, in the early part of the liturgical movement. Häring explicates how external expression is fundamental to religion, but does not go beyond that to consider particular actions. The one action he does consider is how human persons use God's name through speaking God's name in prayer and worship. The act of speaking God's name is fundamental to his conception of the virtue of religion because it combines both receiving and knowing God's name and responding to the divine initiative through the use of God's name.

The Use of God's Name

Häring takes the final category in Aquinas' analysis of the external acts of religion and places it as the central external act of reli-

[56] Ibid., 1:471.
[57] Ibid., 1:476–77.
[58] Ibid., 1:481.

gion. The third set of actions that make up the external acts of religion consists of acts by which something is used to honor God, such as oaths, the use of God's names, and sacraments. Aquinas mentions the sacraments as an external act by which things are used to honor God, but defers his discussion of the sacraments to the third part of the *Summa*. Aquinas and the manualists' begin with oaths and adjuration, which is the major portion, and ends with a brief description of the use of God's name in praise and song. Häring reverses this order and makes the use of God's name the central external act of religion by linking God's name to God's revelation throughout salvation history. The revelation of God's name and the response to God's name constitute the very character of religion. Häring makes this argument by using both biblical material and personalist philosophy.

Aquinas identifies three ways in which the divine name is used: through the making of oaths, adjuration, and the use of God's name in worship. Oaths, according to Aquinas, are promises made to other persons in which the name of God is invoked to assure the truth of the claim: "Now to call God to witness is named *jurare* (to swear) because it is established as though it were a principle of law (*jure*) that what a man asserts under the invocation of God as His witness should be accepted as true."[59] An oath must have three conditions: it must be just or lawful, it must be true, and it must not be frivolous or unimportant, therefore it requires good judgment. Dispensations from oaths may be granted for the same reasons as vows, that an act may in some cases be morally evil or hurtful. Adjuration consists of invoking the Divine name when a person is "beseeching his superiors, or by commanding his inferiors."[60]

Using the Divine name in praise, either through words or song, is a good action, according to Aquinas, because it incites devotion in the heart. It is not necessary for God to hear words or songs of praise, since God already knows what is in the human heart, but it is necessary for humans to use words and songs because they incite affections and the affections of others toward God. Further, in praising God a person is "withdrawn from things opposed to God."[61]

[59] *ST*, II-II.89.1. Aquinas makes a further distinction between declaratory oaths (regarding present or past actions) or a promissory oath (regarding future actions).
[60] *ST*, II-II.90.1.
[61] *ST*, II-II.91.1.

The manualists give more attention to the question of oaths than to either adjuration or praise.[62] As with adoration, they retain Aquinas' categories and definitions with some additional distinctions. For example, McHugh and Callan distinguish between internal and external praise of God, a simple distinction that is actually the same as the difference between devotion and adoration. They also assert that praise of God is "due to" God because of "his essence and attributes" and that praise is "advantageous to man" in that internal praise "lifts the soul on high and prepares it to receive benefits from God" and external praise "helps the mind to keep its attention fixed on God."[63]

Häring's personalism and biblical theology shape his understanding of the relationship between the essence of God, the revelation of the name of God, and the use of God's name by human persons. The use of God's name is profoundly related to the reality and essence of God, God's revelation to human persons, and the experience of God by people. The name *is* the reality and so encounter with the name *is* encounter with the divine person. The use of God's name, then, is grounded not in moral obligation but religious encounter, an I-Thou experience, and response to the divine name means nothing less for Häring than participation in the divine life.

Häring places the use of God's name at the center of the virtue of religion because for him the "name is the expression of the essence or of the pre-eminent characteristic of that which it designates."[64] Ancient peoples, including the Greeks and the Israelites, understood this phenomenon and Häring interprets the revelation of the name of YHWH (Exod 3:13) as the "most solemn moment in the history of salvation" because in this revelation Moses and the Israelites experience the "uniqueness" of this God. The revelation of the name is the revelation of the "God of sacred history and the Lord of the ages" so that the Israelites must forsake all other gods for this one. For Häring, "to invoke the name of the Lord is to call upon Him as present."[65]

[62] For example, McHugh and Callan give 18 sections to oaths, 6 to adjuration, and 4 to the use of God's name.

[63] McHugh and Callan, 2:358. Davis discusses oaths, vows, and adjuration under the second commandment, but does not discuss the use of God's name under a separate category. "The Holy Name of God must be used reverently always, and therefore if it is consciously used as a mere expletive, at least a venial sin is committed unless there is contempt added, when it would be grievously sinful" (Davis, 2:42).

[64] *LC* 2:269; *CE*, 40. See also Guardini, *Sacred Signs*, 91–97; the small book ends with a meditation on the name of God, which is the symbol of divine essence.

[65] *LC* 2:269–70.

The revelation of the name, of who God is, creates a new relationship, one marked by dependence and protection. By dependence Häring means that when God's name is invoked by the Israelites over the people, the ark of the convenant, the temple, the kings, and Jerusalem, these things then belong to God and they become "holy, consecrated to the Lord; they belong to Him." By calling upon the name of the Lord, the Israelites express both their dependence upon YHWH and their need for "special protection" from God.[66] Thus, the receiving of God's revelation and name and the invoking of God's name as an expression of dependence and need for protection express the full dialogical character of religion. In fact, Häring points out that the experience of God's name and reality evokes a particular response symbolized by the taking of a new name, e.g., baptism, religious vows. Taking a new name symbolizes the new identity of the person. "This means the inauguration of a new world order. To receive a new name from God implies an entirely new relation of dependence, of sovereign protection and interior assimilation."[67]

The revelation of the name "Jesus" points to the reality that Jesus is the Messiah. The names given to the Messiah in the Old Testament, such as Emmanuel, Wonder-Counselor, God-Hero, Father-Forever, Prince of Peace, reveal the "most characteristic qualities and activities" of the "Anointed One." In the New Testament the revelation of the name "Jesus" points to the essence of God's revelation as one who saves.

The revelation of God's name is the revelation of God's love and, according to Häring, a revelation that reaches its full "climax" in Jesus Christ. Jesus, as Word of God, reveals God's essence by revealing the name of God, "Abba," to his followers. Jesus both calls his disciples by name (John 10:3) and invites the disciples to invoke God's name in prayer (John 17:1-6). This is the absolute sign of "our intimacy with God through grace" because by calling God "Father" the Christian is "admitted to the inner community of divine love which is the Trinity itself."[68] John's Gospel serves again as the central text for Häring's understanding of Jesus' revelation of God's name and glory to his followers.[69] Häring states that the "name of

---

[66] Ibid. Häring also cites New Testament passages that express this idea, such as Acts 2:21, Rom 10:13.

[67] Ibid.

[68] Ibid., 2:271; *CRCW,* 292.

[69] See Ibid., 269–70.

God, which is associated essentially with the love of God for men and the revealed will of God inviting men to a community of fellowship with Him, also connotes something of the honor and glory *(dóxa)* of God. This is particularly apparent in the Gospel according to John. 'Father, glorify thy name!' 'I have both glorified it, and I will glorify *(doxázein)* it again' (John 12:28). The heavenly Father glorifies His name most of all through the manifestation of His Fatherly love in Christ, particularly in the passion and resurrection."[70]

In revealing the divine name through the visible acts of creation and Jesus' life, death, and resurrection, the continuing invocation and veneration of God's name by the community demonstrates the "bond between the name of God and divine worship." The Israelites give praise and honor to God through prayer, ritual, and sacrifice, and in this sense respond to the revelation of God through God's name. At the heart of worship, then, is the invocation of God by God's name. Häring states that "the divine name, which is an epitome of all that God has revealed about His essence and activity, is a hymn of praise of God's goodness, presence, power, and majesty. Therefore the proper use of the divine name is an important act of the praise and worship of God."[71] Therefore to invoke the name of God in worship, prayer, and service means to act "in the name" of God, to represent and make manifest divine love and will. The revelation of God's name, glory, and honor invites a response that also implies an obligation. The revelation of God's name in love evokes a loving response of adoration for God's name; the obligation upon the Christian is to embody God's name in such a way that the whole person offers "homage to the majesty of God." Häring writes:

> If that which is ultimate in the revelation of the divine name is the manifestation of God as our Father, it must follow that every divine name can be properly spoken and truly honored only through the expression and inner spirit befitting the name of one's Father. In every name of God we must honor Him as our Father: this means, pronunciation with loving reverence. We pronounce every divine name, including the names which reveal the loving majesty and glory of God (particularly the words, *Cross* and *Holy Sacrament*) with this veneration and love.[72]

---

[70] *LC* 2:272.
[71] Ibid.
[72] Ibid.

The Christian community prays in the "name of Jesus" because through baptism the Body of Christ is joined together with him. The prayer of the believer joins with Christ's prayer to the Father and in this sense prayer is "participation in the love and glory of the triune God." To pray in Jesus' name is a sign of the inner conformity to the imitation of Christ so that "we pray only for the things which are in agreement with His loving will."[73]

Häring does not dismiss the other two categories—adjuration and oaths. The two topics follow his theological discussion of the meaning of God's name in the Scriptures, through Christ, and in the sacraments. The adjuration is to call upon God's name or to pray in the name of Jesus and expresses faith and trust in God's love and will.[74] The essence of the oath also expresses faith in God's faithfulness and the willingness of a person to pledge himself in God's name expresses his faithfulness to the truth.[75] These two acts are secondary, however, to the more primary use of God's name in prayer and worship, which encompass the full dialogical pattern of receiving from God and responding to God through the name. The name also allows Häring to place emphasis on the unique individual who is called and known by name and responds and knows the divine person by name.

* * * *

As I argue throughout this study Häring retains and reinterprets the neo-Thomist manuals most creatively through his analysis of the virtue of religion. The virtue of religion is largely a forgotten concept in moral theology, but Häring places it at the center of his moral system in order to highlight religion as dialogical, cultal, and social; the practice of religion as a moral virtue requiring external expression in the world; and the reciprocal relationship between interior and exterior acts of religion in the "ongoing conversion" of the Christian life. Each of these emphases points to further possibilities for integrating moral and sacramental theology.

Häring seeks to reclaim an understanding of religion as relationship, rather than legal requirement, although he does not relinquish the category of obligation. Religion as encounter and dialogue with

---

[73] *CRCW*, 293.
[74] *LC* 2:274.
[75] Ibid., 2:274–76.

God includes both being grasped by the divine presence and the dual response of love and obedience. The very nature of response binds one to God and a relationship that imposes an obligation to respond and live in such a way as to be an "adorer" of God's holiness and name. This understanding of religion provides a way of thinking about the foundation of religious acts—both personal and interior as well as communal and exterior—as embodying a direct response to God's initiation.

Häring retains the virtue of religion within the category of the moral virtues, even though he is not fully convinced of the traditional distinction between the theological and moral virtues. However, by calling the virtue of religion a moral virtue he creates the theoretical conditions for conceiving of moral actions as sacramental. In the terms of sacramental theology moral actions could be understood as "signs of faith" that are at once dialogical, cultal, and social: that is to say, they are performed in response to God; they are acts of adoration and worship; and they are expressed externally in the world in relationship to the neighbor.

Further, Häring explicates the virtue of religion as a moral virtue through a retrieval of the ancient tradition of *imitatio Christi*. His treatment of imitation stresses how both interior and exterior conformity to Christ are integrated and maintained. For Häring, *imitatio Christi* chiefly involves an imitation of Christ the High Priest—the true worshipper. This line of thought can be extended beyond Häring's own christological commitments as well. Given different interpretations of the person and work of Jesus Christ, interior conformity to Christ can be linked to following Christ's moral example through non-priestly exterior acts.

The virtue of religion, by incorporating religious, spiritual, and moral acts, may also provide a way of drawing together three theological disciplines that have grown apart in Roman Catholic theology: spiritual theology, which focuses primarily on the individual; liturgical theology, which focuses primarily on the community; and moral theology, which is concerned about the moral person and act.[76] The mutual-relatedness between interior and exterior actions in Häring, for example, provides an opening for a systematic understanding of the religious or spiritual self as constituted by disposi-

---

[76] Mahoney (254) argues that combining spiritual and moral theology will enrich the categories of moral theology and correct its long standing "preoccupation with law, commandments, and sin."

tions, intentions, thoughts, and emotions as well as by external actions that involve verbal, bodily, and communal expressions.

While Häring's sacramental-moral theology, and in particular his articulation of the virtue of religion, is a potentially rich resource for contemporary moral theology, nonetheless two limitations of his thought present obstacles to those who would expand on his achievements. As many of Häring's students have noted, his doctrine of sin does not provide compelling answers to questions concerning social sin and radical evil.[77] Any adequate account of sacramental-moral theology requires attention to structural as well as personal sin. Yet even in terms of personal sin, Häring does not analyze sin's power to distort the self. Häring incorporates biblical and personalist terms in his definition of sin in order to move beyond the manualists' notion of sin as law-breaking. For Häring, sin is essentially refusal to worship.[78] Yet, as suggestive as this formulation might be, Häring does not incorporate into his system an account of the pervasive power of sin as part of the daily reality of the Christian life. His categories of virtue, growth, and perfection highlight the positive side of the life of faith, but he does not seem concerned to consider more deeply how sin can become rooted in the dispositions, thoughts, emotions, as well as the words and acts, of many Christians.

Ironically as a pastoral theologian, Häring's failure in this regard presents a pastoral problem to those who would learn from him. Ministers and lay persons need assistance in responding to the reality of sin as it manifests itself in small but persistent ways in daily life.[79] To be sure, Häring stresses God's grace as an ever-present

---

[77] Curran (*Critical Concerns*, 38) claims that Häring lacks attention to structural sin and does not see the "radical discontinuity" between the present and the Kingdom of God. See also O'Keefe's study of Häring's concept of sin, which includes an extensive critique.

[78] In *LC* (1:342–50) Häring examines the threefold understanding of sin in John's gospel: *hamartía*, loss of God, *anomía*, opposition to divine will, and *adikía*, the violation of justice, in order to show that disobedience to the law stems from a deeper renunciation of God that is manifested in the refusal to worship God. He also relates sin to value theory (1:365): "Up to this point we have explained the nature of sin in so far as it is common to all sin as an offense against the holiness of God. The root is always the one same evil disposition of aversion from God, but it admits of very diverse degrees of malice and culpability. . . . Sin, therefore, not only offends the infinite value of God's holiness under many aspects, but also the manifold created values. Accordingly, the diversity of the domains of value violated creates a diversity of kinds of sin, or diverse species of sin." In *FFC* 1:69, Häring defines sin as "uncreative freedom"; see also, 1:379–426, for a discussion of sin and conversion.

[79] McCormick ("Moral Theology 1940–1989," 20) has raised a similar point that the attention given to social sin has left personal sin aside: "Many of the quite personal problems

transformative power in each believer's life, but the question remains: to what extent is moral theology a pastoral aid for the sacrament of reconciliation, particularly in helping people to understand the rightness or wrongness of specific acts and how to overcome a disposition to them. Again, ironically, the manualists may, in the end, have more useful things to say about what Christians should and should not think, say, or do. (At least they were willing to say something about these matters.) Moral theology began as an aid for the sacrament of confession and without argument became overly concerned with sinful acts. But in dropping its emphasis on the sacrament of reconciliation, moral theology may have lost its pastoral role in helping ministers and lay people in understanding, identifying, and repenting of sin.[80] The task is not to return to the manualists, however, but to deepen and extend Häring's trajectory of thought in the area of reconciliation.

A second area of Häring's work that requires further exploration has to do with the extent to which his understanding of religious experience bears up under the weight of secularization. Häring believed that the processes of secularization—recognized, among other things, in atheism, alienation, and individualism—were becoming the hallmark of western societies. His response to the problem: the Church should encourage a more vibrant and meaningful liturgy. Modern persons would find their true self and the true community (not exclusively but primarily) through the sacramental dimension of the Church's life. The encounter with God through the sacraments and liturgy constitutes the fullest expression of God's invitation and humanity's response because it is dialogical, cultal, and social. Liturgical renewal, and subsequently moral renewal, offers persons an experience of the sacred through symbol and word within a community of faith.

Häring is characteristically optimistic in his response to secularization. He admits that liturgical forms through which the sacred is

---

that so engaged the manualists are, obviously, still problems. Indeed, there is a pastoral wisdom there that remains somewhat undervalued, largely because it is unknown. Yet the focus has shifted. We are much more concerned about the rights of people that are denied by social structures."

[80] Richard McCormick, "Self-Assessment and Self-Indictment," *Religious Studies Review* 13 (1987) 37. "Within the sacramental perspectives of the times the confessor was viewed as exercising a fourfold office: father, teacher, judge, physician. Specially necessary to effective ministry were charity (of a father), knowledge (of a teacher and judge), and prudence (of a physician)."

encountered are broken and diminished; nevertheless he assumes at the same time that religious experience remains relatively unproblematic for modern persons. He does not consider that secularization may have generated a radically new context that throws religious experience itself into question. Louis Dupré, a Catholic philosopher, offers an interesting counterpoint to Häring when he argues that secularization has indeed created new conditions which radically alter the traditional forms and vehicles of religious experience.

In an article published in 1982, "Spiritual Life in a Secular Age," Dupré argues that due to modernity's "self-sufficient humanism," large aspects of life—science, social structures, morality—is now viewed as fully autonomous to religion. This development, Dupré explains, has thus created a "fragmented world view" in which religion becomes one more aspect of life alongside every other aspect. No longer does "the dynamic opposition between the sacred and the profane always secure some measure of integration with transcendent ultimacy to *all* facets of human existence."[81] This new situation does not spell the end of religious experience, according to Dupré, but it does signal the end of a time when "experience, interpretation and decision" were part of one "continuous act." Religion becomes a matter of personal choice so that people "hold" sacred persons, objects and events as sacred, but no longer "perceive" them to be sacred. Thus, religion will be organized "from within rather than from without" and only when faith is experienced and accepted on the other side of secularity's brokenness will a person "readily join their efforts with those of fellow believers."[82]

The most viable avenue for authentic religious experience in contemporary world, according to Dupré, leads inward. Within the self the individual can gain awareness of God's absence from the secular world and so pass through this "darkness" to a new integration of the self that does not depend on cultural forms.[83] Interestingly, Dupré's analysis resonates with views of a theologian whom Häring once criticized—Jacques Maritain. For example, in language remarkably close

[81] Dupré, 22.

[82] Ibid., 23–25.

[83] Dupré (25–27) relies on the spiritual masters who emphasize the absence of God such as Pseudo-Dionysius, Meister Eckhart, the author of the *Cloud of Unknowing*, St. John of the Cross, John Henry Newman, and Simone Weil, in order "to show that if the believer, who shares in fact, if not in principle, the practical atheism of his entire culture, is left no choice but to vitalize this negative experience and to confront his feeling of God's absence, he may find himself on the very road walked by spiritual pilgrims in more propitious times."

to Maritain's, Dupré follows Pseudo-Dionysius in saying that all language must be "reduced to silence" and spiritual perfection can only be found by abandoning "all experience, all concepts, and all objects" in order to find the transcendent presence. As Dupré recognizes, this kind of mystical experience is ephemeral, and he acknowledges that beyond such experience many spiritual masters seek a "new analogy" or some "partial identity" between the divine and the human. In stark contrast to Häring's emphasis upon a Christian's inescapable need to speak God's name in worship, Dupré warns that "We must not expect to come up with a *new name* for the emerging transcendent, but only to acquire a new perceptiveness for detecting it (italics mine)."[84]

The outward forms of religious expression are not lost for Dupré, they are adopted by the individual when he "joins a community" that provides "him with sacraments, scriptures, and a whole system of representations" so that the community of faith "enables the individual to incorporate his attitude into a living union with his model." These traditional paths of "symbolic gestures and doctrinal representations" have lost their cultural power to convey the transcendent and are only accepted by "deliberate decision" that must be "replenished by a rather intensive and deliberate spiritual awareness." Without this, sacraments, doctrines, and sacred texts are "empty shells."[85]

Given the resemblance between Dupré and Maritain on religious interiority, it seems warranted to suggest that Häring's criticism of Maritain might form a template for his response to Dupré's claims. Religion, according to Häring, requires external expression, not only because human persons are bodily creatures and need external signs, but because God is a God who expresses "transcendent presence" through external cultural forms. It is precisely because modern life is marked by fragmentation and alienation, Häring has said, that religious encounter needs to be seen as arising from and returning to the community. Incorporation into the Body of Christ, for Häring, is participation in the divine community of the Trinity; hearing and speaking the name of God is the encounter with the ineffable one.

Yet Dupré's spirituality in a secular age cannot be entirely ignored by sacramental or moral theologians who assume, like Häring, perhaps too quickly, that bad liturgy accounts for depressed states of religious experience. It may well be, as Dupré points out that religion

---

[84] Ibid., 29.
[85] Ibid., 30.

no longer holds the power to integrate all of life and that, correlative to this cultural diminishment, is a diminishment of human self-hood. A sacramental-moral theology would need to explain further how the encounter with God and the community in the liturgy interprets and integrates all of human experience under the conditions of the contemporary world.

Conclusion

Bernard Häring and Contemporary Proposals in Liturgy and Ethics: Critique and Contributions

A few liturgical reformers of the early twentieth century saw the emerging reform movements in liturgy and Catholic social action as directly related. In Europe, Dom Lambert Beauduin argued that participation in the liturgy was inseparable from the cause of workers' rights in Belgium, and in North America Virgil Michel proposed that a just society would emerge from renewed liturgy.[1] The liturgical reformers believed that greater lay participation in the liturgy would deepen and enliven the Church's self-understanding as the Mystical Body of Christ, carrying with it obvious social inferences.

This same biblical image served as the basis of various social action movements of the time: most social reformers affirmed the notion that a community which understood all relationships in and through Christ would overcome the individualism that plagued modern societies as well as unite people in the cause for social change. Most moral theologians did not join either reform movement; aside from Bernard Häring and a few other alternative manualists, moral theologians remained within the neo-Thomist framework where such questions would not be addressed until after the Second Vatican Council.

---

[1] See "Lambert Beauduin" in *How Firm a Foundation: Voices of the Early Liturgical Movement*, 23–28; and "Virgil Michel," 186–89, in the same volume. For a biography of Virgil Michel, see, R. W. Franklin and Robert L. Speath, *Virgil Michel: American Catholic* (Collegeville: The Liturgical Press, 1988).

The changes introduced by the Council were nothing short of revolutionary in terms of both Catholic worship and morality. The Constitution on the Sacred Liturgy affirmed the central tenants of the liturgical movement, in part by calling for greater lay participation; *Gaudium et Spes* turned the Church's theological tradition toward full engagement with modern social problems. As promising as the new directions might have been, the Council failed to draw together and articulate a relationship between the Church's liturgy and its moral and social vision. Liturgists and ethicists, following the Council, pursued separate agendas: liturgists prepared revisions of the sacraments and a new *Sacramentary*, while ethicists turned their attention to the pressing social problems of the times in medical and bioethics, population, pollution and the environment, and sexual ethics. Many ethicists looked specifically for points of contact between Roman Catholic social teaching and secular or non-religious ethical thought, drawing them further from traditional concerns of sacramental practice. In the North American context each discipline grew in identity and focus, furthered by academic specialization, with the unintended consequence that moral and sacramental theology lost a direct connection. In one sense the decline of the neo-Thomist system marked the end of a systematic expression between sacraments and morality.

Gradually, however, both liturgists and ethicists realized the fragmented nature of their respective theological tasks as well as the separation between worship and social life among faithful Christians. In 1976 Monika Hellwig's small but powerful book, *The Eucharist and the Hunger of the World*, posed the question in new terms: what does the Eucharist have to do with world-wide hunger? By 1979 ethicists joined the conversation, devoting an entire issue of the *Journal of Religious Ethics* to the topic of liturgy and ethics. John J. Egan, upon the twentieth anniversary of the Constitution on the Sacred Liturgy in 1983, stimulated conversation among Catholic liturgists when he claimed that the "unfinished agenda" of the liturgical reformers—the link between liturgy and social justice—remains a significant challenge today.[2]

[2] "The importance of liturgical reform for the renewal of the church life is openly acknowledged in the opening paragraph of the Constitution on the Sacred Liturgy, and yet the document never returns in any explicit way to the problem of the connection between liturgy and the social life of the faithful. The same break is only confirmed by the otherwise splendid achievement of the Pastoral Constitution on the Church in the Modern

Since 1976 conversations between liturgists and ethicists have emerged among both Protestant and Catholic theologians. In general, Catholic theologians have examined the relationship between liturgy and social justice, while Protestants, particularly narrative theologians, have turned attention to how worship forms Christian virtue. Häring's insights into the relationship between worship and the moral life can make important contributions to both of these conversations; likewise, these discussions provide a helpful critique of his position. In these concluding remarks, I will sketch out a few comparisons between Häring's sacramental-moral theology and Catholic liturgist Mark Searle's writing on the topic of liturgy and justice, and with the work of Stanley Hauerwas, who has in recent years championed the renewal of virtue ethics in Protestant moral thought.

Liturgy and Social Justice: The Catholic Conversation

After the Council, Catholics took up the task of renewing the liturgy and transforming society with great energy. Three groups of Catholic thinkers— liberation theologians, feminist theologians, and North American liturgists—began to realize that the liturgical and social justice movements were evolving in too great an isolation from each other. Liberationists, especially those in Latin America and Asia, in developing the biblical principle of justice as a central category for critiquing unjust social and economic structures, extended their critique to church structures, theological systems, and religious practice. For liberationists, the Church cannot lead the cause of justice if it does not itself embody justice in all its teachings and practices, most particularly in the liturgy.[3]

World—its broad vision of the heights and depths of the human condition and the role of the church in forwarding the redemptive work of God for the benefit of all humanity utterly omits any mention of the place of the liturgy of the church as source and summit of this process." John J. Egan, "Liturgy and Justice: An Unfinished Agenda," *Origins* 13/15 (September 22, 1983). See also R. Kevin Seasoltz, "Justice and the Eucharist," *Worship* 58/6 (November 1984) 508; Rembert G. Weakland, o.s.b., "Liturgy and Social Justice," in *Shaping English Liturgy: Studies in Honor of Archbishop Denis Hurley*, ed. by Peter C. Finn and James M. Schellman (Washington D.C.: Pastoral Press, 1990) 343–57.

[3] See: Rafael Avila, *Worship and Politics* (Maryknoll, N.Y.: Orbis Books, 1981); Tissa Balasuriya, *The Eucharist and Human Liberation* (Maryknoll, N.Y.: Orbis Books, 1979); Leonardo Boff, *Sacraments of Life, Life of the Sacraments* (Washington DC: Pastoral Press, 1987); Albert F. Gedraitis, *Worship and Politics* (Toronto: Wedge Pub. Foundation, 1972); Joseph A. Grassi,

Likewise, feminist theologians turned the question of the just treatment of women in society to the Church and its liturgy. They have critiqued the language, symbols, and roles that exclude women from full participation in the sacramental life of the Church.[4] The liturgy cannot "work" if it does not embody the full reality of Jesus' call to justice for all persons. Liberation and feminist theologians have raised questions about the relationship between liturgy and justice quite beyond what the early liturgical reformers envisioned. In their discourse justice becomes the central Christian principle that judges and critiques all human relationships and religious expression. If the liturgy does not promote justice, it most likely is conspiring with unjust and oppressive powers.

In turn, North American Catholic liturgists have taken up Egan's challenge to connect liturgy and the Church's social tradition. Issues raised by liberationist and feminist regarding the ways in which the liturgy mirrors unjust relationships within the ecclesial community and society has received considerable attention from liturgists.[5] In addition, some have explored the "intrinsic relationship" between liturgy and justice by reflecting on the ways justice is already expressed in and through the liturgy.[6] One of the enduring challenges of liturgical reform in this century has been helping the community realize *what* the liturgy proclaims about God and God's justice, and the implications of "full participation in the liturgy" for the social mission of the Church.[7]

Compounding the challenges of catechizing the community, contemporary liturgists have recognized that post-conciliar liturgical changes in theology and practice took place in the midst of rapid social change, some of which profoundly shape the way people expe-

---

Broken Bread and Broken Bones: The Lord's Supper and World Hunger (Maryknoll, N.Y.: Orbis Books, 1985); Juan Luis Segundo, *The Sacraments Today, Vol. 4: A Theology for Artisans of a New Humanity* (Maryknoll, N.Y.: Orbis Books, 1975).

[4] Barbara Reed, "Liturgy, Scripture, and the Challenge of Feminism," *Living No Longer for Ourselves: Liturgy and Justice in the Nineties*, ed. H. Kathleen Hughes, R.S.C.J., and Mark R. Francis, C.S.V. (Collegeville: The Liturgical Press, 1991) 136. See also Susan A. Ross, *Extravagant Affections: A Feminist Sacramental Theology* (New York: Continuum, 1998).

[5] See for example the collection of essays in *Living No Longer for Ourselves* that address issues such as gender exclusivity, inclusive language, and inculturation.

[6] H. Kathleen Hughes, R.S.C.J., "Liturgy and Justice: An Intrinsic Relationship," in *Living No Longer for Ourselves*.

[7] Mark Searle, "Serving the Lord with Justice," in *Liturgy and Social Justice*, ed. Mark Searle (Collegeville: The Liturgical Press, 1980) 16.

rience and participate in the liturgy. Liturgical reforms placed great emphasis on individual participation, yet failed to recognize the ways in which individualism functions in American culture; cultural models of individualism have inadvertently shaped perceptions and impressions of social responsibility and commitment. In this brief discussion, these two issues—understandings of justice and individual participation—provide interesting points of comparison between Bernard Häring and contemporary liturgists involved in dialogue regarding liturgy and justice.

Catholic liturgist Mark Searle's writings on justice and liturgy offer a helpful comparison to Häring. It is important to begin this discussion by noting that justice is not a central category for Häring in terms of defining the relationship between morality and worship as it is for Searle. Häring treats justice as a moral virtue in rather traditional terms, whereas liturgists have focused almost exclusively on justice as a social principle. For Searle justice is both a theological and social reality; it expresses how persons stand in relationship to God, others, and the material creation. In terms of liturgy, justice is expressed primarily as a theological reality because the liturgy proclaims the reality of God's justice at work in the world, which is not to be confused with human forms of justice. God's justice, according to Searle, is "ultimately God himself, just as he is" and "the justice of God is satisfied when things conform to the purpose for which he made them."[8] God's justice is revealed through creation, history, and most fully in the life and ministry of Jesus, the "Just One." Jesus' teaching on the Kingdom of God, in continuity with the prophetic tradition, expresses God's justice in terms of God's mercy and care for the poor, oppressed and the sinner. The liturgy proclaims the Kingdom of God as the manifestation of God's justice in both the present and the future.

Likewise for Häring, justice is what determines right relationship with God and persons, but unlike Searle, his interpretation of God's justice is Pauline rather than prophetic or liberationist. Consistent with his eclectic method in *The Law of Christ*, Häring mixes Thomist understandings of reward and merit with Paul's theology of justification, drawing out some biblical understandings of justice into the word-and-response model. For example, he distinguishes between God's justice, which is manifest in wrath and punishment as well as

---

[8] Searle, 16.

mercy and pardon, God's justification of the sinner, and the Christian practice and expression of justice that follows from and is a response to God's justice:

> The justice of God is superabundant justice. It bestows its blessings, distributes justice. It justifies sinners through grace wherever something of good will still is present, even though it may appear utterly lost in the immensity of guilt which only merits punishment. . . . The reverence of the creature for his creator, of the child for God its father, is due in the strictest sense of justice. It is payment of the most absolute debt. Many should also be conscious of this debt, conscious of his utter incapacity to attain the measure of justice for which he must constantly strive, since he can never give God the honor He really merits.[9]

Häring's interpretation of justice emphasizes the dynamic relationship between the sinner and God, yet it does not draw upon the Kingdom of God as a defining paradigm for God's justice in history.

Häring would agree with Searle's claim that it is "a matter of justice" that the community gathers in the liturgy to give thanks and praise to God. Searle acknowledges Aquinas' connection between the virtue of religion and the virtue of justice, though he goes no further than acknowledging the ideas. For both, it is fundamental to the liturgy that the assembly acknowledges who God is and what God has revealed in creation and history. Such acknowledgment has bearing on "the cause of justice," for Searle, because it points to God's "absolute claims" of justice over any particular social or political program. The proclamation of God's justice reminds the community that they participate in God's work of liberation and reconciliation, but that all human forms of justice fall short of the full manifestation of God's justice. In that sense, the liturgy proclaims the ideals of justice to which the reality of particular social situations can only approximate.

Both Searle and Häring point out the ways in which God's justice informs person's relationship to each other and to the creation. Both persons and creation are received as gift and responsibility. Again for Searle, the liturgy expresses in ideal form the "right relationship" persons have to each other and creation. Christians are called to live a new life expressed in loving service to the neighbor and to use the

---

[9] *LC* 1:524.

material goods of creation with prudence and stewardship. For Searle the liturgy is an "enacted parable" insofar as it gives the community a "new point of view" in which they are "free to decide how to act." The liturgy, like a parable, opens up new ways of seeing the world, though it does not impose precise moral imperatives or social programs. Though human forms of justice fall short of the gospel imperative, the reality of the Kingdom of God gives content and shape to the Christian community's social engagement. The liturgy does not put forth precise formulas for exacting justice in society, but rather enables the community,

> with a sense of the overall meaning and direction of the struggle for justice and with an ideal (the Kingdom) which, while its positive dimensions may be difficult to spell out in specific terms, at least enables us to evaluate critically the direction and value of our work and the attitudes out of which we operate. The liturgy provides a model or ideal in the light of which all human justice is judged and all mere lip service to God is itself denounced as injustice.[10]

Because Häring treats justice as a moral virtue, he does not connect liturgy with justice as a social principle; similarly, Searle treats justice as a social principle, but does not describe how the liturgy forms justice as a virtue. In *The Law of Christ* justice is a virtue, but it is not first among the Christian virtues, and as a moral virtue it does not extend into social analysis. Häring retains Aquinas' definition of justice, "to give to each one his due," and he examines the traditional moral categories of commutative, legal, distributive, and social justice, but these are treated in largely neo-Thomist terms and are not integrated with his virtue ethic or word-and-response model. Later, when Häring abandons the Greek virtues for the eschatological virtues, he interprets justice as part of the virtue of charity and religion—justice never stands apart. This is not to say that Häring is not concerned with just social conditions, as his writings on peace, nonviolence and liberation from sin for free and faithful living demonstrate. But justice is not a defining feature of his system in the way that religion, adoration, freedom, and faithfulness serve as anchors for the moral life.

Religion, rather than justice, is the primary way Häring defines the relationship between the moral and the religious. It is through the virtue of religion that the divine-human relationship gives

[10] Searle, 30.

content and shape to the Christian life. In other words the virtue of religion is the fundamental moral category in relationship to prayer and liturgy and likewise to all the moral virtues, including justice. He has articulated a liturgical anthropology as his fundamental moral theology, asking first what it means to be a worshipper of God, and secondly how the virtue of religion is formative of moral virtue. In most instances his ideas about religion mirror Searle's ideas about justice: the virtue of religion, which is first among the moral virtues, is expressed most fully within the liturgy, to some extent in ideal form, which gives shape and content to the moral virtues that are expressed in the world. The virtue of religion links the life of prayer with the Church's social mission, but Häring goes no further in explaining how a moral virtue like justice is formed through religion and the difference it makes in moral actions toward a just society. Like many virtue ethicists, he is interested in the formation of virtue, but is less concerned with demonstrating how that formation makes a difference when Christians face the concrete realities of unjust social conditions and decisions for what can make such conditions more just in Christian terms.

Of course, Häring did not pose the question in terms of liturgy and justice as has been the case for post-Vatican II thinkers. He sought to develop an integrated liturgical ethic in which the systematic categories are defined in terms of sacramental theology. He does not, therefore, place liturgy and justice alongside each other and ask how they are related, but rather develops a liturgical anthropology and its implications for a fundamental moral theology. Häring's system, however, has the potential to incorporate as well as expand contemporary understandings of justice. First, justice presupposes a prior set of virtues: charity, religion, obedience, and adoration—the justice that extends to one's neighbor is shaped by one's relationship with God, defined in terms of justification that is experienced as both gift and obligation.

Using Häring's own claim that "all moral tasks are at the same time religious tasks," justice could be defined in terms of both a response to God's justice and love toward the community, and the community's response (both love and obedience) to repair unjust social conditions. Häring could argue that justice must be subordinate to religion, as are all the moral virtues; the virtue of religion places persons in right relationship to God, and justice follows as an act of worship, a reversal of Aquinas' idea that religion proceeds from justice. If religion is the bridge that connects the theological and moral virtues, justice would be one aspect of religious and moral response: all acts of justice toward the neighbor, and for the social good, are primarily acts of worship in response to God's justice. Likewise, Searle's interpretation of Jesus as the Just One could be viewed in Häring's terms as one dimension of Jesus' response as the perfect worshipper to God.

Searle, and other liturgists who have drawn upon liberationist interpretations of justice, have advanced the conversation beyond notions of justice found in the early liturgical reformers and Häring. On the one hand, Häring's system could be strengthened by more attention to the social justice tradition as expressed in the prophetic and Synoptic traditions. On the other hand, he has demonstrated most aptly the idea that "we face the world with a moral task that flows from the virtue of religion."[11] Those interested in liturgy and justice may find it useful to expand the conversation beyond justice as a social principle to consider the full range of moral virtues and their formative power in the moral life.

In addition to the topic of liturgy and justice the virtue of religion might contribute some insight into contemporary concerns for cultural patterns of individualism in the liturgy. Some liturgists have identified the impact of cultural individualism on the expression and experience of the liturgy as an additional problem in post-conciliar efforts to draw out the implications of the connection between liturgy and justice. Early reformers realized that individual devotions practiced during the liturgy inhibited participation and its efforts to advance the Mystical Body of Christ ecclesiology. Liturgists, therefore, sought to eliminate personal devotions from the liturgy as one means of highlighting the sense of the community's gathered prayer and, likewise, overcoming privatized and individualistic conceptions of Catholic worship. But as Ralph Keifer notes, "The liturgical movement may have grasped the right issue and proposed the wrong solution—or at least proposed a solution that does not go to the heart of the matter." The reforms of the liturgy "put the private piety" into hymns, prayers, and the entire service, emphasizing a more "individualistic and privatistic character not at all foreseen by the agents of liturgical reform."[12]

---

[11] *LC* 2:124.

[12] Ralph A. Keifer, "Liturgy and Ethics: Some Unresolved Dilemmas," *Living No Longer for Ourselves*, 72.

In effect, the changes moved the liturgy from a corporate exercise that included individual devotion, to a quasi-collective experience that was in fact suffused with strong privatistic tendencies. Not only does the liturgy stress the individual's participation and interaction within the liturgy, but changes in the presider's relationship to the congregation inadvertently causes "idiosyncrasies and personal tastes" to shape the liturgy, which is further evidence that the revised liturgy has absorbed the "individualism of our culture, rather than stand against it." Despite the Mystical Body of Christ image, liturgy leapt from the private individualism of neo-scholasticism into the arms of the culture's individualism. The liturgy continues to struggle in shaping people who are already formed by overwhelmingly powerful cultural forces. Culture, in other words, far more determines how liturgical participation is understood than liturgical or theological principles.[13]

Failure to take into account the ways in which culture shapes and influences the liturgy, early liturgical reformers' may have been naïve about the ability of the liturgy to transform society. The reformers' emphasis on the communal character of the liturgy, along with their discouragement of private devotions in the liturgy, may have inadvertently led to a failure to articulate how the liturgy shapes the person as both individual and social. They may have overlooked or failed to articulate the way devotion and adoration, as individual acts, are formative and participatory of the social self. Of course, when they discouraged the practice of devotions in the liturgy, they were not trying to rid the Christian community of private devotions wherever they might occur. But perhaps labeling as "private" individual devotional practices, both within or outside of liturgy, is precisely the problem and betrays a deficient understanding of the self as inherently social. Therefore, in light of their anthropological deficiencies, liturgical reformers' efforts to incorporate new reforms into the liturgy did not give sufficient attention to the individual's proper interior and spiritual development and its necessary relationship to social and communal participation.

Like the liturgical reformers of his time, Häring is concerned that private devotions practiced during the liturgy separate the individual from full participation in the community. However, his interpre-

---

[13] M. Francis Mannon, "Liturgy and the Present Crisis of Culture," *Worship* 62/2 (March 1988) 98–123.

tation of the virtue of religion attempts to unite the interior and exterior aspects of religion, and the individual and social aspects of the person, without collapsing one into the other. By emphasizing the two aspects of the virtue of religion he acknowledges the way in which worship forms the spiritual, ethical, and social dimensions of persons *in* community. All aspects of the virtue of religion are dialogical (in communion with God), cultal (bearing external expression), and social (in community); even "private" devotions must bear these marks regardless that the person's prayer is interior. Häring's interpretation of the virtue of religion may provide a way of conceiving prayer as well as liturgy as embodying both interior and exterior aspects of the self as well as personal and social dimensions. The interior and individual, however, is not private, but essentially social, because persons are always social creatures in relationship to God and community.

While Häring's theory of justice may not be adequate for today's social ethic his primary question is the relationship between the moral life and worship; he did not focus on one aspect of the moral self or one moral virtue. In that regard perhaps the focus on liturgy and justice among Catholic liturgists and ethicists has been too narrow, not taking account of the whole moral self in relationship to liturgy. The liturgy is not to be defined in terms of justice alone, but the entire moral-religious life, and the virtue of religion may more adequately achieve this than justice, since it incorporates all moral virtues as external expressions of dialogue, response, and imitation of Christ. Häring offers one model for considering how a fundamental moral theology stands in relationship to the Church's liturgy.

Virtue, Narrative, and Worship in Protestant Ethics

Catholic liturgists and theologians may need to look beyond justice to the full range of Christian virtues, particularly the virtue of religion, in order to both strengthen their treatment of justice and demonstrate how liturgy relates to other Christian virtues and the moral person. Here Protestant theologians, especially narrativists such as Stanley Hauerwas, may be helpful.[14] Hauerwas has explicitly

---

[14] Another narrativist theologian to include is Don Saliers, a Methodist liturgist, who examines how prayer and worship "both forms and expresses dispositions" that form the basis for Christian affections and virtues. His essays on liturgy and ethics include "Liturgy and

examined the relationship between character, virtue, and worship. He retrieves character and virtue in Protestant ethics largely to counter what he views as an excessive and misguided emphasis on "quandary ethics" and the search for universal moral principles and rules to guide moral actions.[15] However, to overcome the long-standing aversion to virtue ethics in Protestantism, he seeks to reconcile virtue with traditional interpretations of justification and sanctification through the categories of character and narrative.[16] I will focus on the ways in which Hauerwas' narrative virtue ethic and Häring's sacramental virtue ethic offer mutually helpful insights to each respective position.

Though his approach to the Christian moral life differs in many respects from traditional Catholic virtue theory, Hauerwas shares many similarities with Häring. Both hold, for instance, that virtue precedes a rule, command, or principle ethic. Virtue is prior to rules because Christian ethics must give an account of what kind of people are formed by Christ before it can claim what rules and principles are to be followed. For Hauerwas, "Christian ethics is more of who we are than what we do."[17] Though Häring would not dismiss the category of moral action and the consequences of human acts as readily as does Hauerwas, his moral theology begins with experience and relationship as the basis for the divine-human encounter, not moral rules.

Though both place virtue prior to rules, Hauerwas is more critical of the attempt to search for universal principles that define ethical choices as good and true; rules and principles are determined by a

---

Ethics: Some New Beginnings," *Journal of Religious Ethics* 7/2 (Fall 1979) 173–90; and "Afterword: Liturgy and Ethics Revisited," in *Liturgy and the Moral Self: Humanity at Full Stretch Before God*, ed. E. Byron Anderson and Bruce T. Morrill (Collegeville: The Liturgical Press, 1998).

[15] Hauerwas's writings on virtue and character depend largely on the writings of philosopher, Alasdair MacIntyre, particularly his ground-breaking work, *After Virtue: A Study in Moral Theory* (Notre Dame, Ind.: University of Notre Dame Press). For his writings on virtue and character, see *Character and the Christian Life: A Study in Theological Ethics*, 3d. ed. (Trinity University Press, 1985); *Vision and Virtue: Essays in Christian Ethical Reflection* (Notre Dame, Ind.: Fides Publishers, Inc., 1974); *Truthfulness and Tragedy: Further Investigations in Christian Ethics* (Notre Dame, Ind.: University of Notre Dame Press, 1977); *A Community of Character: Toward a Constructive Christian Social Ethic* (Notre Dame, Ind.: University of Notre Dame Press, 1981); *The Peaceable Kingdom: A Primer in Christian Ethics* (Notre Dame, Ind.: University of Notre Dame Press, 1983). *Christians Among the Virtues: Theological Conversations with Ancient and Modern Ethics*, with Charles Pinches (Notre Dame, Ind.: University of Notre Dame Press, 1997).

[16] See especially Hauerwas, *A Community of Character*, 1981.

[17] Hauerwas, *The Peaceable Kingdom*, 35.

community's particular narrative. In contrast, Häring, consistent with the Catholic tradition, provides a place for moral law and principles in his system, though he argues that they are secondary to virtue; to avoid either rigid legalism or a lax casuistry, they must be placed in proper relation to the whole of the moral life. He does not eliminate categories of law, natural law, and conscience, as does Hauerwas, though it should be noted that these concepts are not fully integrated into Häring's understanding of virtue. Häring uses Scheler's value theory as a way of explaining the good and true value inherent in rules and principles that draws persons to fulfill the command. It is precisely these values that persons are attracted and attached to when following rules and commands—such value has objective worth in and of itself, but it is also relational in that it calls forth a response and imposes an obligation. Hauerwas, in contrast, does not hold to a general theory of value or human goodness that might explain the relationship between virtue and principle precisely because he views general theories as misbegotten attempts to explain away, through the illusory categories of "the general," the specific moral realities of a concrete community's distinctive narrative.[18]

In formulating Christian virtue, both Häring and Hauerwas reject attempts to explain Christian virtue based solely on the Greek tradition. Both lend a Christian interpretation to virtue from a particular reading of the Christian story—Häring explains the theological and moral virtues through the categories of sacramental theology, and later adopts the eschatological virtues, derived from the Sermon on the Mount; Hauerwas, on the way to building an ethic of nonviolence as the basis of Jesus' teaching, focuses on the virtues of patience, peace-making, and joy.[19] In a certain sense, both recognize that moral

[18] Hauerwas, *A Community of Character*, 117ff. Jean Porter points out that Hauerwas's virtue theory borrows generously from Aquinas' system, but does not connect virtue with Aquinas's general theory of goodness. Hauerwas, she notes, denies that it is necessary to identify criteria external to the Christian story to explain its reasonableness or plausibility. The criteria for determining Christian virtue lie within the Christian narrative and any theory of human goodness or reason external to that narrative is impossible to determine. Jean Porter, *The Recovery of Virtue* (Louisville, Ky.: Westminster/John Knox Press, 1990) 28, 36.

[19] Hauerwas's list of virtues includes peace-making (the virtue of remembering and telling Jesus' story), patience, hope, and joy (the presupposition of all virtues). See *The Peaceable Kingdom*, 102ff., 147. It is interesting to note that for all his claims about the centrality of the Christian narrative, Hauerwas has spent considerable time in conversation with ancient Greek and contemporary virtue theorists, drawing insights on happiness, friendship, obedience from Aristotle. He gives much less consideration to what Jesus or Paul says about these same virtues. See, for example, *Christians Among the Virtues*.

virtue is narrative- and context-dependent; different communities and traditions will emphasize virtues particular to their identity, history, and story. Neither is interested in deploying, as do Aristotle and Aquinas, a theory of virtue that applies to all humanity.

Häring and Hauerwas both claim that what makes Christian virtue distinctive is the movement of on-going conversion and sanctification in relationship to Jesus Christ. Häring understands conversion as a process that takes place in and through the sacraments of baptism, Eucharist and reconciliation. Hauerwas understands conversion in narrative, rather than sacramental terms: it takes place by coming to know the Christian story and by viewing reality from its perspective. Through the Christian narrative Christians come to know what sin is and what is necessary to follow Jesus. He claims that:

> the convictions that form the background for Christian growth take the form of a narrative which requires conversion, since the narrative never treats the formation of the self as completed. Thus the story that forms Christian identity trains the self to regard itself under the category of sin, which means we must do more than just develop. Christians are called to a new way of life that requires nothing less than a transvaluation of their past reality—repentance.[20]

Häring and Hauerwas each employ different metaphors for expressing Christian conversion and the process of acquiring and practicing virtue. Häring chooses the metaphor of dialogue in order to heighten attention in Catholic moral theology to the dynamic interplay of divine word and human response, as opposed to ontological explanations found in scholastic theology. As noted throughout this study, dialogue forms the basis for Häring's interpretation of each moral and theological category, emphasizing the experiential and relational dimensions of religious and moral encounters. Hauerwas prefers the metaphor of "journey" to that of "dialogue" because dialogue connotes divine command followed by simple, repetitive response. Dialogue cannot completely capture the unfolding character of the sanctified life, whereas the image of journey points to the gradual transformation that takes place over time in relationship to life's teleological end.[21] The idea that "virtues are the dispositions one ac-

---

[20] Hauerwas, *A Community of Character*, 131.

[21] See *Christians Among the Virtues*, 114ff. It is interesting to note that Hauerwas does not connect the theme of "journey" to the biblical narrative in any extensive way. He

quires on the journey" follows closely from Wesley's notion of sanctification rather than from Luther's radical doctrine of justification, though Hauerwas maintains that an ethic of virtue is compatible with both.[22] Justification is God's act of radical forgiveness; sanctification is the effect of God's transformation on the "whole person."

Hauerwas is more interested in how persons proceed from the point of justification than he is in explaining how grace, through justification, transforms persons. Justification, he claims, is best understood in relationship to the entire Christian narrative, especially in relationship to God's eschatological promises. Justification both changes a person's status as well as provides them with a vision of their journey, one that is now defined by hope. According to Hauerwas, his account of character and virtue overcomes the Protestant aversion to virtue ethics that might hint of works righteousness by emphasizing the way in which virtue is a matter of *being* rather than *doing*. Virtue arises from a character that is already formed through justification.[23]

In essence, Häring and Hauerwas' interpretations of dialogue and journey are not radically different. Both understand that virtues are acquired through habit and practice over time. Häring is concerned that Catholic theology begins with Paul's doctrine of justification, understood as the divine gift of grace that transforms the person into a disciple of Christ, and thereby overcome any Pelagian tendencies in Catholic moral and sacramental practice. Justification and sanctification are defined in terms of God's word that is first spoken to persons, and the free response to divine grace by the community. Hauerwas is reacting to the Protestant tradition's exclusive reliance on a divine command ethic to explain the divine-human relationship; the idea of character explains concepts such as justification and sanctification as the way in which the Christian person, not just acts, is transformed.

Hauerwas' virtue theory contains two important ideas that are not fully developed in Häring's work. First is the idea that virtue is determined by the interaction between the historical contingencies of

---

briefly notes that the biblical ethic is one of growth and development insofar as the Decalogue follows from the covenant, but he does not fully explore the biblical basis for this claim, especially in relationship to the New Testament and Paul. See *The Peaceable Kingdom*, 77ff. and 94–95, for a brief discussion.

[22] Hauerwas, *Christians Among the Virtues*, 19.

[23] See the new introduction to the third edition of *Character and the Christian Life*, 1985.

life and a particular narrative; and, second, is the idea that suffering and tragedy are crucial aspects of virtue formation. Hauerwas' virtue theory is based on the idea that persons are self-determining and narrative-dependent creatures. A person makes choices in relation to the conflicting values, roles, and goods that define the particular circumstances of his or her life. Christians acquire virtue and develop character by understanding and interpreting these choices through the Christian story. What makes for good and true choices is the fact that they arise from a good and true narrative, as opposed to a universal rule, and for Christians that narrative is the Christian story.

Narrative, then, shapes character, which makes a person who he or she is; virtues are the skills, habits, and capacities that arise from character. Character is "our ability to make our actions our own—that is to claim them as crucial to our history—even those we regret, turns out to be a necessary condition for having a coherent sense of self—that is, our character. But such a coherence requires a narrative that gives us the skill to see that our freedom is as much a gift as it is something we do."[24]

Virtues do not "add up" to character, but rather character is the foundation for virtue—as a person accepts their choices from the past and integrates them into the world of the narrative they develop capacities, habits, and ways of seeing reality that are consistent with that narrative. Virtues are the skills and capacities that are acquired through the formation of the self, so that "virtues finally depend on our character for direction, not vice versa."[25] Virtue is a "second nature," a power of self-possession acquired through choice. "The only way to be human is to be habitual—which is to say, historical. Indeed the virtues are the prerequisites illuminating our history as our destiny rather than our fate. Virtue provides the power of self-possession necessary to avoid the parameters of life that others would impose."[26]

According to Hauerwas, the virtuous person does not acquire all the moral virtues, as Aristotle and Aquinas thought; rather particular virtues arise out of particular narratives in relation to life's contingencies. Hauerwas views virtue as context-dependent because the particular values and historical circumstance that give shape to a

---

[24] Hauerwas, *A Community of Character*, 147.
[25] Ibid., 143.
[26] Ibid., 125.

human community and tradition will influence the kind of people that are formed in that context. Just as universal moral rules do not exist independent from a narrative, there is no universal set of virtues that applies to all persons. The diversity of virtue within various communities and traditions, and the variety of definitions of the same virtue, points to the radical historical character of human life: "For the meanings of courage and temperance vary depending on what society considers paradigmatic examples of temperance or courage. The diversity of meaning and kinds of virtues does not imply, however, that all attempts to depict the virtues are arbitrary. For rather than revealing there is no human nature, it reveals the historical nature of our human existence, which requires virtues for the moral life of the individual and society."[27]

Hauerwas critiques Aristotle and Aquinas's virtue ethic for failing to recognize that virtue is "narrative-dependent" and historically and socially conditioned. Their argument about the unity of virtue is also based on a faulty circular argument: the possession and practice of virtue resides in the unity of all virtues, and yet the acquisition and practice of the moral virtues depend on prudence, which is itself a moral virtue that cannot exist without the other virtues. Hauerwas claims to break this circular impasse by arguing for a concept of the unity of the self, rather than a unity of virtue wherein the moral person acquires all the virtues. Rather a person achieves a "unity of the self" through the development of character, which in turn is the basis of virtue. Each person, then, will not cultivate every virtue for the unity of the self does not reside in the unity of all the virtues; rather the "unity of the self is therefore more like the unity that is exhibited in a good novel. . . . Substantive narratives that promise to me a way to make my self my own require me to grow into the narrative by constantly challenging my past achievements."[28] It is the narrative that provides the unifying ground for the acquisition and development of character—how a person responds to life's joys and tragedies. Particular virtues will develop from particular historical and social circumstances in relation to a narrative interpretation of those particular experiences.

Häring and Hauerwas share the modern notion that persons are historical, social creatures, though Hauerwas integrates this idea into

---

[27] Hauerwas, *A Community of Character*, 123.
[28] Ibid., 144.

his virtue theory in ways that Häring does not. Häring advances a historical understanding of the human person, though the historical and social dimensions of his personalist philosophy are not integrated into his virtue theory. Even though Häring defines virtue in biblical and theological terms, it remains largely in the realm of the non-historical scholastic framework. In his early attempts to resolve the tension between the moral and theological virtues he was concerned to demonstrate how both kinds of virtue are divine gifts enabling religious and moral response to God and neighbor. Hauerwas places greater emphasis on the contingent quality of response; Häring describes response in nearly universal terms as though historical and social conditions do not qualify the capacity for and variety of human responses.

A second idea that is prominent in Hauerwas' virtue theory, but is largely absent from Häring's work, is the role of tragedy, pain and suffering in the formation of character and virtue. Hauerwas finds important parallels between the Greek idea that virtue emerges through adversity, risk, and tragedy and the Christian understanding of suffering as a school for virtue. In the Christian story, virtue can be seen from the point of view of heroic action.[29] The virtuous person is made in and through adversity—from personal tragedy as well as resistance to violence—and both require the Christian virtues of patience and peacemaking. Hauerwas highlights the contingent, tragic and complex dynamics of human existence and the ways in which the self is formed in and through a myriad of choices. A person understands and reconciles past choices as they come to understand the Christian narrative; likewise future choices in the face of tragedy and suffering are shaped by Christian interpretations of endurance. The Christian narrative transforms suffering and endurance from "fate into calling."[30]

Häring's formulation of growth and conversion is more optimistic in many respects than Hauerwas's, not because of what persons can achieve, but because of the power of grace to transform the person away from sin toward life in Christ. Häring's sacramental-moral theology would be strengthened by particular attention to the ways in which adversity, tragedy, and suffering constrain and limit human life and challenge a person's capacities to hear and respond to God's

[29] *Christians Among the Virtues*, 32.
[30] Ibid., 118ff.

initiative. And, as noted in previous chapters, by highlighting the positive side of the life of faith in terms of virtue, growth, and perfection, he does not consider fully how sin and vice can become rooted in the dispositions, thoughts, emotions, as well as the words and acts, of many Christians. A theology of virtue seems to require a corresponding theory of vice.

Both Häring and Hauerwas attempt to enlarge the Christian moral life beyond a rule-based set of propositions that determine behavior to a richer and deeper anthropological claim about the kind of human persons Christians become by *virtue*. Persons who are initiated and participate in the Christian community become people of Christian virtue—something is different, then, about whom people *are,* not just what they *do.* The central difference between Häring and Hauerwas is their explanation regarding how virtue develops in relationship to worship: a sacramental versus a linguistic and narrative virtue ethic.

Häring rejects the manualists' understanding of virtue because it is too anthropological. Virtue makes little sense in Christian terms, he claims, unless it is integrated with "true adoration of God." Virtue, for Häring, must be understood theologically—it has Christological, pneumatological, sacramental, and ecclesial dimensions. Because the theological virtues form the inner capacity for dialogue, response and imitation, they orient the person in true and right relationship to God as a worshipper. Häring develops a theological understanding of virtue in relationship to sacramental grace, giving virtue a biblical and theological foundation.

Hauerwas' virtue theory makes important anthropological claims ("for the subject of virtue can be none other than the self, which has its being only as an agent with particular gifts, experiences, and history"); the theological claims, however are either implicit or absent.[31] Hauerwas has not sufficiently answered Häring's question: How, and in what ways, is God related to virtue? Hauerwas's theological position rests on the claim that the narrative—the story of God's relationship to the Israelites and to the early Christians as known through Jesus—forms and shapes character. Persons grasp and understand this story primarily in linguistic terms, and they understand their choices, history, and future within a narrative context. He states: "to be a person of virtue involves acquiring the

---

[31] Hauerwas, *A Community of Character*, 116.

linguistic, emotional, rational skills that give us the strength to make our decisions and our life our own. The individual virtues are specific skills required to live faithful to a tradition's understanding of the moral project in which its adherents participate."[32] While his position, in many ways, is consistent with the central claims of the Protestant tradition regarding the centrality of the Word, he has not fully considered how grace and sacrament are also determinative of Christian virtue.

Hauerwas claims that "nature and grace," "acquired and infused grace," and "incarnation" are abstract concepts that can be understood only from within the narrative, but not as general concepts external to the story.[33] For instance, he interprets nature and grace, and acquired and infused grace, as a way of explaining the reality of possessing two selves and living in a world of "divided narratives," represented by the narratives of the Church and the world. Christians choose to be determined by the Christian narrative, not the false narrative of the world.[34] He acknowledges that virtue is "responsive to a love relation with God in Christ" and that the idea of infusion points to the source and ongoing formation of character in grace, but he is more concerned with understanding the nature of that transformed character, than with how the action of grace occurs.[35] He states, "To be sanctified is to have one's character formed in a definite kind of way. What distinguishes Christian sanctification from the ways men's lives are generally shaped and formed is not the process of formation itself but the basis and consequent shape of that formation."[36] In contrast, this is precisely the point Häring seeks to make about the relationship between the sacraments and the moral life: it is the process of Christian formation in and through the sacraments that is distinctively Christian not just the outcome.

Hauerwas has not written extensively on the topic of virtue and worship, but two essays given some indication of how his narrative

---

[32] Ibid., 115. Hauerwas's primary theological claims about God are narrative: "There is no more fundamental way to talk of God than in a story." See *The Peaceable Kingdom*, 25ff.

[33] Thomas O'Meara notes that Hauerwas uses Aquinas's virtue theory without any reference to his theology of nature and grace. "How this happens, the secondary role of charity, and the real milieu of a supernatural order, life and telos, are not explained; Christian life, character, and virtues lack a real ground or, at least, the source and ground of Aquinas." "Virtues in the Theological of Thomas Aquinas," *Theological Studies* 58/2 (June 1997) 256. Hauerwas offers a brief interpretation of grace in *The Peaceable Kingdom*, 27.

[34] Hauerwas, *Christians Among the Virtues*, 126–27.

[35] See Ibid., 68–69.

[36] Hauerwas, *Character and the Christian Life*, 194–95.

and virtue ethic relate to worship. He makes two important claims about worship. First, Hauerwas stresses the public and political dimension of both virtue and worship, challenging any notion that these are private or individual matters. Christians come to know God through the Christian narrative, which allows them to discern knowledge of the true God as distinct from the false gods of the world. Liturgy is the way in which the Church does its "social work" insofar as it proclaims that the Church is distinct from the world. Baptism and Eucharist are "the essential truths of our politics," according to Hauerwas; they are not only "religious things" but also claims about who Christians are in the world. Likewise virtue is not a private ethic, but rather it is public and political. Formation in Christian virtue is a political act by the Church, so worship is political because communities of virtue are political and public. Worship is the way "the Church has both evangelized and gone about its moral formation" in history. Worship is not intended to directly cause moral behavior; rather worship places all human life before God and teaches Christians to praise the true God.

A second point raised by Hauerwas is the narrative dimensions of worship and the sacraments. The liturgy and sacraments are understood in narrative terms because they "enact the story of Jesus and form a community in his image." Worship shapes character because the Christian narrative is proclaimed and enacted in the sacraments allowing the community to enter the story and be shaped by it. Again, the emphasis on narrative stresses a linguistic and cognitive approach to worship, with less emphasis on the experiential and symbolic. The symbolic and aesthetic dimension of worship and sacraments are not fully explained and developed in Hauerwas' narrative approach.

Häring's sacrament-moral theology could certainly incorporate Hauerwas' claims about the importance of narrative, since the dialogue that takes place in the sacraments is based on the Christian narrative as expressed in salvation history. In addition, the Word is a central category in Häring's anthropology and Christology; the sacraments are a primary way in which persons listen to the Word spoken by God and respond to it. But Häring's Word theology is not limited to the linguistic and the narrative, but embraces the entire person in terms of body, affect, reason, and spirit. Sacraments are the primary context for divine-human encounter because they are dialogical, cultal, and social. They shape virtue and character because they bestow a gift and call forth a response through both the theological and moral virtues. Sacramental grace—understood as God's divine life and gift—remains the center of his virtue theory.

* * * *

Toward the end of his life, Bernard Häring returned to his hometown, Gars, Germany, to resume pastoral work in a local parish. His vocation as a missionary had been averted when his religious superiors called him from pastoral duties to academic work in moral theology. He retained his vocation as a missionary, however, by becoming, in the words of Charles Curran, "a missionary for renewal." His contributions to the renewal of the Church and to moral theology called for by the Second Vatican Council are numerous. I have argued that a significant and under-appreciated contribution is the way he sets forth the relationship between worship and morality. In focusing on this one issue, however, I have not attended to other important ideas in his work, such as the role of conscience and freedom in the moral life, and the role of the Eucharist in his sacramental theology. In other words, for those interested in Häring, there is certainly more to be uncovered than is offered here. In further consideration of his contributions to moral theology and to the dialogue between liturgy and ethics today, two aspects of Häring's approach to moral theology are especially significant: a pastoral impetus and focus as well as a systematic and comprehensive response.

The question Häring brought from his pastoral work to moral theology—How can the Christian respond to the love of God through Christ?—is worked out in what I have called his sacramental-moral theology. Like the liturgical reformers of his time, Häring sought to make the insights of his discipline accessible to lay persons as well as priests, in order that moral theology might aid Christians in understanding and living the Christian life. The manualists too had a pastoral concern, though it was too narrowly defined for Häring, focusing "almost exclusively toward the sacrament of penance, a species of 'confessional moral,' whose principal ideal is the guidance of the confessor in the correct exercise of his role as judge in the tribunal of penance." His focus is primarily on the positive dimensions of religious, spiritual and moral formation through the sacraments, in contrast to the manualists whose focus is almost exclusively on what hinders Christian formation—of course attention to both are required for both good pastoral work. Häring envisions a broader understanding of the minister's role beyond the confessional in shaping and forming the "'school of life' whose purpose is the formation of all spiritual domains in the mind and heart of Christ."[37]

Jean Porter, in the introduction to *The Recovery of Virtue: The Relevance of Aquinas for Christian Ethics*, argues that contemporary Christian ethics is a fragmented discipline insofar as "today's Christian ethicists have seized on fragments of what was once a unified moral tradition as the basis for their interpretations of Christian ethics."[38] Porter's solution is to retrieve Aquinas' theory of the moral good as one account of a unified moral theory, an account to which today's ethicists, including Häring, are indebted, despite their apparent theoretical divisions. Certainly Häring would not be a source for contemporary ethicists like Porter who want to define a philosophically and methodologically coherent foundation for morality; he chooses the experiential and relational over the metaphysical, and the descriptive and explanatory over the philosophical. In this sense Häring's is a pastoral moral theology rather than a philosophical defense for the reasonableness of the Christian way of life.

Nonetheless Häring does offer a systematic approach to moral theology that is comprehensive and thematically-integrated in contrast to those who would, as Porter points out, take up only one aspect of the moral life. Häring's approach calls us to consider the ways in which moral theology is premised on dogmatic theology, how a moral system accounts for both personal and social dimensions of the moral life, and finally how moral persons and communities are formed through prayer, worship, and the sacraments. In pursuing the relationship between worship and morality, much could be gained by a more systematic treatment of the topics by both liturgists and ethicists. Bernard Häring's sacramental-moral theology is certainly one system to be considered in the conversation.

---

[37] *LC* 1:468.
[38] Porter, 15.

Bibliography

I. The Works of Bernard Häring (Complete list of books in English.)

Häring, Bernard. *Das Heilige und das Gute: Religion und Sittlichkeit in ihrem gegenseitigen Bezug.* München/Freiburg: E. Wewel Verlag, 1950.

_____. *The Sociology of the Family.* Cork, Ireland: Mercier Press, 1959.

_____. *The Law of Christ.* 3 vols. Trans. E. G. Kaiser. Westminster, Md.: Newman Press, 1961, 1963, 1966.

_____. *Le sacre' et le bien.* Trans. Robert Givord. Paris: Editions Fleurus, 1963.

_____. *The Johannine Council: Witness to Unity.* Trans. Sr. M. Lucidia Häring. Dublin: Gill and Son, 1963.

_____. *Christian Renewal in a Changing World.* Trans. Sr. M. Lucidia Häring. Rev. ed. New York: Desclée, 1964.

_____. *Theology in Transition.* Trans. Ed. O'Brien. New York: Herder and Herder, 1965.

_____. *Marriage in the Modern World.* Westminster, Md.: Newman Press, 1965.

_____. *Christian Renewal in a Changing World.* Trans. Sr. M. Lucidia Häring. New York: Desclée de Brouwer, 1965.

_____. *A Sacramental Spirituality.* Trans. R. A. Wilson. New York: Sheed & Ward, 1965.

_____. *The New Covenant.* London: Burns & Oates, 1965.

_____. *The Liberty of the Children of God.* Trans. Patrick O'Shaughnessy. Staten Island, N.Y.: Alba House, 1966.

_____. *Road to Renewal: Perspectives on Vatican II.* Staten Island, N.Y.: Alba House, 1966.

_____. *This Time of Salvation.* Trans. Arlene Swidler. New York: Herder and Herder, 1966.

_____. *Toward a Christian Moral Theology.* 2 vols., Notre Dame, Ind.: Notre Dame University Press, 1966.

_____. *Confession to Happiness.* Derby, N.J.: St. Paul Publications, 1966.

_____. *The Nobility of Marriage.* Chawton, Alton: Redemptorist Publications, 1966.

_____. *Christian Maturity.* Trans. Arlene Swidler. New York: Herder and Herder, 1967.

_____. *Shalom: Peace. The Sacrament of Reconciliation.* New York: Farrar, Strauss and Giroux, 1967.

_____. *Bernard Häring Replies.* Staten Island, N.Y.: Alba House, 1967.

_____. *Acting on the World.* New York: Farrar, Straus and Giroux, 1968.

_____. *The Christian Existentilist: The Theology of Self-Fulfillment in Modern Society.* New York: New York University Press, 1968.

_____. *New Horizons of the Church in the World.* Notre Dame, Ind.: Ave Maria Press, 1968.

_____. *What Does Christ Want?* Staten Island, N.Y.: Alba House, 1968.

_____. *New Horizons for the Church in the Modern World: A Commentary on Vatican II's Pastoral Constitution on the Church in the Modern World.* Notre Dame, Ind.: Ave Marie Press, 1968.

_____. *Acting on the World.* Tenbury Wells, Worcs. England: Fowler Wright Books, 1969.

_____. *Celebrating Joy.* New York: Herder and Herder, 1970.

_____. *Love Is the Answer.* Trans. D. White. Denville: Dimension Books, 1970.

_____. *Married Love: A Modern Christian View of Marriage and Family Life.* Chicago: Argus Communications, 1970.

_____. *A Theology of Protest.* New York: Farrar, Giroux & Strauss, 1970.

_____. *Road to Relevance: Present and Future Trends in Catholic Moral Teaching.* Trans. Hilda Graef. Staten Island: Alba House, 1970.

_____. *The Church on the Move.* Staten Island: Alba House, 1970.

_____. *Morality Is for Persons: The Ethics of Christian Personalism.* New York: Farrar, Straus and Giroux, 1971.

_____. *Hope Is the Remedy.* New York: Doubleday, 1972.

_____. *Medical Ethics.* Notre Dame, Ind.: Fides, 1973.

_____. *Faith and Morality in a Secular Age.* Garden City, N.Y.: Doubleday, 1973.

_____. *Evangelization Today.* Notre Dame, Ind.: Fides, 1974.

_____. *Sin in the Secular Age.* Garden City, N.Y.: Doubleday, 1974.

_____. *Prayer: Integration of Faith and Life.* Slough, United Kingdom: St. Paul Publications, 1974.

_____. *Manipulation: Ethical Boundaries of Medical, Behavioral, and Genetic Manipulation.* Slough, United Kingdom: St. Paul Publications, 1975.

_____. *Embattled Witness: Memories of a Time of War.* New York: Seabury Press, 1976.

_____. *Ethics of Manipulation.* New York: Seabury Press, 1976.

_____. *The Sacraments and Your Everyday life: A Vision in Depth of Sacramentality and Its Impact on Moral Life.* Slough, United Kingdom: St. Paul Publications, 1976.

_____. *The Beatitudes: Their Personal and Social Implications.* Slough, United Kingdom: St. Paul Publications, 1976.

_____. *The Eucharist and Our Everday Life.* Slough, United Kingdom: St.Paul Publications, 1978.

_____. *Free and Faithful in Christ.* 3 vols. New York: Seabury Press, 1978, 1979; Crossroad Publishing Co., 1981.

_____. *Discovering God's Mercy: Confession Helps for Today's Catholic*. Liguori, Mo.: Liguori, 1980.

_____. *Called to Holiness*. Slough, United Kingdom: St. Paul Publications, 1982.

_____. *The Healing Mission of the Church in the Coming Decades*. Washington, D.C.: Center for Applied Research in the Apostolate, 1982.

_____. *Christian Maturity*. Slough, United Kingdom: St. Paul Publications, 1983.

_____. *Dare to Be Christian: Developing a Social Conscience*. Liguori, Mo.: Liguori Publications, 1983.

_____. *Timely and Untimely Virtues*. Slough, United Kingdom: St. Paul Publications, 1983.

_____. *Healing and Revealing: Wounded Healers Sharing Christ's Mission*. Slough, United Kingdom: St. Paul Publications, 1984.

_____. *The Healing Power of Peace and Nonviolence*. Slough, United Kingdom: St. Paul Publications, 1986.

_____. *The Song of the Servant*. Slough, United Kingdom: St. Paul Publications, 1988.

_____. *My Witness for the Church*. Intro. and trans. Leonard Swidler. Mahwah, N.J.: Paulist Press, 1992.

II. Articles in Books and Periodicals by Bernard Häring

Häring, Bernard. "Social Importance of the Sacraments." *Lumen Vitae* 13 (July–September 1958) 410–17.

_____. "Liturgical Piety and Christian Perfection." *Worship* 34 (October 1960) 523–35.

_____. "The Christian Message and Apologetics and the Modern Mentality." *Lumen Vitae* 16 (September 1961) 425–34.

_____. "A Closer Look at the Breviary Obligation." *Worship* 37 (April 1963) 274–85.

_____. "Christian Morality as a Mirror Image of the Mystery of the Church." *Catholic Theological Society of America Proceedings* (June 1963) 3–24.

_____. "The Church: Not a Kind of Monopoly." *The Critic* 22/3 (January 1964) 9–12.

_____. "A Modern Approach to the Ascetical Life." *Worship* 39 (December 1965) 635–48.

_____. "Normative Value of the Sermon on the Mount." *Catholic Biblical Quarterly* 29/3 (July 1967) 375–58.

_____. "Dynamism and Continuity in a Personalistic Approach to Natural Law." In *Norm and Context in Christian Ethics*. Ed. Gene H. Outka and Paul Ramsey, 199–218. New York: Scribner's, 1968.

_____. "The Encyclical Crisis." *Commonweal* 88 (September 6, 1968) 588–94.

_____. "Freedom and Authority in the Catholic Church." *Dialogue* 7 (Spring 1968) 96–102.

_____. "Morality: Underlying and Unchanging Principles." In *Dynamic in Christian Thought.* Ed. J. Papin, 125–51. Villanova, Penn.: Villanova University Press, 1970.

_____. "A Theological Evaluation." In *The Morality of Abortion.* Ed. J. T. Noonan, 123–45. Cambridge, Mass.: Harvard University Press, 1970.

_____. "Pastoral Work among the Divorced and Invalidly Married." In *The Future of Marriage as Institution.* Ed. F. Böckle, 123–30. New York: Herder and Herder, 1970.

_____. "Man in Quest of Liberation in Community." In *Human Rights and the Liberation of Man in the Americas.* Ed. L. Colonnese, 247–58. Notre Dame, Ind.: University of Notre Dame Press, 1970.

_____. "Some Theological Reflections about the Population Problem." In *Population Problems and Catholic Responsibility.* Ed. L. Janssen, 156–63. 1975.

_____. "New Dimensions of Responsible Parenthood." *Theological Studies* 37 (March 1976) 120–32.

_____. "In Libertatem Vocai Estis." *Studia Moralia* 15 (1977) 13–30.

_____. "A Distrust That Wounds." *The Tablet* 247 (23 October 1993) 1378–79.

III. Secondary Works on Bernard Häring

Boelaars, Henri, and Real Temblay, eds. "Libertatem Vocati Estis: Miscellanea Bernard Häring." *Studia Moralis* 15 (1977) 13–30.

Bourdeau, F., and A. Danet. *An Introduction to the Law of Christ.* Cork, Ireland: Mercier Press, 1966.

Cahalan, Kathleen A. "The Sacramental-Moral Theology of Bernard Häring: A Study of the Virtue of Religion." Ph.D. diss., University of Chicago, 1998.

Clark, Michael. "The Uses of Sacred Scripture in the Moral Theology of Bernard Häring, C.Ss.R." S.T.D. diss., Gregorian University, 1979.

Corbett, T. Mary. "The Concept of Conscience in the Writings of Bernard Häring." Ph.D. diss., New York University, 1978.

Curran, Charles. "Härring reflects on ministry in *Priesthood Imperiled.*" *National Catholic Reporter.* November 8, 1996.

Farrell, Dermot. "The Dogmatic Foundations of Bernard Häring's Thought on Christian Morality as a Sacramental Way of Life." Th.D. diss., Gregorian University, 1988.

Gustafson, James M. Review of *Faith and Morality in a Secular Age*, by B. Häring. In *Commonweal* 100 (April 12, 1974) 140–41.

Hamel, Ronald. "Methodological and Substantive Development in Catholic Medical Ethics: A Critical Study of the Work of Bernard Häring." Ph.D. diss., Fordham University, 1982.

MacEoin, Gary. "Härring, having met death, does not fear CDF." *National Catholic Reporter,* June 16, 1989.

O'Keefe, Mark James. "An Analysis and Critique of the Social Aspects of Sin and Conversion in the Moral Theology of Bernard Häring." S.T.D. diss., Catholic University of America, 1987.

Omoregbe, Joseph. "Evolution in Bernard Häring's Ethical Thinking." *Louvain Studies* 7 (1978) 45–54.

Piraro, Don Anthony. "A Program for Spiritual Growth for Married Couples, Utilizing Their Lived Experience and the Biblical Image of Marriage as Covenant of Conjugal Love." D.Min. diss., Catholic University of America, 1985.

Schurr, Viktor. *Bernard Häring: Die Erneuerung der Moraltheologie.* Salzburg: Otto Müller Verlag, 1970.

St. Wesolowsky, O. "Bernard Häring." In *Modern Theologians: Christians and Jews.* Ed. T. E. Bird, 64–83. London: Notre Dame Press, 1967.

Zosso, Terisse. "A Dynamic and Ego Developmental Christian Value System: A Comparative Analysis of the Ethics of the Law of the Spirit in Haering's Ego Development in Loevinger." Ph.D. diss., Marquette University, 1976.

IV. General Works

Adam, Karl. *Christ Our Brother.* London: Sheed and Ward, 1931.

_____. *The Spirit of Catholicism.* Garden City, N.Y.: Doubleday, 1935.

Alles, Gregory D. *Rudolf Otto: Autobiographical and Social Essays.* New York: Mouton de Gruyter, 1996.

Augustine. *The City of God.* New York: Penguin Books, 1984.

Aquinas, St. Thomas. *Summa Theologicai.* Trans. Fathers of the English Dominican Province. New York: Benziger Brothers, Inc., 1947.

Avila, R. *Worship and Politics.* Maryknoll, N.Y.: Orbis Books, 1981.

Boney, William Jerry, and Lawrence E. Molumby, eds. *The New Day: Catholic Theologians of the Renewal.* Richmond: John Knox Press, 1968.

Boyle, Leonard, O.P. "The Setting of the Summa Theologiae of St. Thomas." *Etienne Gilson Lecture Series 5.* Toronto: Pontifical Institute of Medieval Studies, 1982.

Brown, Raymond E. *The Gospel According to John, I–XII.* Garden City, N.Y.: Doubleday, 1966.

_____. *An Introduction to New Testament Christology.* New York: Paulist Press, 1994.

Buber, Martin. *I and Thou.* Trans. Walter Kaufmann. New York: Charles Scribners' Sons, 1970.

Burghardt, Walter. "A Theologian's Challenge to Liturgy." *Theological Studies* 35 (1974) 233–48.

Collins, James. "Scheler's Transition from Catholicism to Pantheism." In *Philosophical Studies in Honor of the Very Reverend Ignatius Smith, O.P.* Ed. John K. Ryan. Westminster, Md.: The Newman Press, 1952, 179–207.

Congar Yves M.-J., O.P. *A History of Theology.* Garden City, N.Y.: Doubleday, 1968.

Connell, Francis J. *Outlines of Moral Theology.* Milwaukee: Bruce Publishing, 1953.

Crossin, John W. *What Are They Saying about Virtue?* Mahwah, N.J.: Paulist Press, 1985.

Curran, Charles E. *Christian Morality Today: The Renewal of Moral Theology.* Notre Dame, Ind.: Fides, 1966.

Curran, Charles E., ed. *Absolutes in Moral Theology?* Washington: Corpus Books, 1968.

_____. *A New Look at Christian Morality.* Notre Dame, Ind.: Fides, 1968.

_____. *Contemporary Problems in Moral Theology.* Notre Dame, Ind.: Fides, 1970.

_____. *Catholic Moral Theology in Dialogue.* Notre Dame, Ind.: Fides, 1972.

_____. *New Perspectives in Moral Theology.* Notre Dame, Ind.: Fides, 1974.

_____. *Ongoing Revision in Moral Theology.* Notre Dame, Ind.: Fides, 1975.

_____. *Themes in Fundamental Moral Theology.* Notre Dame, Ind.: University of Notre Dame Press, 1977.

_____. *Transition and Tradition in Moral Theology.* Notre Dame, Ind.: University of Notre Dame Press, 1979.

_____. *American Catholic Social Ethics: Twentieth Century Approaches.* Notre Dame, Ind.: University of Notre Dame Press, 1982.

_____. *Critical Concerns in Moral Theology.* Notre Dame, Ind.: University of Notre Dame Press, 1984.

_____. "Horizons on Fundamental Moral Theology." *Horizons* 10/1 (1983) 86–110.

_____. *Critical Concerns in Moral Theology.* Notre Dame, Ind.: University of Notre Dame Press, 1984.

_____. *Directions in Fundamental Moral Theology.* Notre Dame, Ind.: University of Notre Dame Press, 1985.

_____. *Faithful Dissent.* Kansas City, Mo.: Sheed & Ward, 1986.

Curran, Charles E., and Richard A. McCormick, s.j., eds. *Readings in Moral Theology No. 1: Moral Norms and Catholic Tradition.* New York: Paulist Press, 1979.

_____. *Readings in Moral Theology No. 3: The Magisterium and Morality.* Ramsey, N.J.: Paulist Press, 1982.

_____. *Readings in Moral Theology No. 4: The Use of Scripture in Moral Theology.* Ramsey, N.J.: Paulist Press, 1984.

_____. *Readings in Moral Theology No. 6: Dissent in the Church.* New York: Paulist Press, 1988.

Dailey, R. "New Approaches to Moral Theology." In *Current Trends in Theology.* Ed. D. Wolf and J. Schall, 162–89. Garden City, N.Y.: Image Books, 1966.

Dallen, James. *The Reconciling Community: The Rite of Penance.* Collegeville: The Liturgical Press, 1991.

Davis, Henry, s.j. *Moral and Pastoral Theology*, 4 vols. London: Sheed & Ward, 1935.

Deeken, Alfons. *Process and Permanence in Ethics: Max Scheler's Moral Philosophy.* Paramus, N.J.: Paulist Press, 1974.

Dru, Alexander. *The Church in the Nineteenth Century: Germany 1800–1918.* London: Burns & Oates, 1963.

Dulles, Avery. *Models of the Church.* Garden City, N.Y.: Doubleday and Co., 1974.

Dunn, James P. *Unity and Diversity in the New Testament.* Philadelphia: Westminster Press, 1977.

Dupré, Louis. "Spiritual Life in a Secular Age." *Daedalus* (Winter, 1982) 21–31.

Egan, John J. "Liturgy and Justice: An Unfinished Agenda." *Origins*, 13/15 (September 22, 1983).

Ellard, Gerald. "The Liturgical Movement in Catholic Circles." *Religion in Life* 18 (Summer 1948) 370–371.

Everett, William W. "Liturgy and Ethics: A Response to Saliers and Ramsey." *Journal of Religious Ethics* 7 (1979) 203–14.

Farley, Margaret A. "Beyond the Formal Principle: A Reply to Ramsey and Saliers." *Journal of Religious Ethics* 7 (1979) 191–202.

Fehr, W. *The Birth of the Catholic Tübingen School: The Dogmatics of John Sebastian Drey.* Chico, Calif.: AAR Scholars Press, 1981.

Ford, John C., and Gerald Kelly. *Contemporary Moral Theology*, 2 vols. Westminster, Md.: The Newman Press, 1958.

Franklin, Ralph William. "Guéranger: A View on the Centenary of His Death." *Worship* 49 (June–July 1975) 318–28.

_____. "Guéranger and Pastoral Liturgy." *Worship* 50 (March 1976) 146–62.

_____. "Guéranger and Variety in Unity." *Worship* 51 (September 1977) 378–99.

_____. "Nineteenth Century Liturgical Movement." *Worship* 53 (January 1979) 12–39.

_____. "Response: Humanism and Transcendence in the Nineteenth Century Liturgical Movement." *Worship* 59 (July 1985) 429–41.

_____. "Johann Adam Möhler and Worship in Totalitarian Society." *Worship* 67 (January 1993) 2–17.

Franklin, Ralph William, and Robert L. Speath. *Virgil Michel: American Catholic.* Collegeville: The Liturgical Press, 1988.

Frings, Manfred S. *Max Scheler: A Concise Introduction into the World of a Great Thinker.* Pittsburgh, Penn.: Duquesne University Press, 1965.

Fuchs, Joseph. *General Moral Theology.* Rome: Gregorian University, 1963.

_____. *Human Values and Christian Morality.* Dublin: Gill and Macmillan, 1967.

Gallagher, John A. *Time Past, Time Future: An Historical Study of Catholic Moral Theology.* Mahwah, N.J.: Paulist Press, 1990.

Gallagher, Raphael. "The Manual System of Moral Theology Since the Death of Alphonsus." *Irish Theological Quarterly* 52 (1985) 1–16.

_____. "Fundamental Moral Theology 1975–1979." *Studia Moralia* 18 (1980) 147–92.

Garrigou-Lagrange, R. *The Three Ages of the Interior Life: Prelude to Eternal Life*, 2 vols. St. Louis: B. Herder Book Co., 1947.

Gilson, Étienne. *Moral Values and the Moral Life.* St. Louis: B. Herder Book Co., 1931.

_____. *The Christian Philosophy of St. Thomas Aquinas.* Notre Dame, Ind.: University of Notre Dame Press, 1956.

Gray, D. "Liturgy and Morality." *Worship* 39 (1965) 28–35.

Green, Ronald M. "Religious Ritual: A Kantian Perspective." *Journal of Religious Ethics* 7 (1979) 229–38.

Guardini, Romano. *The Spirit of the Liturgy.* New York: Sheed and Ward, 1935.

_____. *Sacred Signs.* London: Sheed and Ward, 1937.

_____. *The Virtues: On Forms of Moral Life.* Chicago: Henry Regnery Co., 1963.

Guibert, Joseph de. *The Theology of the Spiritual Life.* New York: Sheed and Ward, 1953.

Gula, Richard M. *What Are They Saying About Moral Norms?* Mahwah, N.J.: Paulist Press, 1982.

Gustafson, James M. *Protestant and Roman Catholic Ethics: Prospects for Rapprochement.* Chicago: University of Chicago Press, 1978.

_____. "Spiritual Life and Moral Life." *Theology Digest* 19 (1971) 296–307.

_____. "Faith and Morality in the Secular Age. *Commonweal* 100 (April 12, 1974) 140.

Harris, Horton. *The Tübingen School: A Historical and Theological Investigation of the School of F. C. Baur.* Grand Rapids, Mich.: Baker Book House, 1970.

Hauerwas, Stanley. *Character and the Christian Life: A Study in Theological Ethics,* 3d. ed. Trinity University Press, 1985.

_____. *Vision and Virtue: Essays in Christian Ethical Reflection.* Notre Dame, Ind.: Fides Publishers, Inc., 1974.

_____. *Truthfulness and Tragedy: Further Investigations in Christian Ethics.* Notre Dame, Ind.: University of Notre Dame Press, 1977.

_____. *A Community of Character: Toward a Constructive Christian Social Ethic.* Notre Dame, Ind.: University of Notre Dame Press, 1981.

_____. *The Peaceable Kingdom: A Primer in Christian Ethics.* Notre Dame, Ind.: University of Notre Dame Press, 1983.

Hauerwas, Stanley, and Charles Pinches. *Christians Among the Virtues: Theological Conversations with Ancient and Modern Ethics.* Notre Dame, Ind.: University of Notre Dame Press, 1997.

Hellwig, Monika. *The Eucharist and a Hungry World.* Mahwah, N.J.: Paulist Press, 1976.

_____. "New Understanding of the Sacraments." *Commonweal* 105 (June 16, 1978) 375–80.

Henry, A. M., o.p., ed. *The Virtues and States of Life.* Chicago, Fides, 1957.

Hildebrand, Dietrich von. *Christian Ethics.* New York: David McKay Co., 1953.

Hirscher, Johann M. *Die Christlichen Moral als Lehre von der Verwirklichung des gottlichen Reiches in der Menschheit.* Tübingen: 1835.

Hoose, Bernard. *Proportionalism: The American Debate and Its European Roots.* Washington, D.C.: Georgetown University Press, 1987.

Hughes, Kathleen, ed. *How Firm a Foundation: Voices of the Early Liturgical Movement.* Chicago: Liturgy Training Publications, 1990.

Husserl, Edmund. *Logical Investigations.* London, Routledge, and K. Paul, 1970.

_____. *Ideas.* London, G. Allen, and Unwin Ltd., 1931.

Jones, Frederick M., c.ss.r. *Alphonsus de Liguori: Selected Writings.* New York: Paulist Press, 1999.

Jonsen, Albert, *Responsibility in Modern Religious Ethics.* Washington, D.C.: Corpus Books, 1968.

Jonsen, Albert, and Stephen Toulmin. *The Abuse of Casuistry.* Berkeley, Calif.: University of California Press, 1988.

Jungmann, Josef. *Liturgical Worship.* New York: Frederick Pustet, 1941.

_____. *Liturgical Renewal in Retrospect and Prospect.* London: Burns & Oates, Challoner Books, 1965.

_____. *The Place of Christ in the Liturgy.* Staten Island, N.Y.: Alba House, 1965.

Kelly, G. "Notes on Moral Theology." *Theological Studies* 10 (March 1949) 70–77.

Koenker, Ernest B. *The Liturgical Renaissance in the Roman Catholic Church.* Chicago: University of Chicago Press, 1954.

_____. "Objectives and Achievements of the Liturgical Movement in the Roman Catholic Church since World War II." *Church History* 20 (June 1951) 10–20.

Krieg, Robert, c.s.c. *Karl Adam: Catholicism in German Culture.* Notre Dame, Ind.: University of Notre Dame Press, 1992.

_____. *Romano Guardini: Proclaiming the Sacred in the Modern World.* Chicago: Liturgy Training Publications, 1995.

LaCugna, Catherine Mowry. "Can Liturgy Ever Again Become a Source for Theology?" *Studia Liturgica* 19 (1989) 1–13.

Leeming, Bernard. *Principles of Sacramental Theology.* Westminster, Md.: Newman Press, 1956.

Lonergan, Bernard. *Grace and Freedom: Operative Grace in the Thought of St. Thomas Aquinas.* New York: Herder and Herder, 1971.

MacIntyre, Alasdair. *After Virtue*, 2nd. ed. Notre Dame, Ind.: University of Notre Dame Press, 1984.

_____. *Whose Justice? Which Rationality?* Notre Dame, Ind.: University of Notre Dame Press, 1988.

Macquarrie, John. *Three Issues in Ethics.* New York: Harper and Row, 1970.

Mahoney, John. *The Making of Moral Theology: A Study of the Roman Catholic Tradition.* Oxford: Clarendon Press, 1987.

_____. *Seeking the Spirit: Essays in Moral and Pastoral Theology.* New Jersey: Dimension Books, 1981.

Maritain, Jacques. *Prayer and Intelligence.* New York: Sheed and Ward, 1943.

_____. *Liturgy and Contemplation.* New York: P. J. Kenedy & Sons, 1960.

Maritain, Jacques, and Raissa. "Liturgy and Contemplation." *Spiritual Life* 5 (June 1959) 94–134.

May, William E. *The Unity of the Moral and Spiritual Life.* Chicago: Franciscan Herald Press, 1979.

McCool, Gerald A., s.j. *From Unity to Pluralism: The Internal Evolution of Thomism.* New York: Fordham University Press, 1989.

_____. *Catholic Theology in the Nineteenth Century: The Quest for a Unitary Method.* New York: Seabury Press, 1977.

_____. *Nineteenth Century Scholasticism.* New York: Fordham University Press, 1989.

_____. *The Neo-Thomists.* Milwaukee: Marquette University Press, 1994.

McCormick, Richard A., s.j. "The Moral Theology of Vatican II." In *The Future of Ethics and Moral Theology.* Ed. D. Brezine, s.j., and J. V. McGlynn. Chicago: Argus Communications, 1968.

_____. *Notes on Moral Theology: 1965–1980.* Lanham, Md.: University Press of America, Inc., 1981.

_____. *Notes on Moral Theology: 1981–1984.* Lanham, Md.: University Press of America, Inc., 1984.

_____. "Self-Assessment and Self-Indictment." *Religious Studies Review* 13 (1987) 35–37.

_____. "Moral Theology 1940–1989: An Overview." *Theological Studies* 50 (1989) 3–24.

_____. "Some Early Reactions to *Veritatis Splendor.*" *Theological Studies* 55 (1994) 481–506.

McDonagh, Enda. "Morality and Prayer." In *Creation, Christ and Culture.* Ed., Richard W. A. McKinney. Edinburgh: Clark, 1976.

_____. *Invitation and Response.* Dublin: Gill & Macmillan, 1972.

McHugh, John A., o.p., and Charles J. Callan, o.p. *Moral Theology: A Complete Course,* 2 vols. New York: Jos. F. Wagner, 1958.

Meilander, Gilbert. *The Theory and Practice of Virtue.* Notre Dame, Ind.: University of Notre Dame Press, 1984.

Möhler, Johann Adam. *Symbolism or Exposition of the Doctrinal Differences between Catholics and Protestants as Evidenced by their Symbolic Writings.* Trans. J. B. Robertson. New York: Crossroad, 1997.

Murnion, Philip J. "The Renewal of Moral Theology: Review and Prospect." *Dunwoodie Review* 3 (1963) 39–65.

Niebuhr, H. Richard. *The Responsible Self: An Essay in Christian Moral Philosophy.* New York: Harper and Row, 1963.

Noldin, H., s.j., and A. Schmitt, s.j., *Summa Theologiae Moralis,* 2 vols., 27th ed. (Oeniponte: Sumptibus et Typic Feliciani Rauch, 1940).

O'Connell, Timothy E. *Principles for a Catholic Morality.* Minneapolis: Winston Press, 1976.

O'Meara, Thomas. *Romantic Idealism and Roman Catholicism: Schelling and the Theologians.* Notre Dame, Ind.: University of Notre Dame Press, 1982.

_____. "The Origins of the Liturgical Movement and German Romanticism." *Worship* 59 (1985) 326–42.

_____. *Church and Culture: German Catholic Theology from 1860–1914.* Notre Dame, Ind.: University of Notre Dame Press, 1993.

Oppitz, Joseph. *Alphonsus Liguori: The Redeeming Love of Christ.* New York: New City Press, 1992.

Otto, Rudolf. *The Idea of the Holy.* London: Oxford University Press, 1923.

Pieper, Joseph. *Justice.* New York: Pantheon, 1955.

_____. *The Four Cardinal Virtues.* Notre Dame, Ind.: University of Notre Dame Press, 1965.

Pinckaers, Servais. "The Revival of Moral Theology." *Cross Currents* 7 (1957) 56–67.

Porter, Jean. "Desire for God: Ground of the Moral Life in Aquinas." *Theological Studies* 47 (1986) 48–68.

_____. *The Recovery of Virtue: The Relevance of Aquinas for Christian Ethics.* Louisville: Westminster/John Knox Press, 1990.

Power, David. "Unripe Grapes: The Critical Function of Liturgical Theology." *Worship* 52 (1978) 386–99.

Preuss, Arthur. *A Handbook of Moral Theology Based on the "Lehrbuch der Moraltheologie" of the Late Antony Koch,* 5 vols., 3d. ed. St. Louis: B. Herder, 1925.

Prümmer, Dominicus M. *Handbook of Moral Theology.* Cork, Ireland: Mercier Press, 1956.

Rahner, Karl. *Theological Investigations*, vol. I. Baltimore: Helicon Press, 1961.

_____. *Theological Investigations*, vol. IV. New York: Crossroad, 1982.

_____. *Theological Investigations,* vol. VI. London: Darton, Longman, & Todd, Ltd., 1969.

Ramsey, Paul. "Liturgy and Ethics." *Journal of Religious Ethics* 7 (1979) 139–72.

Regan, George M. *New Trends in Moral Theology: A Survey of Fundamental Moral Themes.* New York: Newman Press, 1971.

Rossi, Philip J., s.j. "Narrative, Worship and Ethics: Empowering Images for the Shape of Christian Moral Life." *Journal of Religious Ethics* 7 (1979) 239–49.

Rousseau, Dom Olivier, o.s.b. *The Progress of the Liturgy: An Historical Sketch.* Westminster, Md.: Newman Press, 1951.

Saliers, D. E. "Liturgy and Ethics: Some New Beginnings." *Journal of Religious Ethics* 7 (1979) 173–90.

Scheler, Max. *On the Eternal in Man.* Trans., Bernard Noble. London: SCM Press, 1960.

_____. *Formalism in Ethics and Non-Formal Ethics of Values.* Evanston, Ill.: Northwestern University Press, 1973.

Schillebeeckx, Edward, o.p. *Christ the Sacrament of the Encounter of God* (New York: Sheed and Ward, 1963.

Schoof, Mark. *A Survey of Catholic Theology, 1800–1970.* Paramus, N.J.: Paulist Press, 1970.

Schweiker, William. *Responsibility and Christian Ethics.* Cambridge: Cambridge University Press, 1995.

Searle, Mark, ed. *Liturgy and Social Justice.* Collegeville: The Liturgical Press, 1981.

Siker, Jeffrey S. *Scripture and Ethics: Twentieth Century Portraits.* New York: Oxford University Press, 1997.

Slater, Thomas, s.j. *A Manual of Moral Theology*, 2 vols., 3rd ed. New York: Benziger Bros., 1908.

Spohn, William C., s.j. *What Are They Saying About Scripture and Ethics?* Mahwah, N.J.: Paulist Press, 1984.

Stevens, Dom P. Gregory, o.s.b. "Current Trends in Moral Theology." *Catholic Educational Review* 58 (1960) 1–11.

Stevens, P. "Moral Theology and the Liturgy." *Yearbook of Liturgical Studies* 1 (1960) 65–122.

Tanquerey, Adolphe. *The Spiritual Life: A Treatise on Ascetical and Mystical Theology*, 2nd. rev. ed. Tournai, Belgium: Desclée, 1930.

Taylor, Charles. *Sources of the Self: The Making of Modern Identity.* Cambridge, Mass.: Harvard University Press, 1989.

Tillman, Fritz. *Die Idee der Nachfolge Christi,* vol. 2. *Handbuck der katcholisen Sittenlehre.* Düsseldorf: Druckund Verlag L. Schwann, 1934.

Tracy, David. *The Analogical Imagination.* New York: Crossroad, 1981.

Tugwell, Simon, O.P., ed. *Albert and Thomas: Selected Writings.* New York: Paulist Press, 1988.

Wolf, Donald J., and James V. Schall, eds. *Current Trends in Theology.* Garden City, N.Y.: Doubleday, 1965.

Yaffe, Martin D. "Liturgy and Ethics: Hermann Cohen and Franz Rosenweig on the Day of Atonement." *Journal of Religious Ethics* 7 (1979) 215–28.

Yearley, Lee H. "Recent Work on Virtue." *Religious Studies Review* 16/1 (January 1990) 1–9.

V. Liturgy and Ethics

Anderson, E. Byron, and Bruce T. Morrill, eds., *Liturgy and the Moral Self: Humanity at Full Stretch Before God.* Collegeville: The Liturgical Press, 1998.

Avila, Rafael. *Worship and Politics.* Maryknoll, N.Y.: Orbis Books, 1981.

Balasuriya, Tissa. *The Eucharist and Human Liberation.* Maryknoll, N.Y.: Orbis Books, 1979.

Boff, Leonardo. *Sacraments of Life, Life of the Sacraments.* Washington, D.C.: Pastoral Press, 1987.

Bouyer, Louis. *Liturgical Piety.* Notre Dame, Ind.: University of Notre Dame Press, 1955.

Bulloch, Jeffrey. "Forum: The Ethical Implications in Liturgy." *Worship* 59 (1985) 266–70.

DeMargerie, B. *The Sacraments and Social Progress.* Trans. M. Carroll. Chicago: Franciscan Herald Press, 1974.

Egan, John J. *Liturgy and Justice: An Unfinished Agenda.* Collegeville: The Liturgical Press, 1983.

Ellard, Gerald, S.J. *Christian Life and Worship.* Religion and Culture Series. Milwaukee: Bruce, 1940.

Everett, William W. "Liturgy and Ethics: A Response to Saliers and Ramsey." *Journal of Religious Ethics* 7 (1979) 203–14.

Farley, Margaret. "Beyond the Formal Principle: A Reply to Ramsey and Saliers." *Journal of Religious Ethics* 7 (1979) 191–202.

Gedraitis, Albert F. *Worship and Politics.* Toronto: Wedge Pub. Foundation, 1972.

Grassi, Joseph A. *Broken Bread and Broken Bones: The Lord's Supper and World Hunger.* Maryknoll, N.Y.: Orbis Books, 1985.

Gray, Donald. "Liturgy and Morality." *Worship* 39 (1965) 28–35.

Green, Ronald M. "Religious Ritual: A Kantian Perspective." *Journal of Religious Ethics* 7 (1979) 229–38.

Grosz, Edward M., ed. *Liturgy and Social Justice: Celebrating Rites—Proclaiming Rights.* Collegeville: The Liturgical Press, 1989.

Happel, Stephen. "Worship as a Grammar of Social Transformation." *CTSA Proceedings* 42 (1987) 60–87.

_____. "The 'Bent World': Sacrament as Orthopraxis." *Proceedings of the 25th Annual Convention CTSA Proceedings* 35 (1980) 88–101.

Hauerwas, Stanley. "The Liturgical Shape of the Christian Life: Teaching Christian Ethics as Worship," in *In Good Company: The Church as Polis.* Notre Dame, Ind.: Notre Dame Press, 1995.

Hellwig, Monika. *The Eucharist and a Hungry World.* Paulist Press, 1976.

Himes, Kenneth. "Eucharist and Justice: Assessing the Legacy of Virgil Michel." *Worship* 62 (May 1988) 201–24.

Hughes, Kathleen, R.S.C.J., and Mark R. Francis, C.S.V., eds. *Living No Longer for Ourselves: Liturgy and Justice in the Nineties.* Collegeville: The Liturgical Press, 1991.

Kadushin, Max. *Worship and Ethics: A Study in Rabbinic Judaism.* Evanston: Northwestern University Press, 1964.

Lane, D. "The Eucharist and Social Justice." In *Eucharist for a New World,* S. Swayne, ed., 55–68. Carlow: Liturgy Centre, 1982.

Mannon, M. Francis. "Liturgy and the Present Crisis of Culture." *Worship* 62 (March 1988) 98–123.

McDonagh, Edna. "Prayer and Politics." *The Furrow* 30 (1979) 543–54.

_____. "Morality and Prayer." In *Creation, Christ, and Culture: Studies in Honor of T. F. Torrance.* Ed. Richard McKinney. Edinburgh: Clark, 1976.

_____. "Morality and Spirituality." *Studia Moralia* 15 (1977) 121–37.

_____. "Liturgy: Expression or Source of Christian Ethics?" In *Remembering and Reforming: Toward a Constructive Christian Moral Theology.* Notre Dame, Ind.: University of Notre Dame.

Meyer, Hans Bernhard. "The Social Significance of the Liturgy." *Concilium* 2 (1974) 34–50.

Miller, Donald E. "Worship and Moral Reflection: A Phenomenological Analysis." *Anglican Theological Review* LXII (October 1980) 307–20.

Mosier, John. "A Promise of Plenty: The Eucharist as Social Critique." *Downside Review* 91/5 (October 1973) 298–305.

Ramsey, Paul. "Liturgy and Ethics." *Journal of Religious Ethics* 7 (1979) 139–72.

Ross, Susan A. *Extravagant Affections: A Feminist Sacramental Theology.* New York: Continuum, 1998.

Rossi, Philip J. "Narrative, Worship, and Ethics: Empowering Images for the Shape of the Christian Moral Life." *Journal of Religious Ethics* 7 (1979) 239–49.

Saliers, Don E. "Liturgy and Ethics: Some New Beginnings." *Journal of Religious Ethics* 7 (1979) 173–90.

Schmidt, Herman, and David Power, eds. *Politics and Liturgy. Concilium* 92 (1974).

Schneiders, Sandra M. "Liturgy—Spirituality—The Widening Gap." *Spirituality Today* 38 (1978) 196–210.

Searle, Mark, ed. *Liturgy and Social Justice.* Collegeville: The Liturgical Press, 1980.

Seasoltz, R. Kevin. *Living Bread, Saving Cup: Readings on the Eucharist.* Collegeville: The Liturgical Press, 1982.

_____. "Justice and the Eucharist" *Worship* 58/6 (November 1984) 507–25.

Sedgwick, Timothy E. *Sacramental Ethics: Paschal Identity and the Christian Life.* Philadelphia: Fortress Press, 1987.

Segundo, Juan Luis. *The Sacraments Today,* vol. 4, in *A Theology for Artisans of a New Humanity.* Maryknoll, N.Y.: Orbis Books, 1975.

Stamps, Mary E., ed. *To Do Justice and Right Upon the Earth: Papers from the Virgel Michel Symposium on Liturgy and Social Justice.* Collegeville: The Liturgical Press, 1993.

Stevens, Dom P. Gregory "Moral Theology and the Liturgy." *Yearbook of Liturgical Studies* 1 (1960) 65–122.

Swayne, Sean, ed. *Eucharist for a New World.* Carlow, Ireland: Irish Institute of Pastoral Liturgy, 1981.

U.S. Catholic Bishops. *Economic Justice for All.* Washington, D.C.: USCC, 1986.

Voll, V. "Contemporary Developments in Sacramental and Moral Theology." *Society of Catholic College Teachers of Christian Doctrine Proceedings* 8 (1962) 122–37.

Weakland, Rembert G., O.S.B., "Liturgy and Social Justice." In *Shaping English Liturgy: Studies in Honor of Archbishop Denis Hurley*. Ed. Peter C. Finn and James M. Schellman (Washington D.C.: Pastoral Press, 1990) 343–57.

Williman, William H. *The Service of God: How Worship and Ethics Are Related.* Nashville: Abingdon, 1983.

Yaffe, Martin D. "Liturgy and Ethics: Hermann Cohen and Franz Rosenweig on the Day of Atonement." *Journal of Religious Ethics* 7 (1979) 215–28.

Author Index

245

Subject Index